BEER

for

PETE'S

SAKE

BEER
for
PETE'S
SAKE

The Wicked Adventures of a Brewing Maverick

PETE SLOSBERG

Siris
Books

An Imprint of Brewers Publications
Boulder, Colorado

ADDRESS: Siris Books, an imprint of Brewers Publications
PO Box 1679, Boulder, CO 80306-1679
(303) 447-0816; Fax (303) 447-2825

Printed in the United States of America

10 9 8 7 6 5 4 3 2 1

ISBN: 0-937381-63-2

Siris Books. Who is Siris? She was the daughter of Ninkasi, the Sumerian
goddess of beer. Anthropologists personify Ninkasi as the filler of the cup, the
one who pours the beer. Siris is the beer itself. Because she represents the presence and cultural importance of beer throughout civilization, this mysterious and little-known deity
seemed perfect as the name of our new imprint.

Please direct all inquiries to the above address.

Permission for use of the following illustrations is gratefully acknowledged:

From *Guinness,* by Peter Walsh. Color plates of Guinness cartoons. Used by permission of
Guinness Brewing Worldwide. From *Brewing for Victory,* by Brian Glover. Photos of World War
II planes carrying barrels of beer. Copyright 1995 by Lutterworth Press. Used by permission.
From *An Uncommon Brewer,* by Berry Ritchie. Porter cartoon. Copyright 1992 by James and
James, Ltd. Used by permission. From *The Hop Atlas,* by Heinrich Joh. Barth, Christiane Klinke,
and Claus Schmidt. Photo of a man stringing frames for growing hops and an illustration of a
hop harvest. Copyright 1994 by Joh. Barth and Sohn. Used by permission.

Permissions for use of copyrighted material are on file with the publisher.

LIBRARY OF CONGRESS CATALOGING-IN-PUBLICATION DATA

Slosberg, Pete.
    Beer for Pete's sake : the wicked adventures of a brewing maverick
/ Pete Slosberg.
        p. cm.
    Includes bibliographical references and index.
    ISBN 0-937381-63-2 (alk. paper)
        1. Slosberg, Pete. 2. Brewers—United States—Biography.
3. Pete's Brewing Company. I. Title.
TP573.5.S55A3   1998
663'.42'092—dc21
[B]   98-9820
                                                                  CIP

To my wife, Amy,

and sons, Eric and Alex,

for putting up with the time I've spent

away from them while developing and growing

Pete's Brewing Company, and for being willing

to stop at every beer store we pass

so I can look for more cans

to add to my collection.

CONTENTS

PREFACE

My first beer was a Pabst Blue Ribbon. I was sixteen, hiding behind the hamburger stand where I worked in Norwich, Connecticut. I hated it. For that matter, I didn't like any alcoholic drinks. I remember when I had my Bar Mitzvah at age thirteen, there was a Friday-night ceremony that included a blessing over wine. Of course, since I was leading the prayer, I had to drink from the cup of wine. I was really nervous because I couldn't stand the taste of wine, and I thought I'd lose it in front of everybody.

I did not learn to like beer until I was twenty-nine.

So how does one become a brewing ambassador given these humble beer/drinking beginnings? You could say it was my wife, Amy, who "drove me" to drink even if it was an introduction to drinking wine. She also taught me to like eggplant. In fact, she has shared many wonderful things with me over the years—things I might have never tried myself because I was afraid to. There were many reasons to be afraid of trying something new. I might fail. I might not like it. It might be a complete waste of time and money. All very good reasons. But is it reason that makes dreams happen?

I never set out to start a company of my own and never anticipated that studying space mechanics and propulsion as an undergraduate — yes, I majored in rocket science—would lead me to live a life focused on beer. It actually was a serendipitous event of home winemaking that led to experimenting with homebrewing. That finally opened my eyes to the delights of the world of beer. Starting a company isn't simple; I had *lots* of good reasons to be afraid.

This book is not a company success story. It's also not a technical book about beer or a compilation of stories about the history of beer.

It's not even about how beer changed my life. Rather, it's about all of these things. Most of all to say that beer is only something to drink is to miss out on so much that makes it come alive. To really understand beer, it takes some knowledge of the beermaking process, as well as the glorious stories of beer.

Some people think beer is just a cheap, tasteless liquid. As I got more involved with it, I realized that there really was more to beer than the beer itself. The same beer can taste okay when you're by yourself and then taste fantastic when you're surrounded by good friends. It is an integral part of our heritage and language. Many words, phrases, and stories find their origin in the lore of beer. While the wide variety of beers from around the world provide great taste and enjoyment, the words and stories bring beer to life. Beer has been a part of civilization from the time nomadic tribes settled down; in fact, anthropologists believe that people started communities specifically to grow grain to make bread and beer!

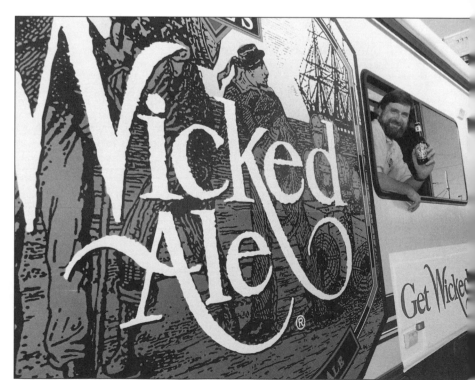

Me in the Wicked Winnebago at the 1995 Great American Beer Festival.

In this sense, you can't judge a beer by its name or by the design on the six-pack, or expect to learn much about it by just reading a book. Although you can know something about a beer from its style and color, you still have to taste it to explore all of its facets. I didn't like the first beer I ever tasted. To be honest, *I* don't even like all of the beers I make. But that's what makes beer so wonderful: There are so many different varieties that it's okay not to like some of them.

I have a rule of thumb about living now. Because time goes by quickly, too quickly, I look for the unique things that people are producing around me. Sometimes I have to go out of my way to find those special things, and sometimes I have to take a chance. I've learned to not always do the convenient thing, but to take the time to search for the unusual and not to be afraid to ask others what's good.

This book is my attempt to show how a couple of small steps at the right time in the right direction can lead to a complete life change. I have found that the more I become involved with beer, the more it interests me and continues to change my life for the better. It's actually pretty incredible that a simple desire like wanting to brew a beer I could enjoy at home would lead to so many amazing things.

Have you ever dreamed of someone walking up to you on the street and telling you that something you made was their favorite in the world? Or perhaps of giving a talk on a subject you feel passionately about and having someone in the audience tell you afterward that he or she actually learned something from you? How about having people come up to you and say that you have the best job in the world? I'm the luckiest guy there is because my answers to those questions are yes, yes, and yes!

Welcome to my wicked world of beer!

ACKNOWLEDGMENTS

Writing a book is not easy, I have learned. I want to thank everyone who stood by me through the process, and most especially: Marla Mulkey, my assistant, for her outstanding ability to keep everything organized, on track, and supporting too many balls in the air at the same time; my publisher, Toni Knapp, for making me aware of how complicated it is to get a book out, and for always being there to help and guide me through it; and my personal editor, Nicholas Cravotta, whose world-class skills helped me see the forest through the trees in the vast amount of information I was able to discover.

Part One

Discovering Wine, Beer, and Eggplant

CHAPTER 1

FROM NEW YORK CITY
CAB DRIVER TO ... WINE?

*A woman drove me to drink, and I didn't even have the
decency to thank her.* —W. C. FIELDS

I went to the Columbia University School of Engineering
and Applied Science because I wanted to go to an engineering
school where you had to take liberal arts. At Columbia, the first two
years you certainly had a lot of science and math classes, but you also
had the same core curriculum as liberal arts. Thus, I got to read many
of the epic books of the centuries. It was a lot of work, but it was eye-
opening, too.

In engineering you didn't have a lot of non-science electives
in your second, third, and fourth years, but I wanted to take an art
history class. Columbia had the typical art history classes with big
lecture halls with slides and all that crap. I didn't want to take that. I
like getting my hands dirty. Fortunately, another benefit of Columbia
was that I could take classes in other divisions of the university. One
of those was the School of General Studies, which was basically a night
school for adults. General Studies offered a class on Rembrandt at the
Metropolitan Museum, but it was never given when I had free time.
One class that met when I did have free time, called "Early Christian
Treasures," caught my eye. I figured, what the hell, I don't know anything about Christianity, but I'll take the class because it's held in the
cellar of the Metropolitan Museum.

I was one of only six people in the class: five art history
majors, all upper-class folks, and me. I asked the professor if it was

a problem that I had never had "Art History 101." She said no, but warned me that I'd still have to write a term paper. "I'd like you to study an object that I studied for my master's thesis several years ago." This scared the daylights out of me since I didn't think I'd be able to handle a term assignment, in my first class in art history, that the professor has done her masters work on. But what the hell, why not give it a shot.

In the course of those classes held in the cellar of the Met, we saw a bunch of pictures and slides of mosaics from cathedrals in Istanbul and churches in Italy. The professor also brought out many art objects, and we were allowed to hold them in our hands. It was great.

My class assignment involved a separate unit of the museum called the Cloisters, a medieval castle in an upper-Manhattan park. I was to go look at an object there, a silver chalice thought to

My 1968 high school student ID, and 1969 and 1970 Columbia University IDs.

have been the holy grail. My professor told me it wasn't, that the date on that chalice was wrong. She challenged me to redate it. If the museum has the wrong date on it, I thought, how the hell was I going to know what to put on it? "When you see the chalice," she said, "you'll see all sorts of representations of grapes and grape leaves, animals, and the apostles. What you need to do is go to all the other museums around New York and assume that the dates on those objects are correct. Do a correlation of the images of grapes and grape leaves, animals, and apostles with objects at the other museums and come back with a date."

So there I was, an engineer, taking to the subways to visit all of these museums I would probably have never gone to otherwise. I really got into it. Of the six of us in the class, I received the highest grade. I dated the object somewhere around the mid-fourth century. My professor asked if I could read French; I couldn't. This comment threw me for a loop. Where did the question of French come from? It turned out that there was a book in the Columbia University Library, written in French, on the Chalice of Antioch, which was the proper name of the chalice I was studying. Information from the book would have led me to date the chalice a little bit later, that is, the mid- to late-fourth century. As it was, she told me I was close enough!

What a great class! That's why I went to New York, to the big city, to expose myself to things that I wouldn't have experienced in other places.

I've worked at many jobs since I was sixteen. While I was at Columbia, I found a job working for Hertz Rent-a-Car on the weekends. Many rental cars were taken out of New York City to surrounding regional airports, like Bradley Field in Hartford/Springfield. Hertz would pay a lump sum per person for five of us to pile into a car in Manhattan and go out to collect those cars. The Connecticut State Police were notorious for catching speeders (the speed limit is still 55 there), so the Bradley run wasn't popular because of the ticket risk. For me it was great. My parents lived in Norwich, Connecticut, so I could go out to Bradley Field (with my laundry in the trunk), pick up a car, and head to my parents' home for a home-cooked meal and laundry services before driving back to the city. And when I wanted to spend the night, Hertz said it was okay to return the car the next day.

The Hertz job was convenient and had its perks, but it wasn't very lucrative. What it did was get the driving spirit into my blood. I knew many other guys who earned money driving a cab, so I thought I'd give that a whirl. This was a real experience! To get my license, I had to take a written test and a medical test. I remember being a little leery of the written test, but having seen the caliber of NYC cab drivers, my nervousness was somewhat mitigated.

Just how hard was the NYC hack-license written test? You had to know the street address of ten of the most famous NYC landmarks. The agency gave you a sheet of paper with the ten addresses on it, including the Empire State Building, the Port Authority Bus Terminal, Grand Central Station, Yankee Stadium, and so on. You just had to memorize the addresses. For the test, you had to identify the address of three of the locations. You did not have to know where these places actually were, nor any of the intricacies required to arrive at them via the New York City street system. The test was classic. Nobody knows these addresses, most people know only what avenue the buildings are on and what cross-streets they're near.

The cab companies must have been desperate for drivers. If for any reason you failed the test, they gave you a second try and, if necessary, a third try. Each time, you got to study the same ten locations before the test. For the record, I passed the test on my first try.

My New York City taxi-cab license, circa 1970, and my 1972 photo ID from working at NASA's Institute for Space Studies in New York City during my senior year.

The medical exam was as rigorous as the written exam. Step one was to roll up my sleeve so the nurse could check for needle marks. Whew. I passed that test on my first try, too. For the final step of the examination, I had to hop up and down on one foot several times. If the nurse detected a pulse after all this, then you became an honest-to-goodness official New York City cab driver! No cap and gown ceremonies here, just a fine-looking license.

For new graduates of the cab license agency, jobs weren't hard to find. They just happened to be pretty much limited to the graveyard shift. It's a relatively quiet time of the night, but there are several reasons why the more experienced drivers avoid this shift: It's late, there are weirdos out there, and you get fewer fares.

Thank heaven that soon after I got my license, I also got a job at an engineering lab at Columbia. The pay was better, and I could name my own hours. It was my first career change, from transportation to engineering. Fortunately, more changes were to follow.

I met Amy, my future wife, back in 1971 while I was a senior in college. At that time the drinking age was eighteen, so most students could drink legally as freshmen. I played on the tennis team my freshman year and joined the rowing team as a junior. Beers were generally available, but the taste of beer did nothing for me. It just didn't taste good.

With a relatively steady income during school, I had some extra money to take Amy around the city. We followed *Craig Claiborne's (New York Times) Guide* to eating out in New York, enjoying the diversity of the city's ethnic restaurants. Our budget of $3.00 for two people actually went a long way since I didn't like drinking enough to spend any money on beer or wine. We loved Brazilian food, and there are still places in Manhattan's Brazilian neighborhoods where you can stuff yourself with great food for about $10.00.

Amy, bless her heart, did not take out a cattle prod and force me to drink. She enjoyed a glass of wine now and then—and a glass of Scotch, not so now and then. There was no way I could tolerate, let alone enjoy, the alcohol burn of Scotch, so I had to turn to wine if I was going to have a drink with her. When sampling reds, usually served at room temperature, I found the taste and aroma way too strong to enjoy. White wines, on the other hand, were served chilled and I found that they weren't too bad. As soon as they warmed up, however, I didn't like them either. Being an engineering student almost ready to graduate, I put two and two together and tried putting some wine in the freezer. If chilled wine didn't have much flavor and aroma, then frozen wine should have close to none. Given our budget, a sweet Lambrusco was our starting wine. Guess what? Thousands of dollars in education, and I finally figured out a way that I could drink wine!

Over the next several years, my taste in wine grew more refined, and I found that the serving temperature could be somewhat warmer than frozen. Continued experimentation with beer at colder temperatures did nothing to change my dislike for it. Even haunting the hallowed halls of McSorley's Pub, the oldest pub in New York City, added little to the appeal of beer for me. I do recall ordering the fabulous plates of cheese, onions, and crackers along with hot mustard at McSorley's. This combination built up an incredible thirst, which their ice-cold beers did make some progress with. Okay, okay, so I did enjoy a beer or two, but it was more to quench a thirst or to be sociable than really enjoying the beer for its flavor.

After graduate school at Columbia's School of Business, Xerox offered me a position as a financial analyst in Rochester, New York. So off to upstate New York I went, without Amy. She had another year to go before she finished her graduate program at the New School for Social Research. What a school! They offered undergraduate courses in any field they could find a qualified teacher for. My favorite listing in their catalog was "How to Survive on Native Plants in New York City."

In upstate New York, I was near the home of Genessee Brewing and close to the wineries of the Finger Lakes region. The people of Rochester went nuts over Genessee Cream Ale and even more crazy over Genessee's spring seasonal beer, Genny Bock, which was available for only a few weeks of the year. I still didn't understand what other people saw in beer, but one thing I discovered with Genny Cream was that it had a faint sweetness to it that I found rather pleasant. If pressed to order a beer, then Genny Cream was my choice because of the sweetness, not because it had any real appealing flavor.

On the wine side, my tastes continued to develop. Chilling wine was no longer necessary. Amy's continued patience had taught me that allowing the liquid to warm first allowed the flavor and aroma to come out. More experimentation led to trying varietals of New York State wines rather than blends like the typical chablis, burgundy, and rosé. Not all varietals were pleasant, but it was fun to try the options.

Weekend trips to the countryside showed us the bounty of the area. We would pass many orchards, including an apple orchard where the farmer had trained the apple trees to grow horizontally along wire frames so that during harvest season, you could pick your own apples by walking around rather than having to use a ladder to get to the fruit. It was an ingenious idea, and it certainly made harvesting easy for customers.

There were also several wineries in the area. Our favorite was Bully Hill, founded by Walter Taylor. Walter was a scion of the Taylor family that had built Taylor wines. The family had sold the business to a large conglomerate and along with the business, the rights to the Taylor name. Walter discovered this when he put his name on the labels of Bully Hill wines and the conglomerate came after him. He had to cross his name out with a black marker on every label. Walter found, as we would later at Pete's Brewing, that big competitors can and do come after smaller competitors. Whether they are in the right doesn't matter—they have the resources to win.

What really impressed us about Walter was the wine he produced. In the early 1970s, New York State required that wines made in the state only had to have 51 percent grape juice. Sugar and water could make up the remaining 49 percent if you so chose. Walter thought this was bullshit and decided to use 100 percent grape juice in his wines. He later fought in the New York State legislature to make all wines produced in New York contain 100 percent juice. It's funny, because today we are facing the same battle in our efforts to make beer with 100 percent traditional beer ingredients like barley and wheat the standard. The major brewers use a large percentage of adjunct grains, like rice and corn, that are cheaper and actually take away flavor from barley and wheat.

Bully Hill Baco Noir wine was nectar from the gods. This fantastic red varietal became our wine of choice. No freezing of this puppy. Open it up, let it breathe, then savor the aroma and flavor. Baco Noir forever changed my opinion of wine. Wine was no longer something I drank only when in an environment where I was expected to have a drink. Wine was now pure pleasure.

Working for Xerox, on the other hand, was not pure pleasure. Overtime was expected! Work weeks of 80 to 100 hours were typical. Some of my friends would actually boast about the number of hours they had worked and would try to set new records. The local paper ran an article about the typical Xerox employee versus the typical employee at Kodak (the other large company in Rochester). The typical Kodak person talked about bowling, whereas the typical Xerox person talked about work.

We spent so many hours together at Xerox that we usually socialized with other Xerox people; there wasn't enough time to meet others in the community.

After my first year at Xerox, Amy finished her master's degree and moved up to Rochester. We were married the following November. The morning of our wedding I cut my neck all over the place while shaving. It was the last time I shaved!

Amy and I resumed our search for great hole-in-the-wall places to eat. Our choices in Rochester were so limited that we had to drive all the way to Buffalo just to get decent ice cream (Baskin Robbins) or up to Toronto for dim sum. We also discovered cooking at home. Amy got me to try eggplant by preparing an old family recipe for an appetizer. She put the eggplant over a low flame, so that it burned and simmered the inside of the eggplant. The outside got kind of crispy, but when it was all soft inside, she scooped the pulp out. After mashing it up, she added oil, grated onions, and salt, then spread it on toast. It was wonderful. Having realized the worth of trying new foods, I even worked my way up to baba ganush, a Middle Eastern eggplant dish.

One night, Amy and I were invited over to eat at the home of our friends, Chris and Paul Hertz. They also enjoyed cooking and eating a wide variety of food. On this particular evening, Paul opened a bottle of wine during dinner. What a surprise! Bully Hill Baco Noir was my ideal wine, but Paul's was every bit as good, if not better. "Who made this wine?" I asked. Paul replied, "I did." Huh? "What do you mean, you made it? I thought you had to have your own winery and all sorts of equipment to make wine." I was sure that Paul didn't own a winery.

Paul took me down to his cellar. There it was. Not a big winery, but it had carboys (five-gallon glass containers which are similar to the five-gallon plastic bottles used by commercial water companies), bottles, and some other tools and tubing. Making wine at home was not only possible but, as Paul showed me, actually easy to do. Based upon the quality of the wine that Paul had made, I realized that not only could I do it, but I could make a world-class product. My mind started spinning as I thought about trying to make some wine as good as Bully Hill's or Paul's. Paul offered to teach me, and I took him up on his offer.

When we got home, however, I saw that our apartment was much too small for this new hobby. My appetite had been whetted, but I didn't have the space for it. Oh well, I thought and proceeded to grind another telescope mirror, which was my current hobby at the time. I built two telescopes and relished watching the stars on clear nights. However, the idea of making wine stayed with me.

Rochester, New York—what a place to live. The city has a huge corporate base, as well as some great universities, and no major heavy industry. What it doesn't have is sunshine. One might expect a lot of cold or a lot of snow—it can actually snow as late as June and as early as September—but no sunshine? The culprit is something called the "lake effect." Rochester, located on the south shore of Lake Ontario, is the cloudiest city in the United States. Clouds form because of the lake effect, and there are days on end when, while driving to work, I could see the ball of the sun as it rose up from the horizon and formed a complete circle, only to have it disappear into the clouds for the rest of the day. At sunset I might get another glimpse as the sun dropped below the clouds on its way to the horizon. How depressing! It was probably one of the reasons we worked so many hours at Xerox. If it wasn't going to be nice outside, you might as well stay inside and work.

I figured that there had to be an answer to my prayers about more sunshine. Xerox had many divisions and its tens of thousands of employees in California. If I could only get a transfer, then the dark, cloudy days of Rochester would be but a distant memory. Alas, Xerox would not post any open positions in California for employees in Rochester to consider, probably in fear of inciting a massive exodus. With some ingenuity, I planned a vacation in California with Amy that would include a job search.

One of the companies I interviewed with there didn't actually have any openings at the time. The interviewer himself had left Xerox, located just down the street, a couple of months earlier, and he knew of a couple of openings there. He offered to help set up an interview for me, and within the day I had an offer to work at that California division of Xerox. Needless to say, my boss in Rochester was furious that I hadn't gone through the "proper channels," but of course there were no "proper channels" for transferring to California. Sometimes you just have to try to make things happen for yourself when the system won't do it for you.

When I left Rochester for California, Xerox gave me the choice of flying at the company's expense or driving. The number of days allowed for the drive was based on covering 350 miles a day. When I asked Amy if she wanted to fly or visit friends that we hadn't seen in years throughout the country, it was really a no-brainer. It was January when we left, and we decided that we would stay with friends in Durham, Nashville, and Dallas. There were also a few sights we wanted to see along the way, so we took the southern route to avoid winter storms.

We shipped a lot of our stuff, but Amy had an avocado tree she wanted to take along. Now, when you live in New York, don't ask me why, but it's almost a rite of passage to take an avocado pit, put three toothpicks in it, and park it in a glass of water. Eventually it develops roots, and you grow it into a full-blown plant. Amy had had her avocado tree all throughout undergraduate and graduate school in Rochester, and the last thing she wanted to do was leave it behind. Her avocado plant was six feet tall, so it really had grown into a tree. We were going to drive across the country in my Ford Mustang—not the original Mustang, but the Mustang 2—which meant the back seat was tiny. Nonetheless, we headed out loaded with suitcases and other junk, and the avocado tree.

Our first day out we hit an ice and snow storm. In Rochester, you get used to ice and snow. Down in North Carolina there were cars spinning off the side of the road. It was freezing, so we couldn't leave the avocado plant out in the car; we had to bring it into our friend's house. The next day, we stopped at Nashville, which had had a high of 5 degrees that day. We had to carry the tree up two stories to our hotel room. When we got to Dallas, it was below 30. In and out. In and out. This bloody tree was driving us nuts!

I don't know why I thought of it, but I asked my friend in Dallas, Carl Anderson, if he knew where the agriculture checkpoints between Texas and California were because after schlepping this tree around I didn't want it to be confiscated. He said there was definitely an agricultural center between Arizona and California, and most likely one between Arizona and New Mexico.

We paid close attention to our map as we were driving across West Texas into New Mexico. We timed it so that we would cross the border between midnight and three in the morning. We also got off the main highway at the last exit before Arizona and took a side road forty or fifty miles out of our way to cross the border before returning to the main highway. It was past midnight as we happily traveled along this back road, going north from the freeway. There was no traffic, nothing, when all of a sudden we saw flashing blue lights. It turns out the road we were on was so remote that many illegal aliens tried to use it to come across from Mexico. The police were looking for refugees, but they didn't care about the plant.

After the police let us go, we looped back around into
Arizona, very pleased with ourselves for having made it past the
agriculture checkpoint. We drove for another half-hour, when we
hit what looked like a toll station. This, we found out it, was the
agriculturel checkpoint. In all our clever dodging, we hadn't passed
it! I said *!#@, what are we going to do? I decided I'd better get out
of the car and go talk to the guy.

A thought hit as I was getting out of the car. I turned to
Amy and said, "If they ask you where we're going, tell them Las
Vegas." She said, "What are you talking about?" I asked her to bear
with me and just say that we were moving to Vegas. I approached the
agent inside his little booth. He asked me if I was carrying any plants.
I said, "Yeah." It was obvious. You could see the plant poking out the
window. What do you have? It's an avocado tree. Where are you
going? Las Vegas. Where? We're moving to Las Vegas; I have a new
job in Las Vegas. The agent eyed me and said, "Are you sure? If you're
going to California, we'll have to confiscate that plant. We don't have
reciprocity with Nevada though." He looked at me and said to stay
right here. Then he went out to the car and knocked on the window.
Amy rolled it down, and he asked her where we were going. She said,
"Nevada." The agent came back to me and said, "Okay. You're on
your way." I don't know where this brainstorm came from, but Amy
played along with it, and we got through.

We knew that the border between Arizona into New Mexico
is all land, so there are many small roads you can use to sneak across.
The border between Arizona and California, however, is a river, and
there are only so many bridges. At the exit before California I got off
and pulled into a truck stop. I asked the waitress where the border
crossings were. I told her we had a tree we wanted to bring in. She
told me there was one close by and another twenty miles up the river;
there really weren't that many options. Then some guy walked by and
told us that just across the border the inspection station was closed.
If we got in our car right that moment, we might get past it. So we

jumped into the car and high-tailed it across the border. As we drove by the inspection station, we could see that it was indeed closed. All right!

In California, we lived in an apartment in a town called Claremont, which was near the Xerox plant I worked at until I transferred to an office in Pasadena. A year later we moved from the apartment into a house. We had kept the avocado tree in its pot, waiting until we had a house of our own and could plant it in our backyard. When we bought the house, we planted the avocado tree. It was great coming full circle, from watering a seed to planting the tree in its own native environment! As irony would have it, two months later there was a frost, and the tree died.

Hallelujah! Out to the Golden State, reveling in its sunshine. However, the new job didn't work out, and I soon got a job in the Bay Area with a company called ROLM, which made computerized telephone systems for businesses. The year was 1979, and the stars were starting to align. ROLM was an incredible company. I had interesting work, and the employees were actually treated like human beings. For example, managers got offices and non-managers got cubicles. That was pretty standard for Silicon Valley. What was different was that the cubicles were at the windows and the offices were in the middle of the buildings.

I couldn't get Bully Hill wine in California, and my friend Paul was still in Rochester, so I had to look for other interesting wines to try. My taste in wines soon gravitated to Stags Leap Cabernet from the Napa Valley. Amy and I bought a house in Belmont, California, on the San Francisco Peninsula, about twenty-five miles south of the city. Belmont is hilly, and the house we bought was part way up one of the hills. Unlike most California homes, it had a partial basement. The basement stayed cool year-round, and it occurred to me that if I was ever going to make my own wine, I now had the perfect conditions for making and storing wine.

Amy agreed to help me make the wine. First I had to find out where to get the supplies—both the equipment and the fruit. I found a place called Wine and the People, a store on University Avenue in Berkeley. Berkeley was just under an hour away, so one weekend we made the trip over to check out the store and see about making wine. The store was pretty nondescript from the outside, but on the inside we found a plethora of materials for making wine and beer. An announcement caught my eye; one of the services the store offered to its customers was buying grapes by the ton from a variety of California vineyards and selling them in one-hundred-pound lots to home winemakers. Cool deal—just sign on the dotted line, and then show up on the date of harvesting when the grapes were delivered to the store. When I finished reading the fine print, I knew it was time for me to make wine. Included in the sources of grapes were cabernet grapes, from Stags Leap in Napa! Make my day! We bought two hundred pounds.

When the grapes arrived, we were so excited that we couldn't just throw the grapes in a tub and stomp on them with our feet. No, this had to be more ritualistic. We wrapped clumps of grapes in cheesecloth and then squeezed the juice into containers. Believe me, there is a reason people stomp on grapes. It's a lot easier than hand-squeezing. I suppose we could have gotten a grape press, but this was our first time, and we wanted to treat the grapes lovingly. The work was long and hard, but we managed to crush all two hundred pounds. Our hands stayed purple for the longest time!

We followed the instructions about adding the yeast to the juice and then watched the building froth of the fermentation. After several days, the froth settled down as the fermentation came to a finish. Allowing another day for the yeast and any other solids to settle at the bottom of the liquid, we then siphoned off the freshly fermented wine into five-gallon glass carboys for secondary fermentation and the beginning of long-term maturation. It seemed like every day something important was going on and that there was variety in the activities. This was a cool hobby!

All of a sudden, after we had put the wine into the five-gallon carboys, it occurred to me that this hobby was not going to be what I had expected. Since this was a cabernet, we were going to have to wait five to ten years to drink this stuff. Who the hell wanted to wait that long? This wasn't a hobby. It was about as exciting as watching rocks erode!

CHAPTER 2

If You Haven't Had a Homebrew, Then You Haven't Had a Real Beer

Listening to someone who brews his own beer is like listening to
a religious fanatic talk about the day he saw the light.
—Ross Murray, *Montreal Gazette,* July 10, 1991

P aul's homemade wine was great, but I hadn't realized that he had been storing it for years. Maybe, just maybe, winemaking wasn't the hobby I had built it up to be in my own head. A call the next day to Wine and the People expressing my frustration got me the following response: If I wanted to do something quicker, I could do a white wine and have it mature in one to two years. Gee, that would be an improvement, but still not good enough. Okay, they said, how about making beer? It only takes a month or two. I liked the idea of a month or two, but I explained that I didn't like beer.

The guy asked me if I ever had a homebrew. I hadn't. Then he said something to me that was really profound: "If you haven't had a homebrew, then you haven't had real beer!" That got my attention. I decided to give it a try. After all, it would only cost about twenty dollars to give it a whirl.

My first batch was pretty much "follow-the-recipe" for a basic amber ale. Few books were available then to help the homebrewer, so I took whatever help I could from Wine and the People. The most basic method for making homebrew is to start with a malt extract liquid, thus avoiding a lot of the complexity of starting with grain. Boil the malt extract, add the hops, and away you go. It is slightly more complicated than boiling water, but not much. The key to good homebrew is cleanliness.

Six weeks later, I opened up a bottle, a couple of weeks before I was supposed to, but I couldn't wait any longer. The amber liquid developed a glorious head as I carefully poured it into a pint glass, and the aroma was actually quite inviting. The first taste surprised me because it didn't taste like anything I had ever had before. Sure it was odd, but the oddness evolved into a realization that this stuff did taste good. Maybe I hadn't had all that many different kinds of beers in my life, but this beer was far superior to anything I had ever tasted. I knew, then and there, that I was going to become a beer lover. Twenty-nine years old, and I finally became a beer drinker. It was a long way from frozen Lambrusco, but I was amazed at how good beer could be if done right.

In hindsight, my first homebrew may not have won gold medals, but the flavor was spectacular. It took me some time to realize why I enjoyed my first homebrew so much: For the first time, I tasted something in the beer—the flavor of barley malt. As a kid, I grew up in Norwich, Connecticut, about ten miles from New London, which is on the shore. We'd go to a place called Ocean Beach lots of days during the summer. On the way back, about a mile from the beach, there was an outlet called Mitchell Dairy, where we'd always stop for ice cream. I tended to ask for an ice cream milk shake and always got the extra spoonfuls of malted milk put in to make it a malted milk shake.

HONEYMOON

In Babylonia, about 2000 B.C., when a couple got married, it was the accepted practice that the father of the bride would supply his son-in-law and daughter with all of the mead (honey-beer) they could drink for a month after the wedding, for reasons of fertility. Because the calendar was lunar-based then, a honey month was really a honeymoon.

Malt powder, made from barley malt, is actually the same basic ingredient used in beermaking. Tasting the malt sent me back to Ocean Beach, summertime, and all of those wonderful memories. If you've never had a malted milk shake, then maybe you've had another favorite of mine, a chocolate-covered malted-milk ball called a Whopper. The center of these candies is made from barley malt. Do you see a pattern forming in my adoration of the flavor of barley malt?

Mass-produced and marketed American lagers do use some barley malt, but the use of rice or corn as additives diminishes the flavor of the barley malt. It wasn't until I made my first homebrew from 100 percent barley malt that I was able to taste the full flavor of malt that I had always loved as a kid.

One homebrew led to another, and there was always another style of beer to try to make. Some were dark, some were light; some were sweet, some were bitter; some were very strong in alcohol, and others were fairly weak. Not every batch had a pleasing flavor to me, but I was astounded to discover the incredible variety of beer styles that existed.

When we got married, Amy and I received a set of wine glasses with our monogram on it: ASP, for Amy and Pete Slosberg. An artist friend of mine did a label for us to use on the wines and beers we were now making at home. Some young wines are sharp, and some hoppy beers have a bite, so I figured, why not do a takeoff on our wine-glass monogram for the labels? Thus was born the ASP Winery and Brewery, employing asps—poisonous snakes from Egypt—on the label to warn unsuspecting drinkers of the "bite."

Our first homebrewed wine and beer label, circa 1981.

After getting the fundamentals of homebrewing down pat, it really takes a lot of effort to make a "bad" beer. Yes, you can make beers that don't appeal to your palate, but as long as you keep everything clean, the beer should come out okay. So what's the real difficulty in becoming a homebrewer? It's not really the brewing. It's acquiring and cleaning bottles! As a homebrewer making five-gallon batches, I would need approximately 55, twelve-ounce bottles per batch.

When there were several batches going at once, I'd scrounge around for bottles that I could use and then reuse. Clear glass and green glass are not appropriate for beer so I had to find brown bottles. Even then, the brown bottles needed to be sturdy for reuse in future batches.

It's funny, in hindsight, but some bottles really didn't work very well. It's not because of the brown glass, but because the brewers had used glue in putting on their labels that was impossible to scrape off. My homebrews would either be in plain bottles or bottles that I put labels on. In either case I had to get the old labels off. This limitation of brown bottles that were sturdy and had labels that were easily scraped off became my mantra for bottle collection.

With bottles in hand, the next difficulty was to make sure they were clean and sterile. Many bottles looked suitable, but had all sorts of things inside from beer residue to other unrecognizable growths. Hours were spent cleaning the bottles. The hardest part in homebrewing is the time to find and clean the bottles!

After months of brewing and rummaging through glass recycling bins for bottles, I determined that my bottle of choice for homebrews was (I can't believe I'm saying this) the Budweiser 12-ounce returnable longneck. The bottle was great, as it was very sturdy and hardly ever broke. Back then 22-ounce bottles didn't exist, except for a small handful of imports that were hard to find.

Within walking distance of my house was a tasty burger joint called Marvin Gardens. It was a small, out-of-the-way place by the railroad tracks with a nice patio for relaxing outside in perfect weather, under tall Eucalyptus trees with their wonderful aroma. They had basic but very good food and offered a large selection of beers for that time (circa 1979). Whenever I went there, especially after starting to homebrew, I could see stacks of empty bottles. Most of the cases of empties were Bud returnable longnecks, bottles that last forever.

I finally asked to see the owner, Chip Truett, and offered him a proposition: a six-pack of my homebrew for cases of Bud empties. It was a great deal for me, and I hope equally good for Chip. He took me up on the offer, so I had found an endless supply of bottles.

At ROLM, a bunch of my friends and I developed a strong appreciation for beer and homebrewing. We also loved barbecue. These dual loves made for a great synergy. It just so happened that right around the corner from Wine and the People in Berkeley where we bought our brewing supplies was—and still is—one of the best barbecue places on the face of the earth: Everett and Jones Barbecue. (As a side note, I have to tell you that I ran a full 26-mile marathon in an Everett and Jones T-shirt. I finished (yeah!), but I was a hurting cowboy. I can't imagine that it had anything to do with not carbo-loading the night before, but eating two portions of ribs and links from Everett and Jones couldn't have helped.) Every month or so, our group of ROLM homebrewers got together to try each other's brews and

Logo of the homebrew club I started at ROLM, circa 1983.

do some barbecuing. We needed a name for our homebrew club, so I came up with "The Worry Worts." (Wort is a brewing term for the sweet liquid you extract from the grain and hot water prior to adding the yeast.) Our meetings took place in a variety of county parks throughout the Bay Area. Spectacular scenery was conducive to making our club meetings terrific, even if most of us did end up on our backs. The majority of our homebrews were higher in alcohol than typical beers, which made for high-octane get-togethers.

ROLM was doing well in the late 1970s and early 1980s. Our stock kept splitting and the company kept growing. Although

ROLMagazine

Volume 1, No. 6
September 1980
Published by and for
the people of ROLM

"Ale-ing" Employee Wins State Prize

"Having a ball doing it" is Peter Slosberg's explanation for his interest in brewing. Recently honored by this state's amateur brewers, Peter has been formulating and fermenting a variety of potable liquids including wine, root beer and a Norwegian soda. A relative newcomer to the art of beer making, Peter was one of more than 100 entrants to the recent competition. He submitted entries in two categories, light lager and brown ale.

Patience is an essential virtue for any vintner or brewer as Peter explains. The initial stage in the fermentation process takes one week to 10 days which must be followed by a secondary stage of approximately a month's duration. Th

PHOTO BY MIKE KING

Brewmaster Peter Slosberg displays his award winning a...bon bestowed upon it at the ...er-making competition.

...wing purists start with a ...hing" which is the boiling ...wers will begin with malt ...e added hops and the ...the desired product. ...for his craft is so con- ...w part of a growing ...who are brewing and ...ng sessions to share ...Prospective brewers ...to contact Peter in ..., Building 5.

Former ROLM employee sticks with alma mater

Pete Slosberg shows off his wickedly famous ale.

Former ROLM employee leaves company. Takes full-time position with firm he co-founded. Not long after, his new company purchases a ROLM telecommunications system. A foregone conclusion, right?

Not in Pete Slosberg's case. When his Pete's Brewing Co. bought a ROLM 9200 CBX with PhoneMail in late 1993, hard-headed financial and performance reasons — not sentimentality — formed the basis for the decision.

"We looked at AT&T, Northern Telecom and ROLM systems," says Slosberg, who spent about a dozen years in marketing and technical positions at ROLM before leaving in late 1992. "ROLM's wasn't the least expensive one, but it could do everything we needed it to do, and had plenty of capacity to accommodate our growth. The ability to upgrade and the support that came with it were very important. Also, it will help us save enough money in certain areas to cover our monthly payments on the system."

Palo Alto-based Pete's Brewing Co., founded in 1986, recently ranked 33 on Inc. Magazine's list of 500 fastest-growing privately held companies in the United States, and is the nation's fifth-largest micro brewery. It needed much more capacity and flexibility than its old key system and outside voice messaging service could provide.

The 9200 system, combined with PhoneMail, T1 links and Dialed Number Identification Service (DNIS), helps outside salespeople nationwide stay in touch with the business more easily. It also reduces the company's trunk and messaging costs, and makes it easier for people calling before or after normal business hours to leave messages.

Hard sell

Was Slosberg an easier or a more difficult sell because of his ROLM background?

"With his history at ROLM, Pete had a level of trust that allowed us to move forward and cut through a lot of the normal sales cycle kind of positioning," Hal Marty, the sales rep who handled the account, notes. "His expectation was high and his level of knowledge was high. So we had discussions at a very intricate level — much more so than with most customers."

"The voice messaging service we used before was costly," Slosberg says. "Under the old setup, it was costing us between 20 and 30 cents a minute for people to check messages. Now, it's about 12 cents a minute. Besides that, having the 800 number routed over a T1 span eliminates the need for direct-inward-dial numbers and separate trunks for each line. We save probably 50 percent compared to our previous trunk costs."

... hard-headed financial and performance reasons — not sentimentality — formed the basis for the decision.

continued on page 16

not every project I worked on was fun, many were. For a while I found myself product manager for something called the USCBX. You have to understand that in the high-tech world, acronyms dominate. ROLM's main product was the CBX, or Computerized Branch Exchange (an automated version of the telephone switchboard like the one comedienne Lily Tomlin uses in her routines). The CBX product line included the VSCBX, SCBX, MCBX, LCBX, and VLCBX. VS stood for very small, S for small, and so on. Pretty creative!

The product family was being reinvented with the code name USCBX, where US stood for ultra secret, but which we wanted our competitors to think was short for ultra small. It was a complete product-line replacement, and we didn't want outsiders to know what was going on, so the ultra-small imagery was heavily promulgated. This new product family was actually made up of three distinct products: U0, U1, and U2. I was the product manager for U0. Another thing I like about high-tech is that engineers don't do things in a way that makes sense to normal people. For example, the standard numbering system doesn't start at 1. With computers, numbering starts at 0. Thus, U0 was the first in the product series.

We had progressed to the point of actually installing a working product in the lab and exercising the equipment. This was known as "going to ROLM Trial." ROLM Trial was a major milestone, and we were going to celebrate when we reached it. I approached the vice president in charge of the program to see if it would be okay to brew a commemorative beer with a special label for the team. His reaction was positive,

My celebratory label for the USCBX product.

but he made a caveat that because the program was still secret, there could be no reference to USCBX anywhere on the label. We took this as a challenge.

One fellow Worry Wort worked in the media department, and we put our heads together to come up with a label that would commemorate the event while not giving away any information about the product. We dreamed up Ewe Zero with a sheep. Unfortunately, the program was killed right at ROLM Trial, and instead of celebrating, we drank the beers at a product wake. I know of only one remaining bottle, and the guy who owns it still won't give me a value on it so I can trade with him.

Beer had become a major focal point for me by that time in my life. Whenever I traveled, I had to try the beers of the local microbrewery or brewpub. I also became a beer-can collector (up to 1,100 and counting). Every liquor store or grocery store that I passed in my travels was a potential source of a can I didn't have. My collection consists almost exclusively of contemporary cans that I can say I have drunk from. I wouldn't dare do that with an older can! My obsession with collecting cans has driven my wife and kids nuts. Even my business associates have had to put up with my wandering inside of stores around the world.

On a trip to Mexico, I went so far as to go to the American Embassy to check on how many beer cans I could bring into the United States. I knew about limits on spirits and wines but had never seen anything about beer. My fear was that I'd buy a ton of beer cans and then have customs either say I couldn't bring them in or slap me with a bill for duty on the beer. The man at the embassy had to look it up, but he came back smiling and said that it wasn't a federal issue, only a state issue. If I was foolish enough to carry the weight of all the beer, that was my perogative. Since major ports of entry were manned by the feds, there would be no issue with beer because, in practice, the feds never cared. I've only had a couple of customs agents make wise-cracks about all of the cans I was carrying.

I told this story to Mark Stutrud, the founder and owner of Summit Brewing in St. Paul, Minnesota, and he laughed. Once, on a trip to Canada, he came back to the States through a small port of entry in northern Minnesota that was manned by state officials rather than the feds. He had to pay extra duty to bring the beers into the United States!

When I give speeches around the country and relate the story of how I got into beer, I love it when some perceptive listener raises his or her hand at the end of the talk to ask whatever became of the cabernet we made that led me into the whole beermaking process. For a birthday gift in 1980, Amy bought me a seven-and-a-half-gallon French oak cask to store it in. The wine had been resting about a year in the glass carboys and was doing extremely well. The cask came with no instructions, but I figured I'd wash it out a couple of times just to make sure it was clean. After all, I knew enough to know that cleanliness is next to godliness when it comes to fermentation. What I didn't realize is that it takes a lot of washings to get the strong oak flavor out of a cask. Unfortunately, I didn't wash it out enough, so the cabernet was not only oaky, it was undrinkable. Years later a friend laughed when I told him that I had cleaned the cask out twice. He told me I really should have cleaned it fifty—yes fifty—times. Thank God I had discovered beer in the meantime!

CHAPTER 3

THE MAGIC OF BREWING

No one "manufactures" great beer. Brewing is a precision craft.
—VACLAV JANOUSKOVEC, day-shift boss at Pilsner Urquell,
from *National Geographic*, September 1993

B eermaking is a relatively simple, if delicate, process. Anyone can make a world-class beer at home. When I started brewing my own beer, I realized that there was a lot more to beer than I had ever thought. By learning what beer really was and how it was made, my appreciation of beer grew, as did my enjoyment of it. If all you know about beer is that it somehow shows up in the cooler section of the grocery store, you're missing out on a lot. When you're picking a beer to drink from a wide selection of beers, how do you know which ones you might like and which ones to avoid?

On the basis of color and style descriptors, you can have a good idea what a beer ought to taste like. You can learn where the flavor comes from and what flavors there are. Many people let their lack of knowledge turn into a fear of trying something new; they buy what they've always bought instead of exploring the world of options available to them. Understanding more about the beermaking process can remove that fear and increase your enjoyment of beer. One common misconception is thinking that beer is made from hops. It's made from grain. Hops are a spice that increases the bitterness and aroma of beer.

This chapter and the next are intended to give you a simplified idea of what goes on during the brewing process, when the taste and aroma of a beer are developed. Knowing something about the

Picture of me in the government cellar at Minnesota Brewing Company in St. Paul, Minnesota.

different steps will help you appreciate the great varieties of beers and the subtle differences among them. Later on, we'll look into a few technological innovations and see how they have affected beer. If you're interested in homebrewing or in learning more about industrial brewing, there are many good technical books available.

1. MALTING THE BARLEY

Malting is sprouting the grain seed in water and then drying it. The brewer must break down the complex starches inside the grain so that during mashing, enzymes in the grain can convert these more simple starches into sugars. The brewer must not let the sprouting seed grow too much because as the seed grows, the starch is consumed by the growing roots and leaves. Brewers have traditionally inhibited growth with heat. In the past, the wet grain was placed on screens over a fire. Nowadays, hot air is blown through the wet grain in very large kilns.

Once the grain sprouts, it's called malt. A low drying temperature will result in a lightly colored malt. The longer the grain is held in the kiln and the higher the temperature is, the darker the resulting malt will be.

People are often surprised to learn that the color of beer comes directly from the types and quantities of malts used. For example, pale malt gives beer a golden color. Caramel malt results in an amber or reddish beer. Chocolate and black-patent malt yield brown and black beers, respectively. By the way, the terms "caramel" and "chocolate" do not stem from flavors, but rather from the color of the liquid produced when the different grains are used.

Another surprise is that the flavor of beer also comes primarily from the kilning of the malt. The pale malt used for golden beers should result in a bready or "crackery" basic taste. Caramel malt, because it roasts longer than pale, gives beer a nutty or slightly roasted flavor similar to Grape Nuts cereal. Chocolate malt gives beer a slightly burnt taste, if used in moderation. If used in greater quantity, chocolate or black-patent malt will result in a very burnt flavor, like that found in a stout.

> **WHY BARLEY?**
>
> If not the oldest, at least the most important ingredient for brewing beer is barley. In fact, the origin of the word "barley" comes from the Celtic word *bere-lec,* which means beer plant. Barley is so well suited for beermaking that it is used in nearly all industrial beer. It tastes good, has a husk that helps filter the wort during the lautering stage, and is one of the few grains that contains enzymes— the chemical "scissors" that cut starch down into sugars. Generally speaking, barley is not, in its own right, very useful as an article of food since it isn't well adapted to bread-making. Indeed, in the Middle Ages many countries prohibited the use of wheat and other grains for beermaking in order to preserve them for food purposes; that left barley for the brewers' use.

One side benefit of being in the beer business was having the opportunity to create an educational video about beer and brewing. The segment on malting was enhanced by a visit to a malt house, where the process could be filmed. After donning a white "clean-room" suit, I was allowed to wiggle my way into the three-foot bed of drying grain in the kiln. The temperature was about 130 °F, but it didn't feel too hot because of the very swift wind blowing through the kiln. The space was filled with the aroma of toasting bread, and before long the temperature began to lull me to sleep. It was a womb-like

THE BREWING PROCESS

STEP	REASONS
Beer Only:	
1. Malting the barley	• Soaking, sprouting, and drying the grain
	• Converting complex starches
2. Milling the barley	• Cracking the malt and separating the husks
	• Maximizing the surface area of the malt
3. Mashing the barley (liquid now called wort)	• Creating amino acids for yeast food
	• Adjusting the acidity of the liquid
	• Creating fermentable and unfermentable sugars
4. Lautering or coarse filtering of the wort	• Creating a filter bed of husks
	• Filtering grain particles from the wort
	• Spraying water in to extract more sugar
5. Boiling the wort with hops in the brew kettle	• Creating bitterness in the wort
	• Sterilizing the wort
	• Driving off grain aromas
	• Caramelizing some sugars in the wort and darkening it
	• Coagulating proteins so they'll drop to the bottom
	• Boiling to concentrate the wort
6. Whirlpooling the wort	• Spinning the hot wort to drop out the solids (trub)
	• Saturating the wort with air (yeast requires oxygen)
7. Cooling the wort	• Cooling to 60 °F before adding yeast
Beer and Wine:	
8. Injecting or pitching the yeast	• Streaming in the yeast for good mixing
9. Fermenting (the wort is now called beer)	• Allowing a three- to seven-day cycle to convert sugar into alcohol
10. Storing or aging the fermented beer	• Transferring beer to new storage tanks
	• Separating the beer from the yeast
	• Allowing the beer to age for weeks or months
	• Mellowing harsh young flavors
	• If desired, adding dry hops
11. Packaging in kegs, bottle, or cans	• Packaging the beer for sale
	• Bottles or cans must be pasteurized at this step
12. Shipping and consuming	• Off to your favorite watering hole for pure enjoyment

experience; the cares of the world just disappeared. I suppose it's sort of like taking a mud bath, but with a much better smell. Get to know your local maltster, and maybe you too might get a chance to experience true relaxation.

2. MILLING THE BARLEY

Milling barley involves putting the malted barley between two rollers and crushing the seeds. Milling cracks open the hard barley husk and exposes the starchy material inside the seed, called the endosperm. The husk is saved for a later process called lautering. The endosperm is cracked into many smaller pieces so that more of the barley's surface area will be exposed to the hot water and enzymes during the mashing process, which then results in more starch being converted into sugars.

3. MASHING THE BARLEY

To make an "infusion mash," the crushed barley is placed in a "mash tun" or large tub and mixed with hot water. The mash tun, usually fitted with a steam jacket, heats the water to a final temperature of about 170 °F. That temperature is held constant to allow for certain chemical reactions to take place. This process, called a "step infusion," is the more typical method of doing a mash.

> **A YARD OF ALE**
>
> When brewers want to gauge the strength of their beer, they use a device called a hydrometer or saccharometer, which was invented in the eighteenth century to measure the density of brewing liquids. Saccharine is another term for sugar, and the saccharometer measures the concentration of dissolved sugar. It looks a lot like a thermometer with weights at the bottom, and it floats in liquid.
>
> In those days, "flint-glass"—a yard long and of sufficient diameter to allow the saccharometer to float freely—allowed for easy readings. A graduated scale on the flint-glass showed what level the saccharometer was floating at and thus the strength of the beer. Once the measurement had been taken, the flint-glass was used as a drinking vessel. (What else would a reasonable brewer do after taking a measurement of the gravity of the beer? Throw the beer out? No way! They drank it. Thus, the ale-yard became today's yard of ale.

Another method is called "decoction mashing." Instead of heating all of the crushed barley and liquid in the mash tun, part of the mash liquid is drawn off and boiled in another vessel, then returned to the mash tun. This step is repeated several times to raise the temperature of the mash.

MALTING

The process of malting, though complex, was documented centuries ago. The following poem, from a thriteenth-century Norman French text, was written by Walter de Biblesworth and is one of the earliest European references to malting:

Ale shall now engage my pen to set at rest the hearts of men.

First, my friend, your candle light; next of spiced cake take a bite.

Then steep your barley in a vat, large and broad, take care of that;

When you shall have steeped your grain and the water let out-drain,

Take it to an upper floor, if you've swept it clean before;

There couch and let your barley dwell, till it germinates full well.

Malt you now shall call the grain, corn it ne'er shall be again.

Stir the malt then with your hand, in heaps or rows now let it stand;

On a tray then you shall take it to a kiln to dry and bake it.

The tray and eke a basket light will serve to spread the malt aright.

When your malt is ground in mill, and of hot water has drunk its fill

And skill has changed the wort to ale, then to see you shall not fail

Miracles and marvels; Lo! Two candles out of one do grow.

Ale makes a layman a good clerk, to one unknown it gives a mark.

Ale makes the strong go on all fours and fill the streets with shouts and roars.

The good ale from the malt at length so draws the barley's pride and strength,

That a royster's figure head needs no dye to make it red.

Here then let the matter rest. To talk of other things were best.

HUSK

The husk is very important to the brewer. After the wort is transferred into the lauter, the husk, which is heavier than water, sinks to the bottom and forms a thick layer. The brewer opens the holes at the bottom of the lauter tun and the sweet wort slowly trickles down through the husk layer, which filters out the particles of grain.

If you use wheat as your grain of choice, there is no husk. Imagine trying to filter the sweet wort through Cream of Wheat cereal; you get a thick sludge that is gummy and just barely lets the wort trickle through. Using oats gives you oatmeal cereal and the same slow filtering.

The barley husk makes the brewer's job much more manageable! Lautering with barley takes about one to two hours. It can take several days for the wort to filter through when wheat or oats are used as the base grain.

Mashing was the key mystery of brewing before the invention of the thermometer and the saccharometer, a type of hydrometer for measuring the sugar concentration of a solution. The brewer's technique is critical at this stage because small variations in temperature can change the very soul of the brew. The temperature of the hot water determines which form of sugar will be produced when the enzymes react with the starches. Depending upon the temperature, some starches become fermentable, some not; some starches become sweet, some not. I learned this the hard way when I tried making homebrews from only grain. The temperature wasn't maintained at the correct level for the right amount of time, which yielded too few fermentable sugars and thus a very weak beer.

Once the sugars have been created in the hot water, the liquid is called wort. The brewer then raises the temperature to 170 °F, killing off the enzymes so they can't cause reactions as the wort cools.

4. "Lautering" or Coarse Filtering of the Wort

Wort contains barley husks, as well as all of the broken-up pieces of the inside of the seed that was primarily starchy material. These crushed pieces don't entirely disappear. The solids don't do the brewer any good from this point on, so how are they eliminated?

HEAT EQUALS COLOR EQUALS FLAVOR

The heat of the fire affects the color of the malt. The lower the temperature, the lighter the color. The higher the temperature, the darker or blacker the color.

There is some correlation between the color of the beer and the flavor of the beer. Malts that have been dried in the least amount of heat are called pale malts. These dried malts are light enough in color that they result in a golden beer. If you were to eat some pale malt, you'd discover that it tasted sort of bready or crackery. If you see a golden beer that's been made from barley, in most cases, it should have that bready or crackery taste.

Using a more-roasted barley malt—let's say a caramel malt—will result in a darker beer. Caramel malt tastes like Grape Nuts cereal, and it darkens or reddens the beer. If you see an amber or red beer, it most likely has a malt like caramel in it, and the beer should have a nuttyness flavor.

The more roasted the barley malt, the darker the grain gets, imparting a brownish or black color to the beer and developing a deep-roasted, if not burnt, flavor. My original beer, Pete's Wicked Ale, has a rich brown color with reddish highlights when you hold the beer to a bright light. Away from the light, it looks brown. The darkness comes primarily from a roasted barley malt known as chocolate malt. Amazingly, only 1 percent of the total grain used is chocolate malt, but this small percentage is enough though to darken the beer.

The wort is moved into a lauter tun, which has grooves cut into the bottom of the vessel that can be opened or closed. The heavier solids and husks settle to the bottom of the tank. At a typical large brewery, the husks form a layer about three feet thick. The brewer opens the grooves at the bottom of the tank and the sweet wort trickles through the nooks and crannies of the husk bed. The edges of the husks filter the malt particles coming down with the wort. Ultimately, you're left with clarified sweet wort and a lauter tun full of husks and other unwanted solids. (These spent grains are actually high in protein and are used in animal feed.)

BODY

Body is a descriptor for how thick a beer feels on the tongue. When you taste Budweiser and Guinness, you should be able to detect how thin in body Budweiser is and how thick and chewy Guinness is. Body is directly related to the mix of fermentable and unfermentable sugars in a beer. During the mashing phase, temperature is critical. There are literally hundreds of different forms of sugar. At 140 °F, the primary fermentable sugars, glucose (chemically speaking the simplest sugar) and maltose (the second most simple sugar), form. Larger chain sugars then form as the temperature goes up. Yeast cannot convert these larger sugars, so they remain in the liquid and contribute to the body, or thickness, of the beer.

5. BOILING THE WORT WITH HOPS IN THE BREW KETTLE

The clarified sweet wort and hops meet in a brew kettle for another round of boiling, so that acids in the hops can be dissolved into the wort. The acid humulone (alpha acid, one of the two resins found in hops) is actually a crystalline solid. If the hops were added to cold wort, the humulone would just drop to the bottom of the kettle and not dissolve. Heat makes humulone soluble, so that it will dissolve into the wort. The sweet wort now becomes bitter.

The good news is that boiling sterilizes the wort, killing off any bacteria or wild yeast it may have harbored. When the bittered wort is cooled and the brewery's specific strain of cultured yeast is added, the yeast completely controls fermentation; the beer won't be affected by other critters that might have changed the character of the beer. The bad news is that boiling drives off the wonderful aroma of hops. Then again, the grain used in mashing has also imparted an aroma to the wort, and many of those aromas aren't pleasant, at

least not if you're trying to enjoy a beer! Boiling acts to drive off
these unpleasant grain aromas. To recover the hops aroma, some
hops may be added at the end of the boil to impart hop oils into
the beer.

The heat from boiling creates browning compounds from the
malt and the sugars. This has a caramelizing effect and helps to slightly
darken the beer. Typical boils in the brew kettle are 1 to 1½ hours.
Anheuser Busch boils for about 30 minutes. (Their beers are very light
in color, aren't they?) Miller boils for about 45 minutes. Coors boils for
about 2 hours, but given that Golden, Colorado, is more than 5,000 feet
above sea level, it takes longer to produce the desired effects of boiling.

Finally, boiling concentrates the
wort through evaporation. A
typical boil in the kettle will
result in a 5 to 10 percent
reduction in water volume. In
this way, the concentration of
sugar is increased.

What has made hops
the most common beer spice?
First, hops are very bitter; second, the aroma is pleasing; and
last but not least, hops contain
a preservative. This last attribute
is very significant. Beer is a perishable product and pasteurization was not invented until the
mid- to late-1800s. Before that,
beer went bad fairly quickly.

SPARGING

During lautering, all the sugars make the wort hot and
sticky. As the wort flows through the husk bed, sugars stick
to the grain and the husks. You've gone through all this
work to create these sugars and a lot of it has ended up
sticking to material that you will soon be throwing out. In
a process called "sparging," these residuals sugars can be
recovered by spraying the husk and malt bed with hot
water. Derived from the French word *asperger,* meaning to
sprinkle, sparging was developed by Scottish brewers in the
middle of the 1800s. Showering too much hot water over
the grain bed can leech out tannins in the husk and turn the
beer astringent or sharply metallic in taste.

In medieval times, brewers would make several classes of
beer: normal beer, table beer, and beer for servants. The difference between them was that normal beer was produced
from the free running of the wort through the grain bed.
After that, table beer would be created by reprocessing the
same grain bed with hot water, making a weaker version of
the beer. Beer for servants came from a third processing of
the same grain. In this way, brewers would extract every bit
of sugar possible from the grain. Each version was progres-
sively weaker and sharper-tasting.

Beer made with some bittering agent other than hops may have lasted
about a week before spoiling; beer made with hops would last two to
three weeks before spoiling. These estimates assume that the brewers

kept fairly good sanitary conditions, which more often than not wasn't the case. Hopped beer, nonetheless, kept longer.

6. WHIRLPOOLING THE WORT

Why whirlpool the wort? It's actually a form of filtration to separate solids formed in the brew kettle during the boiling process. While the wort is boiling away, small solid particles of tannins and proteins are sloshing around. As they hit one another, they tend to stick together and form larger particles. The whirlpool is just a round tank, but hot wort from the brew kettle is streamed around the outside curvature of the tank, creating a whirlpool. Solids in spinning liquid tend to aggregate in the middle of the bottom of the tank. A cone of solids, called "trub," will ultimately accumulate. The clarified wort will be drawn off, away from the trub.

RULE OF THUMB

Before the invention of the thermometer in the 1760s, brewers had to judge when to add yeast to the sweet liquid made from barley and water (called the wort). If yeast is added while the wort is still too hot, the heat kills the yeast. If the wort cools off too much, the yeast will have a tough time propagating, and that will stall fermentation. Brewers measured the wort's temperature by dipping a thumb or finger into the cooling wort. When it felt like the correct temperature (close to body temperature), they added the yeast and could be fairly confident about getting a proper fermentation. In short, "rule of thumb" means, when it feels good, do it.

7. COOLING THE WORT

Before boiled wort is ready for fermentation, it must be cooled to 60 °F through the use of a heat exchanger. A heat exchanger is similar to a car's radiator. The hot wort is pumped into the heat exchanger, which has a setup of tubes within tubes. The hot wort tubes are surrounded by cold water tubes. The heat is absorbed by the cold water and the wort is cooled. After cooling, the wort is saturated with air because the yeast requires oxygen for its growth prior to fermentation. Before the invention of the thermometer, brewers stuck their thumbs in the wort to determine if it had cooled sufficiently for fermentation to begin without killing the yeast.

8. INJECTING OR "PITCHING" THE YEAST

Yeast is a microscopic fungus and needs to be evenly distributed throughout the wort for optimal fermentation. In general, the amount of yeast added or "pitched" is about 12 million cells per milliliter. As the yeast propagates during fermentation, the density of yeast cells multiplies dramatically (by about six or seven times).

Yeast is a unicellular fungus that comes in two basic forms, top- and bottom-fermenting. The scientific name for the genus of yeast used in brewing beer, is *Saccharomyces,* from the Latin "Saccharo," meaning sugar and "myces" meaning fungus. The mysterious entity that ferments beer literally means "sugar fungus."

Yeast can cloud beer, but it also adds a flavor and aroma I'll call yeastiness! Yeast is high in B vitamins, but our government, in its infinite wisdom, does not allow brewers to put any nutritional information on beer labels. They don't want the public to see that beer is actually good for you.

MAKING BEER VERSUS MAKING WINE

When I'm on the road, wine advocates (we call them "winos") sometimes tell us "beer geeks" that wine is more elegant and much more difficult to make than beer. There are points to be made on both sides of the debate, but being a beer guy I think beermaking is more difficult. Why? To make any fermented beverage you have to have a sterile sweet liquid in which the yeast can ferment. In winemaking, God delivers that liquid neatly packaged in a grape. All the winemaker has to do is crush the grape. To make beer, you have to create that sterile sweet liquid yourself, which involves all the steps of malting, mashing, lautering, and boiling. After we cool the wort, in a metaphoric sense, we have finally achieved the juice of the grape.

9. FERMENTING — THE WORT IS NOW CALLED BEER

Fermentation takes place when yeast converts the fermentable sugars—glucose and maltose—into alcohol, carbon dioxide, and a few other by-products. There are thirteen distinct metabolic steps yeast goes through to produce alcohol, so the yeast has to work very hard. It's been estimated that a typical yeast cell will eat about 60 million glucose molecules per second during fermentation. Now *that* is serious work!

The rate of fermentation is fairly constant, but results will vary based on the particular strain of yeast and the particular by-products

Kegging beer at Minnesota Brewing Company.

it's known for. Temperature is also a key factor in fermentation. In general, ales ferment for three to four days while lagers ferment for about seven days. The higher temperature of the ale fermentation accelerates the overall process.

10. STORING OR AGING THE FERMENTED BEER

Eventually the yeast from fermentation either rises to the top or drops to the bottom of the tank. The yeast is harvested, and the beer is transferred to another tank. In the new tank, the beer is allowed to "ruh," or sit, for a length of time at cold temperature. (In German *ruh* means "to rest"; *lager* means "to store.") During this time, the aging and development of the beer takes place. Yeasty, grassy, and sulfury flavors decrease and the beer mellows. Ales are stored usually up to a maximum of a month; lagers can be aged for several months.

11. PACKAGING IN KEGS, BOTTLES, OR CANS

Once beer has been properly aged, diatomaceous earth (DE) is used to filter and clarify the beer. (DE is the fossilized skeletons of microscopic diatoms. These skeletons have sharp nooks and crannies that do a great job of grabbing any remaining solids in the beer.) The beer is then sent to the "government cellar." From here, beer has to be packaged in order to be sold. Some beer may be pumped into kegs, and the kegs are then bunged. That sounds simple, but it's actually a lot of work. The kegs are kept ice-cold from then on. Because cans and bottles are not necessarily kept cold all of the time like kegs, that beer must go through an additional step called pasteurization.

During pasteurization, the beer is heated to a point at which any potential bacteria in the beer will be killed off. This keeps the beer stable; that is, it won't go bad due to any live critters left in the liquid. That's great news; the down side is that the heat needed to kill off the bacteria quickens the aging of the beer. So what does pasteurization mean to the average drinker? It just means that right after packaging unpasteurized keg beer will have a fresher taste than pasteurized beer. After a couple of weeks, the differences won't be as obvious: Pasteurized beer of the same age as unpasteurized beer will taste like it's a couple of weeks to a month older.

KRAEUSENING

"Kraeusening" is a process whereby new, one-day-old fermenting beer is added to already fermented beer, usually with the new beer making up 15 percent of the total mixture. Yeast will work on the newly fermenting beer, which will still have a high sugar content, and the carbon dioxide given off will "naturally" carbonate the beer.

Kraeusening demands exacting timing, for it should only be done when the yeast in the newly fermenting beer has reached the stage at which it is ready to metabolize diacetyl, sulphur compounds, and metabolic mistakes in the already fermented beer that it has been added to. Although the resulting carbonation may be nice, the main purpose of kraeusening is to clean up flavors in the beer. Unless the timing is correct, you will get carbonated, but not necessarily cleaner, beer.

12. SHIPPING AND CONSUMING

Drink beer as "young" as you can get it. Don't pass "Go," and collect $200 dollars, and store the beer at home. The only exceptions to this rule are beers that are high in alcohol or hops. Alcohol is a preservative,

The engraving from the Universal Magazine *of 1748/9 shows contemporary brewing in detail.* **A** *is the big copper heated by the furnace,* **C. D** *is described as a mash-vat or tub, and* **E** *is the mashing oar. Below this,* **F** *is a receiver to under-vat and, at the top,* **B** *is a "rudder, lead, or pump" to pump up the wort out of the receiver into the copper to boil. On the floor,* **G** *shows two ladles, one with a long and one with a short handle.* **H** *marks the coolers and* **I** *is a pump at the back of the copper that fills it with cold water. The water from* **I** *is also used to wash the casks,* **K**, *as well as the working tubs, tuns, and barrels.*

and hops also contain a natural preservative, so high hop bitterness carries with it a higher level of preservative. Also, if a beer still has live yeast in it, then any oxygen that got in during packaging will be absorbed by the yeast and thus extend, or push off, the aging process. Beers that combine high alcohol, hop bitterness, and yeast, like some Belgian Trappist ales, will last a long time. I just had such a bottle of a beer from 1986, and it tasted great!

NOT ALWAYS SO SCIENTIFIC

Making beer hasn't always been such a scientific process, but the lack of biochemical knowledge has never prevented humans from making it! Whenever people ask me how hard it is to do homebrewing, my answer is simple: Anyone can make an incredible, world-class beer at home. Use decent ingredients, keep everything clean, and you should be able to make some great beer. The difficulty is in being able to create a given taste more than once. There are so many variables in brewing that it's very hard to consistently brew good beer. In medieval England, the brewing guilds were called "The Mystery of Brewing." These brewers made beer even though they had no idea what was actually happening. Thank heaven they never gave up!

THE GOVERNMENT CELLAR

Historically, the government cellar was where the government took its measurements of how much beer a brewery produced. The government now levies an excise tax of $18 per barrel (about 14 cases). Small brewers only pay $7 per barrel on the first 60,000 barrels. More important to today's beer drinkers, the government cellar is home to the freshest beer on the face of the earth. This is the ideal place to go grab a cold one. The finished beer has not been exposed to light or heat or air, so the aging process has not started yet. This beer is incredible—I can't rave about it enough. Having access to the government cellar is the main benefit of working for a beer company. Even beers from the big guys are very drinkable when they arrive in the producers' government cellars.

CHAPTER 4

KEEPING IT SIMPLE:
BEER, ALE, AND LAGER

The best beer in the world is the one in my hand.
—CHARLIE PAPAZIAN

In the United States alone, beer retailers sell on the order of 60 billion 12-ounce bottle equivalents each year. That's over 300 six-packs a second. That's a lot of beer. With the advent of the specialty beer movement, brewing companies have invented and re-invented many different Old World styles and flavors. This wide range of choice is a relatively new phenomenon. Until about ten years ago, the only choices you had were the few the big guys saw fit to offer; alternatives didn't really exist, or if they did, they were hard to find.

As I traveled around, I began to wonder if the proliferation of all of these "new" styles was causing confusion. I asked retailers all over the country how they dealt with customer questions about beer. Were people confused about porters, stouts, Trappists, or *bocks?* What I discovered was that the variety of styles was not where people were getting confused; it was the common terms people hear and use all the time that caused most of the misunderstandings. I love getting up in front of large audiences of beer retailers and beer wholesalers and asking them questions about beer. These folks have been selling beer for decades, so you'd think they'd know something about it by now.

My initial question to these groups is, "How would you explain the difference between a beer, an ale, and a lager in terms that any customer can understand?" Beer, ale, and lager—these are the most common words in the brewing industry, and yet most people neither know how to define nor how to explain the differences between them. Many people believe that an ale must be dark, strong, and bitter. A smaller number of people believe lagers have to be dark and bitter. Both beliefs are so far from correct that it is obvious that the general public lacks some of the most basic information about beer.

The definitions are actually quite straightforward. The hard part is being extremely careful not to let preconceived notions get in the way of reality.

THE TASTE OF BEER

"Beer" is a generic term for a fermented liquid made from grain. It doesn't matter what the grain is. Most specialty brewers utilize barley and, to a much lesser extent, wheat. Large industrial brewers use rice and corn as adjuncts to a smaller amount of barley in their beers. African beers are made from sorghum and millet. Other beers can be made from rye and oats.

I like to use the term "specialty brewer" to refer to those who make beers with distinctive color, taste, and aroma. These characteristics differentiate many of the new beers coming onto the market from the widely available light golden beers produced by the mass-market brewing concerns.

Taste is very subjective. To call barley the best-tasting beer grain is going out on a limb. Fortunately for me, I've loved the taste of barley malt since I was a kid. When I first tried beer, though, I couldn't help but wonder why people were so into it. There really wasn't much flavor, or aroma, and the little there was wasn't that enticing. To me, beer just smelled and tasted weird.

As I've come to find out, the big brewers utilize a variety of grains in their beers, including rice and corn, which diminish the color, flavor, and aroma that barley imparts. What caused this conversion from all-barley to brewing with added grains like rice? By the

FIRST U.S. LAGER

The first U.S. lager was brewed in 1840 by John Wagner, who had a small brewery in the back of his house on St. John Street in Philadelphia. Wagner brought the first lager yeast to the United States from a brewery in Bavaria where he had worked as a brewmaster.

The first U.S. brewery to routinely make cultured lager yeast was the Joseph Schlitz Brewing Company of Milwaukee. Other American brewers began to accept this practice starting in 1886. Using cultured yeast was probably one of the most important steps in putting the American brewing industry on a scientific basis and moving it away from the haphazard methods employed before this time.

BRITAIN MEANS BEER!

You know that beer has to be important to a civilization when there's an outside chance that the very name of the country may have come from beer! Several sources have indicated that "Britain" may have been derived from the Ancient Greek word, βρυτον. According to an ancient Greek dictionary, βρυτον means malt liquor made from barley. As a judge at the Great British Beer Festival in London, I had the opportunity to meet with the British Guild of Beer Writers. None of the writers had heard about this Greek word or the possible derivation of "Britain." At least some of the people I've mentioned this to in the United States know that "America" comes from the name of the New World explorer, Amerigo Vespucci. Wouldn't it be terrific if Great Britain actually means "Great Beer"?

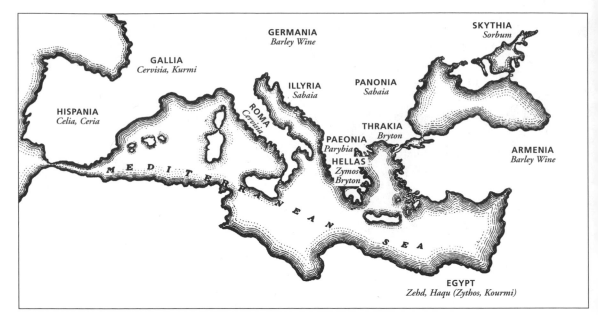

GERMANIA
Barley Wine

SKYTHIA
Sorbum

GALLIA
Cervisia, Kurmi

ILLYRIA
Sabaia

PANONIA
Sabaia

HISPANIA
Celia, Ceria

ROMA
Cervisia

THRAKIA
Bryton

PAEONIA
Parybia

ARMENIA
Barley Wine

HELLAS
Zymos
Bryton

M E D I T E R R A N E A N   S E A

EGYPT
Zehd, Haqu (Zythos, Kourmi)

Geographical distribution of beermaking peoples in pre-medieval times.

1870s, most American beer drinkers had opted for lager beers over ales, porters, and other English styles. Moreover, American taste tended toward the Pilseners (light golden) over the darker Munichs. Brewers of the time discovered that barley containing less albumen (a protein) than starch made a more popular beer. Unfortunately, the barleys that were the most widely available then were high in albumen and low in starch. Brewers made up for this imbalance by using rice, and to a lesser extent corn, to increase the level of starch. Using such raw grain adjuncts also brought down the cost of production, something that was not lost on the brewers.

Using grain adjuncts, the big guys are able to produce very pale liquids with minimal flavor and aroma, which are likely to offend fewer drinkers. When a beer has definitive color, taste, and aroma, not everyone is going to like it. To maximize sales, the big brewers have taken more and more out of their beers over time. That was why I never really got into beer until I started homebrewing with just barley malt—the amazing ingredient that can make milk shakes taste even better, that flavors the to-kill-for center of Whoppers, and as it turns out, that makes beer the most magical of all beverages.

The Mystery of Chicha

In 1985, my wife and I were on vacation in Peru, traveling south from Lima to the Nazca desert to see a set of lines and shapes laid out on the desert floor. The whole design is only visible from the air, so some believe the patterns were made by visiting space travelers a long, long time ago. I had been doing some background reading on Peru and a native Indian corn beer called Chicha. This unusual beer is somehow fermented in the ground.

On the long drive to Nazca, our driver wouldn't speak to us (maybe because we were gringos) even though we knew enough Spanish to get by. About halfway to the Nazca area, I asked him where I could get some Chicha. His eyes lit up, and he started talking. I guess no gringos had ever asked about Chicha before. He immediately pulled off the main road into a small village, saying, "No problema" (probably the most commonly used phrase in South America, but that's another story). All I needed to do, he said, was to look for a red flag or cloth hanging on a pole. I was reminded of the descriptions of bushes and ale-stakes signifying pubs in early England. Once you knew what to look for, the red flags were everywhere.

We stopped by a street vendor and got out of the car. The vendor had a small cart with a couple of large, clear old-style, glass Pepsi bottles. They were not capped, and flies hovered around the opening. Through the clear glass of the bottle, I could see a cloudy golden liquid with pieces of grain floating in it. When we requested some Chicha, the vendor grabbed a couple of dirty glasses. At this point I asked myself, is this going to fun, interesting, or deadly? Well, Amy and I are still here. And it was a delightful-tasting beer. Not too alcoholic and about medium body, but very different from the taste of barley beers. For the rest of the trip, we saw red flags in

THE ORIGINS OF THE WORDS "ALE" AND "BEER"

The word "beer" appears to come from a technical term used in monasteries in the eighth century. Derived from the old High German form of *peor* or *bior,* it also corresponds to the old English-Saxon *beor.* The derivation of the German Benedictine word is most likely from the Latin word *bibere.*

"Ale" is derived from the Saxon word *alu* and the Danish *ol.* There is even a German word, *alufal,* that means beer jug.

the desert, on the coast, in the high Andes, literally everywhere. Chicha fascinated me.

When we returned to California, it dawned on me that corn lacks the enzymes necessary to break down starches into sugars. Enzymes are complex chemicals essential for processing barley malt in the making of beer. Enzymes break starches in the grain down into sugars that the yeast later converts to alcohol and carbon dioxide. Barley is rich in these enzymes. Wheat has some, but other grains have none.

How did they make Chicha without enzyme-laden barley? After some more research, I learned that native peoples around the world had discovered that we humans possess a very interesting natural ability: Our saliva has the enzyme necessary to break starches down into sugars. In Peru, native Indian women literally sit around and chew the fat, or should I say, the corn. In a process called mastication, the women chew the grain to get the saliva working on the corn and then spit the results into the brew pot. Although the process isn't exactly sanitary, the brew is boiled. I'm glad I found out about the process after we got back. Otherwise, I probably wouldn't have tried Chicha!

You can perform your own experiment to see how this process works. Take a piece of plain white bread or a cracker, put it in your mouth, and leave it there for about five minutes. Yes, it's hard to leave it there and it'll get real mushy. After five minutes, you'll discover that this mush turns sweet. That's from the enzymes in your saliva converting the starch in the bread or cracker to sugar.

If that isn't crazy enough, try to imagine how this process was discovered. If you accept that beer originated in gruel, then the process of chewing grain to convert it makes sense. Here's the scenario: Youths and adults with sufficient tooth strength could actually chew and eat the grain in the gruel. Infants and old people who had

THE DERIVATION OF "BERSERK"

The term "berserk" is from the Norse for "bare shirt." After consuming a bucket or two of a vibrant brew they called aul (ale) before going into battle, the Vikings would feel invincible and go berserk, literally going off to fight bare shirted, without any armor.

lost their teeth would have had to depend on others to chew the grain down to the point where they could eat it. Obviously, the initial chewing of the grain would have allowed the enzymes from saliva to start their magic. As the grain steeped in the gruel, the enzymes would have continued to do their thing, converting the starch to sugar in the warm gruel. Wild yeasts would have settled on this sweet liquid and started the fermentation process.

I'm sure it was a great pleasure for those people who first had access to barley, to discover that enzymes in the grain would do the work, rather than having to chew the grain to get things going.

A Simple Answer

Now then, if beer is the generic term for a fermented liquid made from grain, then what are ales and lagers? They are actually the two main types of beer. There are many technical ways to differentiate them, including the type of yeast used and the temperature of fermentation, but here's a definition of the difference in terms that any drinker can understand:

ALES HAVE A FRUITY, OR SOMETIMES SPICY, AROMA, AND LAGERS DON'T!

SAKE ISN'T REALLY WINE—IT'S BEER

Beer is a fermented beverage made from grain. Wine is a fermented beverage made from fruit. One general misconception is that sake, the popular beverage from Japan also known as rice wine, is actually a beer. In reality, sake is a rice beer, since it's made from grain —even if it does have the alcoholic strength of wine.

Wow. The difference really doesn't have to do with color, sweetness, bitterness, alcohol, or body? Wait a second, you're probably saying, that can't be right. There are lots of ways that ales and lagers are different. Ales have to be dark and bitter, don't they?

Debunking the Myths of Color and Bitterness

Color comes from the degree to which the grain is roasted and bitterness from the emphasis on hops. Brewers can make any beer range in color from light golden to very dark. Beers can also have a sweet or bitter emphasis. Ales and lagers both have sub-styles that demonstrate these different attributes. The simple fact is that ales do not have to be dark and bitter.

When I first developed Pete's Wicked Ale, an American brown ale, the only way I could get the word out about it was to go to as many tastings as possible. Given that Pete's Wicked Ale was my only beer at the time, everyone who came to the booth got a taste of it. I would pour a sample into the festival's commemorative cup. The visitor would hold it up, take a look, and say, "yuck!" This is a dark beer—I hate dark beers." After a lot of festivals, it finally dawned on me that these people were really saying, "Yuck! This looks like Guinness, and the one time I drank that, it tasted too bitter and burnt."

The only way I could get these people to try my beer was to offer them their money back if they didn't like the sample. Fortunately for me, 99 out of 100 people would try Wicked Ale and say, "Wow! I didn't know that dark beer could taste this good!" There really weren't any dark beers on the market at the time other than Guinness. Stouts are made from burnt malt and have a very strong burnt flavor and bitterness. Although, Wicked Ale was dark but not as dark, I had used only a small fraction of the burnt grain you'd find in a stout recipe. Wicked Ale had a sweetness to it as well as a bitterness.

The point is that often preconceived notions about beer are wrong. Ales don't have to be dark and bitter. They can be anything the brewer wants them to be.

Disproving the Yeast Myth

Other people have told me that ales are top-fermented and lagers are bottom-fermented. These terms don't mean anything to the vast majority of people and, even if they did, the differentiation between ales and lagers as being top- or bottom-fermenting has begun to disappear over the past decade or two. Contrary to popular belief "top-fermenting yeast" does not ferment at the top of the fermentation tank nor does bottom-

MAY POLE

The origins of the May pole and May games are rooted in ale. Ale-stakes, which ultimately became pub signs, date back to Roman times, when a bush or a sign of a bush outside a tavern indicated that ale or beer was available. The bush or sign of a bush later became a pole hanging from a building with a bush on it. If you ran a public drinking house, you were required to have an ale-stake to show that you were conducting a business where ale was being brewed for sale. This sign told the ale-stake conner (a city official) where to go to inspect and certify newly brewed ale. Ultimately, the ale-stake was transformed into a sign hanging off a pole on the side of pubs.

Up until the 1200s, the clergy participated heavily in Scot Ales and Church Ales, but then the bishops prohibited these drinking parties on church grounds and elsewhere. In any case, the ale-stake or May pole at the Scot Ales or Church Ales indicated the availability of hootch for the party! Scot Ales and Church Ales, by the way, are celebrations. The term *ale* in old England also meant a party or chance to drink beer. Party-goers generally had to pay for the beer and the recipient of the payment more or less defined the name of the ale. If the church got the money, it was called a Church Ale. Scot, in this case, means a tax, so a Scot Ale was a means to raise money for the local government.

WHEAT BEERS

If beer is based on barley, then how is it that so many wheat beers are becoming available? This is actually a case of mistaken identity. Remember the old joke, Who's buried in Grant's Tomb? Obvious answer, right? Not really. Both Grant and his wife are buried in Grant's Tomb. Well, wheat beers are not made from just wheat; they are made from wheat and barley. Most wheat beers contain about 50 percent wheat malt. The maximum amount of wheat you can use is about 80 percent because you need at least 20 percent barley malt to get enough husks in the lauter tun to allow sufficiently efficient filtering.

fermenting yeast ferment at the bottom. In reality, both kinds of yeasts ferment throughout the fermentation tank. "Top" and "bottom" refer to the ultimate destination of the yeast.

Top-fermenting yeast is distinguished by a protein on its cell wall. When the yeast converts sugar to alcohol and carbon dioxide, molecules of carbon dioxide accumulate until they form bubbles and begin floating to the surface of the fermentation tank. The protein on the top-fermenting yeast cell wall acts as an adhesive, allowing the yeast cells to literally stick to the bubbles that rise and form a layer at the top of the fermentation tank.

Bottom-fermenting yeast *does not* have this protein on its cell wall. During fermentation when the carbon dioxide is given off and the bubbles rise to the surface of the tank, the lack of the protein on the bottom-fermenting yeast cell wall means no free ride to the top. Gravity pulls these yeast cells to the bottom of the tank. Remember, it is the presence of the protein that determines whether the yeast is top- or bottom-fermenting—whether it rises to the top of the tank or sinks to the bottom.

So what's happened in last decade or two for there to be both top- and bottom-fermenting ales and top- and bottom-fermenting lagers? Suppose that you've been a bottom-fermenting lager brewery forever and have been very successful at it. All of a sudden, your marketing and sales departments come to you and say that, for competitive reasons, you have to start brewing ales (a top-fermenting yeast process). You immediately think to yourself, gee, it's going to cost us a lot of money to modify our fermentation tanks. Since we've been a very successful lager brewer, our equipment for harvesting the yeast at the end of fermentation has been designed to harvest the yeast from the bottom of the tank. If we try to ferment ales in the same tank, we're screwed, because the existing equipment can't harvest the yeast from the top. So what does the successful lager brewer do? It calls in the biochemical engineers. If you can't modify the equipment easily, why not modify the yeast—genetically engineer a top-fermenting lager yeast that won't have the protein on the cell wall? Then, your top-fermenting ale yeast becomes a bottom-fermenting lager yeast and your existing equipment doesn't have to be modified. Pretty slick!

When we started brewing Wicked Ale at Palo Alto Brewing Company (an ale brewery), we used a top-fermenting yeast. When we moved production to August Schell Brewing, we utilized a Whitbread bottom-fermenting ale yeast because Schell's was a lager (bottom-fermenting) brewery. Which brings us back to the main question: What, then, is the difference between an ale and a lager?

A TECHNICAL ANSWER

The answer should be given in terms that are understandable, measurable, and accurate. One major difference between ales and lagers comes from the temperature used for fermentation. Ales typically ferment in the 50 to 60 °F range; lagers ferment in the high 40 to 50 °F range. Does this temperature make a difference that is noticeable? You bet!

Fermentation produces many end-products. The most commonly known are alcohol and carbon dioxide. Yeast also creates chemicals called esters. Esters give fruity aromas to fruit and spicy aromas to spices. The higher the temperature, the more esters created during fermentation. The concentration of esters is critical because if it is not high enough, you can't smell them, even if they're there. The lower temperature of lager fermentation does produce esters, but not enough of them to be detected by the human nose. The higher temperature of the ale fermentation produces a much higher concentration of esters, enough for us to detect.

Xs ON BARRELS

When monks and monasteries were the main brewing entities, the heads of the casks were marked with single, double, triple, or more crosses to indicate the strength of the brew. The crosses were originally in the shape of a crucifix and were an indication that the monks had sworn an oath by the Cross that the ale was of the correct quality and strength, making the crosses one of the earliest forms of trademark. Over time, the coopers who made the casks took over this custom, and later the tax man took it over to levy the correct amount of tax.

Each individual strain of yeast creates its own set of esters, which produce the special aroma and flavor that brewers try to develop in their products. That's why brewers jealously guard their strains of yeast, and that's why homebrewers don't fare too well when trying to recreate commercial brews. A homebrewer may get the ingredients right and possibly some of the temperatures and timings of the mashing and boiling, but the beers don't come out the same as the commercial ones because a different yeast strain gives the beer a much different character.

Sometimes you'll hear about citrus or passion fruit aromas. The most incredible one I've experienced is from a Belgian ale called Rodenbach Grand Cru. This ale has the aroma of cherries, although no cherries are used in the beer. The aroma is strictly a by-product of the particular yeast strain used. Some German wheat beer yeasts give off the aroma of cloves or bananas or both. Again, there is no fruit or spice in these beers, just the unique esters that are developed by the yeast strains.

SO, WHICH CAME FIRST: ALES OR LAGERS?

Before the 1800s, yeast was a mystery. Originally, wild yeast carried on the winds would settle on the sweet liquid created from the grain and spontaneously ferment the liquid. Wild yeast was essentially a top-fermenting yeast, so for thousands of years beers were top-fermented —even the lagers of what would someday become known as Germany. The peoples of Germania fermented their beers at colder temperatures at an earlier stage, but, in general, they used top-fermenting yeast. As a matter of fact, one style of beer from Germany is called *altbier,* or "old beer," so named because it's a top-fermented beer conditioned at the colder temperatures of a lager.

LAGER YEAST HAS A NAME
The scientific name for lager yeast is *Saccharomyces carlsbergensis* (later renamed *Saccharomyces uvarum*) in honor of the pioneering work done at the Carlsberg brewery.

The creation of true lager beer is credited to Gabriel Sedlmayr of Munich and Anton Dreher of Vienna. They traveled around Britain in the 1830s studying British techniques. (At the time, Britain was the center of the brewing world. Most scientific advances relating to beer were made in Britain; it took decades for Germany to become a brewing powerhouse.) Sedlmayr and Dreher brought back to Germany two valuable instruments—the saccharometer and thermometer, which led to more scientific brewing. Sedlmayr applied these technologies to brewing with bottom-fermenting yeast in the late 1830s, Dreher in 1840.

In 1883, a brewer by the name of Emil Hansen, working at the Carlsberg brewery in Denmark, became the first person to utilize an absolutely pure yeast culture. He was able to propagate the yeast culture from a single selected cell. Until then, brewers like Sedlmayr and Dreher used bottom-fermenting yeast but always as mixtures of various yeast strains. Different strains might dominate from one batch to another, depending upon the environment. Hansen designed practical equipment that allowed him to culture pure or pedigreed families of yeast. That monumental effort made it possible to brew a consistent product, freed from the vagaries of other yeasts and bacteria that might change the final product.

So, one more time: How does one generally tell the difference between an ale and a lager? By the aroma!

Part Two

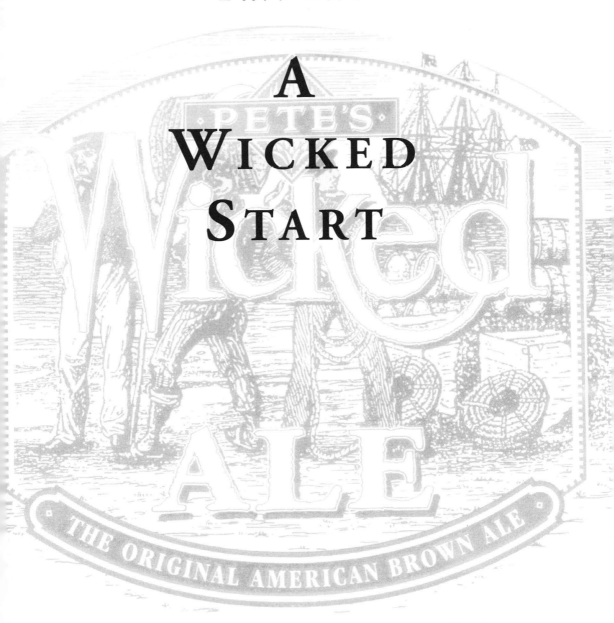

A
WICKED
START

CHAPTER 5

HAVING FUN IS SERIOUS BUSINESS

Of Doctors and medicines we have more than enough. What you may, for the love of God, send is some large quantity of beer.

—Dispatch from the Colony of New South Wales, Australia, 1859

Mark Bronder and I met at ROLM in 1979. Mark, a nondrinker then and now, left ROLM in the early 1980s for a venture capital firm. In 1984, he started bugging me about starting our own company. He had seen so many business plans go across his desk that he thought there was no reason that the two of us couldn't do our own thing and be successful. To be honest, at the time the idea of starting a company was not a priority for me.

One of the incredible employee benefits at ROLM was a twelve-week paid sabbatical every seventh year, and 1985 was to be my sabbatical year. I was tired and thought of nothing else but making it to the sabbatical. Imagine twelve weeks off with pay. Sounds good, doesn't it? Well, I made it even better by adding four weeks of vacation I hadn't had time to take, which gave me a total of sixteen weeks off. Amy couldn't take that much time off, but she did go on two four-week trips with me. I spent the time in between trips doing odd jobs around the house and improving my basketball skills.

Our first trip was to Europe. We spent just about all of our time in the Alps of Germany, Switzerland, and Austria. We had brought our four-year-old son along and took a leisurely route along back roads; we were having a beautiful time. Since I'd never been to the Alps before, I didn't know what to expect. I had this image of spending every afternoon sitting on the deck of an Alpine chalet with a first-rate European beer in one hand and a good cigar in the other. Although this didn't happen every day, it did come true many, many times. What a great way to relax! We especially loved Switzerland, where trams took us to mountaintops that sported welcoming restaurants with huge outdoor decks. The views of green valleys, clear blue skies, and snow-covered peaks were glorious. I can't describe how basking in the sun with a beer and a Cuban cigar hit the spot. Those afternoons seemed pretty close to heaven, literally as well as figuratively. Slow down, relax, and enjoy! Stop and think about what's really important and where you get your greatest satisfaction in life. I began to suspect that maybe corporate life wasn't where it's at.

After the first trip, Mark began to bug me again about starting a company. The idea was beginning to sound interesting, but I was engrossed in planning a four-week trip to the South American Andes. One thing was for sure: ROLM had been purchased by IBM, and already I could see the Big Blue bureaucracy in action. Our ROLM beer busts—and many other things—quickly became memories of a bygone past. Although the thought of starting a company to bring enjoyment to others began to form in my mind, traveling was still first on my sabbatical agenda.

We crossed the Andes from Argentina to Chile and spent time in the high Andes of Peru and Bolivia. This part of the world has its own fantastic scenery and interesting people, as well as some incredible beers. Sitting on top of a mountain overlooking Machu Pichu was one of the most amazing experiences I've ever had. Infused with the hauntingly beautiful music of Andean pipes, the scene had an other-worldly air about it. I certainly wasn't thinking of working at IBM/ROLM. I kept returning to the idea of starting a business with Mark.

My visit to South America taught me to slow down. When we started out, we had a fairly tight schedule to keep if we were going to make it to every place we planned on seeing. The problem is, South American planes, trains, and busses don't always run on schedule. One of the most frequently used words in South America is "soon." When does the plane leave? Soon. When does the train leave? Soon. There was absolutely nothing we could do to hurry things along. We just had to live with it. Getting pissed off and complaining would accomplish absolutely nothing. There are things I can stress over and change, but there are other things outside my control that I simply needed to let go of. So, why stress over it? I began to look forward to hearing that the plane would be departing "soon." I'd pull out a paperback, get relaxed, and start reading. This was actually very calming. Before long, the thought of going back to all that bureaucratic paperwork at IBM was a major turn-off. Why waste time on things that you can't really change? Maybe doing something on my own *was* the way to go.

> **MIND YOUR Ps AND Qs**
> In old England, when customers in pubs got out of hand, the owners or bartenders would yell out to the crowd to mind their *p*ints and *q*uarts and keep it down.

As amazing as the sabbatical benefit was for ROLM employees, I suspect that it wasn't an overall success for the company. A huge percentage of employees never came back from sabbatical for a variety of reasons, including whole lifestyle changes, career "readjustments," or even just a change of job or scenery. Certainly it motivated some people to stay at ROLM if they were within a year or two of their time off. As for me, I had worked ever since I was sixteen. Having sixteen weeks off gave me the opportunity to really reflect on what I enjoyed doing.

I finally decided to talk to Mark and see what we might do together. Mark wanted to start a company; I wanted a beer I could drink at home. Our thoughts went down the path of a beermaking company, but we also had some other criteria. First and foremost, we wanted to get in on the ground floor of a growing industry. We also wanted to have fun doing it.

Mark, Amy, and I used to go to comedy clubs in the city a lot. One night at The Other Café, we saw two comedians who called themselves the Booger Brothers. It was painfully obvious that this was their first night on stage. They had a routine that was so bad—I mean, so *incredibly* bad—that I burst out laughing. And then Mark couldn't stop laughing because I was laughing. Soon the whole club was laughing, just watching these two guys dying up there. It was hilarious. So when we talked about having fun, we wanted to make sure we had fun, but not the way the Booger Brothers came across.

We thought it would be hard to decide what we were going to do, but it was actually pretty easy. The Bay Area was the first hotbed of microbrewing. Anchor Brewing in San Francisco was ressurected in 1965. New Albion, in Sonoma, California, was the first real microbrewery, starting up in 1977. Sierra Nevada was started in Chico, California, about 1980. Mendocino Brewing and Buffalo Bill's were also among the original brewpubs. As a homebrewer and discriminating beer drinker, I could appreciate what these companies were doing. Even though they were making good beers and getting a lot of word-of-mouth recommendations, their beers remained relatively hard to find. However, slowly but surely, these beers were being seen in more and more places.

There were also microbreweries in the Pacific Northwest, New York, Massachusetts, and a few other locations. We thought,

A-ha! this may be the industry for us. The thought of building a company dedicated and devoted to making beer appealed to both of us. It was probably a little presumptuous, but I had won some awards with my homebrew, and we thought we had as good a chance as anybody else to make world-class beer. The other companies—and there were only a couple of dozen in existence at the time—were making good beers, but they were serious about their business. We saw an opportunity to make great beer while having great fun. We intended to develop a world-class product, but we were determined not to take ourselves too seriously.

We were impressed by how consumers seemed to get behind companies named for the people who founded them, like Ben and Jerry's or Mrs. Field's. We decided we'd use our names in the company name, maybe Mark and Pete's Brewing Company, or maybe Pete and Mark's Brewing Company. Ultimately, Mark thought we ought to use just my name because he wasn't a drinker and I was the brewer of the beer.

I suspect Mark may regret this decision, given the notoriety we achieved as a company—and, hound dog that he is, he's discovered it's harder to impress women if your name isn't on the label. For example, in 1994, I met twins Debbie and Lisa Ganz through our sales manager, David Glasser, in New York. They were planning on opening a restaurant called "Twins," and they wanted help with their beer menu. They've since become quite successful. Their concept is all the members of their staff who are visible to the public must be identical twins. You can't stop looking around when you're there because twins are all over the place! Debbie and Lisa are wonderful, very gorgeous women, and good friends of mine now. But when I told Mark about them he went over to Twins. Mark is not shy, so he goes in and says, "Hi, I want to introduce myself. I'm the cofounder of Pete's Brewing Company." Debbie and Lisa basically ignored him. We're considering starting up a new company, one focused on barbecue, and trust me, Mark *will* have his name on it!

Back to our story. Many strategic decisions had to be made, not the least of which was brewing the beer. We did our homework and discovered that many breweries had the capacity to make a lot more beer than they were actually producing. This led us to the intriguing idea of not building our own brewery. Amazingly enough, on our first phone call, we hit paydirt. About six miles from my house was the Palo Alto Brewing Company of Mountain View, California, one of the earliest microbreweries in existence.

Bob Stoddard had bought the place from its original owners in the mid 1980s, and he produced two wonderful beers there: London Real Ale and California Golden Ale. It was through Stoddard and his London Real Ale that I first witnessed the power of government regulation. The Bureau of Alcohol, Tobacco, and Firearms (BATF) in Washington, D.C., regulates many aspects of the brewing industry, including label

On the right is Bob Stoddard from Palo Alto Brewing Company, on the left is Bob's friend Vladdie, and that's me in the middle.

approval. Since Bob's London Real Ale wasn't made in London, the BATF made him change the name to London-Style Ale.

Mark called Bob in early 1986 and asked if we could use his equipment for our brewing when he wasn't using it (for a fee, of course). Bob was amenable and encouraged us to move forward with the idea. This eliminated lots of planning and red tape for us. We didn't have to expend incredible amounts of energy deciding what equipment to purchase, what capacity to build, where to locate the brewery, or how we'd raise the large amount of capital required. Our

PETE'S SPECTRUM OF BEERS

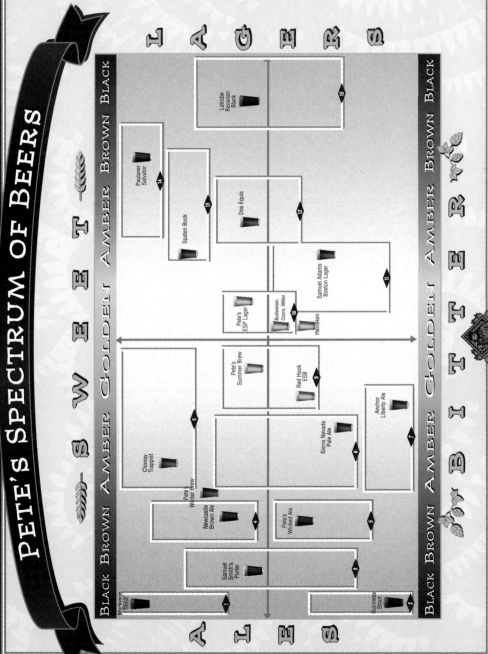

LAGERS

BLACK BROWN AMBER GOLDEN AMBER BROWN BLACK

←— SWEET —→

←— BITTER —→

BLACK BROWN AMBER GOLDEN AMBER BROWN BLACK

ALES

- McKenzie Stout — 1
- Guinness Stout — 2
- Samuel Smith's Porter — 3
- Newcastle Brown Ale — 4
- Pete's Wicked Ale — 5
- Sierra Nevada Pale Ale — 6
- Anchor Liberty Ale — 7
- Chimay Trappist — 8
- Pete's Winter Brew — 8
- Pete's Summer Brew
- Red Hook ESB — 9
- Pete's ESP Lager
- Budweiser, Coors, Miller — 10
- Heineken
- Samuel Adams Boston Lager — 11
- 12
- Dos Equis
- Spaten Bock — 13
- Paulaner Salvator — 14
- Latrobe Bavarian Black — 15

PETE'S

BEER TASTING TERMS

Beer A fermented cereal beverage which traditionally is made from malted barley, hops, water and yeast. Most beer styles are derivatives of ales and lagers. Other ingredients such as wheat, fruit and spices are used for unique styles of beer. Corn and rice are used as adjuncts but primarily as cheaper sources of fermentable sugar.

Ale Ales are fermented at higher temperatures. Fruity aromas are a common characteristic.

Lagers Lagers are fermented at lower temperatures and are aged for a longer period of time. Lagers do not have a fruity aroma.

Color Color comes from the amount and type of roasted barley used. Caramel, Chocolate and Black Patent are "color" descriptions of roasted barley. In these cases, the colors range from golden to amber to brown to black.

Taste The tastebuds that concentrate on sweet are located at the front of the mouth and pick up the malt tastes in the beer. Bitter tastebuds are located in the back which emphasize the hoppy characteristics. The aftertaste is also an important factor in beer tasting. The lingering taste should be pleasing, not sour or harsh.

Aroma Beer should be a savory experience for your senses. Begin enjoying the beer by inhaling deeply. A variety of scents should be detectable based on the beer's ingredients. The aroma of malted barley is sweet and roasted with dark beers. Hops impart a pleasant, flowery, bitter aroma that balances the sweet smell of malt. Fruity aromas add to the complexity of ales' bouquet.

Body As beer rolls across the tongue, the beer can feel watery (light in body) all the way through thick and chewy (full body).

KEY

- 1 Sweet or Cream Stout
- 2 Dry Stout
- 3 Porter
- 4 English Brown Ale
- 5 American Brown Ale
- 6 Pale or Amber Ale
- 7 India Pale Ale
- 8 Strong Ales
- 9 Wheat Beer and Golden Ales
- 10 American Lager
- 11 European Pilsner
- 12 Oktoberfest
- 13 Bock
- 14 Double Bock
- 15 Dark or Black Lagers

* This spectrum is a broad generalization. Not all beers will fit into these 15 particular style boxes.

Thanks for Your Support

THE TOPGUN BRO'S

Me and Millie.

Governor Wilson accepting the T-shirt I gave him in 1992 . . .

. . . and in 1996 wearing the Pete's jacket.

Some fun promotional shots.

The tenth anniversary Millie label.

Me and my beer-can collection.

back-of-the-envelope calculations indicated that we could start our
company with far less money than we had anticipated. Who'd have
thought it? You didn't have to own your own brewery to make great
beer! I guess some people have to hug their very own vessels and pipes
every day in order to feel good, but it wasn't a requirement for us.

We incorporated in April 1986 and proceeded to get licensed by
the appropriate government agencies. Our first stop was the San Jose,
California, office of the State Alcoholic Beverage Commission. We
were told by a bureaucrat there that it was absolutely not possible to use
someone else's equipment to make our beer. We couldn't be brewers if
we didn't have a brewery. So we told him that was bullshit and went
over his head to the agency headquarters in Sacramento. We were trying
to do something new that wasn't on the prescribed list of official options,
and if it's not on the list, it must be prohibited. We had to work our
way up through the organization, explaining what we were attempting
to do, why our approach actually fit within the scope of licensing, and
how the license could be issued without having to turn the commission upside down. It took perseverance, but we finally got our license
to operate.

We determined that we could get our company going,
at least through the initial phase of producing our first batch of beer,
for $16,000. To give ourselves a cushion, we invested $21,000 in this
start-up phase. We knew it would take more money over time, but we
didn't know exactly how much. When our investment in the company
reached $50,000, I remember sitting in a restaurant talking with Mark
about the business. Some guy, overhearing our conversation, approached
the table and asked if we'd tell him more about what we were doing.
When he heard how much money we had raised, he laughed and told

us it would take five years and a million dollars to get to cash-flow break-even—that is, to the point when our monthly income would cover our monthly expenses. I thought the guy was just giving us a hard time, but it *did* take us five years and $1.4 million dollars. He wasn't far off at all!

We started work on what beer to produce, what to call the beer, and what the labels and six-packs would look like. I focused on developing the beer on Bob's equipment, and Mark worked with a friend of his on the label. Having agreed that the company would be called Pete's Brewing Company, Mark's friend proceeded to draw a picture of me for the label. We were both shocked when we finally got a look at the artwork. I looked like a Middle Eastern terrorist! We knew we had to have a label that would get people's attention, but this wasn't the way. My dog, an English bull terrier named Millie, was in my opinion the best-looking dog on earth. Mark thought Millie was the silliest looking

Picture of Dave Miller, my friend whom I named Millie after, and me at a promotion we did at the Fleet Center in Boston.

dog on earth. Together, we figured that putting an English bull terrier on the label would certainly get people's attention, whether they loved the dog or hated her.

The artist came up with a caricature of Millie, a white dog on a purple background. It stood out! We decided to put a banner under the dog with a Latin motto, mirroring the way universities have Latin mottoes. I wanted our motto to be funny, though. Searching through the dictionary, I discovered a section that had a bunch of Latin mottoes. Several caught my eye, but the one I thought had the most potential was *Cave canum,* which means "beware of the dog." Since Millie was white, I turned to Bill Stensrud, a friend who had gone to school in the heavily Catholic state of Massachusetts. I figured he'd probably studied Latin, and I asked him what the adjective for "white" was in Latin. He thought it was probably a form of *alba,* or something like that. The correct form turned out to be *album.* Now we had "beware of the white dog"— *Cave canum album.*

Just to make sure *album* was correct, I checked with a fellow Worry Wort homebrewer at ROLM, Mark Housely. Housely

An original Millie six-pack carrier.

truly knew something about everything. I didn't know whether he knew Latin or not, but I figured I had nothing to lose by asking. Right off the bat he said that *album* wasn't the correct way of saying "white" in Latin. It means absence of black. The correct adjective would be *nidentum,* which means "shining white." Why Housely had this trivia stored in his memory was beyond me; I was blown away by the ease with which he answered my odd question! But was he right?

I checked with another friend, John Driscoll, whom I grew up with in Connecticut. Both he and his brother were lawyers, two of the most brilliant guys I've ever met. They searched through several books before they finally found "shining white" as a third definition of *nidentum.* I finally had the motto I wanted for the label with Millie on it: *Cave canum nidentum,* Beware of the Shining White Dog. It still amazes me that Housely pulled *nidentum* from the recesses of his mind, but we Worry Worts, we're a different breed!

The question of what beer to make was a big dilemma for me. Despite the plethora of beer styles available and the handful of recipes I had successfully brewed over the last seven years, nothing seemed to leap to the top of the list. One thing that most people don't realize is that a beer recipe that works for a certain batch size doesn't necessarily scale up to larger sizes. If you use different equipment, it's even more complicated to scale the recipe. At home, I made 5-gallon batches. At Palo Alto Brewing the equipment made a 10-barrel batch (310 gallons), so whatever I did at home wouldn't scale up exactly. A new formula might be the way to go.

I considered the possibility of failure. If we couldn't sell the beer, I at least wanted something I could enjoy at home. In the end, I tried to replicate my favorite commercial beer at that time, Samuel Smith's Nut Brown Ale from Tadcaster, England. I tried four test batches, all failures at replicating Sam Smith's Nut Brown. The last test batch, however, produced a beer I liked even better. Talk about serendipity! A failure in one perspective became a total success from another. It was dark beer, with a nice brownish-reddish color and great aroma and flavor. This darker beer was also different from most of the other specialty brewers' beers. Their flagship products were either golden or amber in color.

So now we had a great label and a great beer, but no name
for it. We wanted to convey that we had a sense of humor and an
attitude. We could have called the beer Pete's Ale or even Pete's Brown
Ale, since it was a dark beer, but that seemed boring. It was time to
go to the chalkboard and list any and all adjectives that could possibly
describe a beer. We tried, but nothing clicked; the names were all so
bad I can't remember any of them.

During this time, Mark was a fan of the comedian Alex
Bennett, who had a morning talk show on a San Francisco radio
station. Besides doing his own rap, he also had comedians come
on his show and do their stuff. One morning, Bob "the Bobcat"
Galthwaite made an appearance. During his routine, he yelled and
screamed about "wicked" this and "wicked" that. Mark told me about
the show and Galthwaite's use of "wicked." He thought it was a brilliant descriptor, and I had to agree. Wicked has so many meanings.
And that's how the name "Pete's Wicked Ale" was born.

Our first batch was produced toward the end of 1986 and yielded
several hundred cases of beer. All the beer was packaged and sold locally
in the Mountain View, California, area. Seeing the first display at the
local Liquor Barn was extremely satisfying after all the work we had
gone through to get that far. We knew we still had a long way to go,
but we also thought we were on a roll. Little did we know that disaster
was about to hit.

While our second batch of Wicked Ale was in the tanks aging,
I got a call from Bob Stoddard, the owner of Palo Alto Brewing. We
knew Bob was having some financial difficulties and had spent a lot of
time getting his equipment debugged. Of course, when you're a small
operation, if you're installing or fixing equipment, you're not selling beer.
Not selling beer limits your cash intake, and your reserves dwindle

away. Bob was going bankrupt. He wasn't going to try and reorganize—he was going into Chapter 7, where the business is shut down and locked up.

Bob called me late Wednesday night to warn me that the sheriff would arrive on Monday to lock the doors. He urged me to

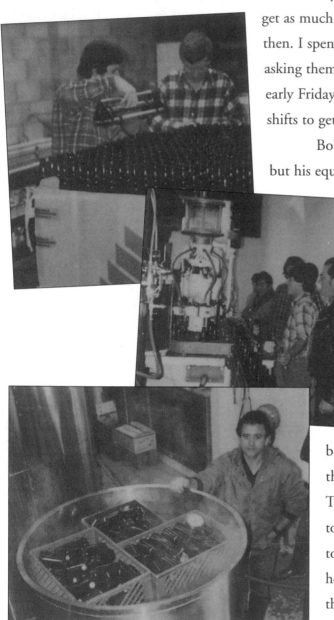

get as much of our beer out as we could before then. I spent all day Thursday calling friends and asking them to come down and help. We started early Friday morning and put in round-the-clock shifts to get the beer out.

Bob is a great person with a big heart, but his equipment back then was not very efficient. The brewery was in a light industrial development, housed in two small, attached buildings. The layout was such that bottles had to go back and forth from room to room in order to be filled and finished. Bob had purchased and installed all of the equipment himself, but the down-side was that packaging the beer was extremely labor-intensive. There was no easy handling equipment to transport the bottles either. We resorted to stealing a good number of those heavy-duty plastic milk carriers from the local Safeway for hauling the bottles around the brewery. It took us nearly

Our 2½-day blitz to get beer out of Palo Alto Brewing Company before the sheriff locked it up.

2½ days to get the beer out, but at least we had something to sell.

In the course of this flurry of work, I went out to get some pizza for our friends, who were working. Hey, if these people were nice enough to take time off from work to help us, the least I could do was to keep them well fed. And of course, they could drink all the Wicked Ale they wanted. All morning long, my stomach had been a little upset. I figured it was from all of the stress I was under. One result of this internal distress was the old passing of gas, breaking wind as I worked.

When I returned from my pizza run, I was expecting to inhale the wonderful aroma of malt and hops, but there was quite another aroma emanating from the brewery, sort of like swamp gas. Turns out the others had the same affliction, but nobody was admitting to it. My guess was that they were all SBDs, silent-but-deadlies. Talk about product attributes. Apparently Wicked Ale caused flatulence! We were now without a brewery and had a product that, when consumed in sufficient quantities, caused flatulence.

We soon solved both problems. We moved production to the August Schell Brewing Company in New Ulm and we reformulated our ale. The original Wicked Ale was made from malt extract instead of barley malt because that had saved Bob from having to purchase and install equipment to process the barley grain. When we made Wicked Ale directly from grain, the undesireable effects were eliminated. Whew!

Frank Chang, friend and investor, at the first display of our Wicked Ale at Liquor Barn in Mountain View, California.

CHAPTER 6

How I Kept Pete Wilson, Governor of California, from Becoming President of the United States (And Other Stories from the Road)

Beer is not a good cocktail party drink, especially in a home where you don't know where the bathroom is.

—Billy Carter

In many ways, running a company has been a lot more challenging and exciting than I expected. I've had some really wonderful jobs over the years; some, I didn't want to leave. When IBM sold ROLM to Seimens, I wound up with an even better job than when IBM had bought ROLM. I went from managing the competitive analysis group to a fairly high-level position making alliances with other companies. Although Seimens was a big company, it still couldn't do everything; my job was to find companies that could do whatever Siemens needed next. I'd negotiate how we could work on some project as a joint effort between our company and theirs. I was also on a track that would get me transferred to Munich for three years. Amy and I both wanted to go. It was an incredible opportunity. It just happened to come up right when I had to decide if I was going to quit my job and work at Pete's Brewing Company full time.

At this point, neither Mark nor I had ever drawn any income from the company. When a new venture is in its infancy, you have to put everything back into the company to "grow" it. We had to keep our "day jobs" if we wanted to maintain our homes and feed ourselves. When the company was relatively young, we managed to keep it going just working nights. I did a lot of PR for the beer when I was on the road. My boss at ROLM was very supportive, letting me schedule a trip to our plant in say, Colorado Springs, the day before the Great American Beer Festival in Denver. He often came with me—I think he enjoyed helping pour the beers.

Now it was time to make a choice. Was I really going to make beer or was I just going to own this company on the side? It wasn't an easy decision. Amy and I wanted to live in Europe. Pete's Brewing Company was tiny (even today it's still not out of the woods). There were so many reasons not to go full time, but I realized I simply had to do it. I told Amy that only God knew whether we'd be successful, but I knew that if I didn't go all-out with the company, I'd regret never having taken the chance. Amy stuck with me, and I left ROLM.

I never have regretted that decision. I like to talk to people—at least until they get drunk—and my role is to evangelize the fun and the more unusual aspects of beer. I try to make it more approachable, to show people that there's more to beer than just what's in the bottle. It has had an intriguing history, and there are lots of words and phrases that you hear without realizing they originated with beer. The fact is, I have a great job. I get to travel around the world talking about my favorite subject and meeting interesting people. This chapter contains stories of some of the adventures I've had as a brewing ambassador.

Back in 1988, Roger Stallmann and I were managing two parts of the competitive analysis group for the ROLM division of IBM. Roger ran the technical group, and I managed the market and business analysis side of things. Collectively we earned a reputation for having one of the best, if not the best, competitive groups within the IBM Corporation. Why? Well, we took the customer's view of the world. As was typical for IBM in those days, most other divisional competitive groups followed what IBM called "Feeds and Speeds," looking at the world from the perspective of how fast and how compact the equipment was.

Roger and I, radicals that we were, first determined what our customers wanted and *then* asked whether our solutions were better than our competitors' at meeting the customer's needs. It wasn't exactly rocket science, but our approach was relatively rare in an environment where engineers tended to lead management and mainly wanted to know whether our equipment was better than the competition's. They really didn't care whether the overall solutions were what the customer needed.

Roger and I spent a lot of time traveling around the United States and other parts of the world to give presentations on our novel methodology at other IBM divisions. We had a lot of fun together and came to be known as the "twisted pair" (in telephony, the wires that lead to your phone are literally a twisted pair of copper wires).

One trip to IBM-Japan was particularly interesting in terms of both a telephony business and beer. For eight days, we spent a great deal of time with IBM people and with customers. Whatever free time we had left, we devoted to exploring Tokyo. This included waking up at 2:30 A.M. one morning to visit the bedlam of the largest fish market in the world. On the weekend, in the middle of our trip, I wanted to go on a brewery tour. The folks at IBM suggested we visit Kirin in Yokohama. They called ahead and reserved us a spot on the 3:00 P.M. tour that Saturday.

Traveling with Roger was a blast; together, we had no fear about going anywhere. We allowed three hours to get to Kirin because even though the trip itself was only supposed to take an hour, we would have to change trains three times to get to the brewery. Since there was virtually no English used in the train system, we wanted extra time in case we got lost. As it turned out, we actually made all the correct connections and arrived in Kirin two hours before our scheduled tour.

The train let us out directly across the street from the entrance to the Kirin Brewery complex. We decided we'd just go to the security entrance and ask where we could hang out until our tour started. We soon found ourselves launched on an incredible adventure. As we walked up to the gate, the two brewery security people stared at us. Roger told them we were there for the 3:00 P.M. tour. They stared at us in a way we interpreted as "what planet are they from?" Actually, they didn't speak any English and didn't have a clue what we were saying.

After a couple of minutes, one of them made a phone call. The only thing we understood in the conversation was *gaijin,* which means "foreigner" in Japanese. The guard handed the phone to Roger. Roger explained that we were early for the 3:00 P.M. tour and asked where we could wait. The lady on the other end of the line told Roger to wait right where he was. A couple of seconds later we saw this woman, in heels, running out of the doorway of a building down the roadway from the entrance. She ran all the way to the entrance, arriving out of breath. "I apologize for keeping you waiting!" she said.

Top: Looking up from the guard's shack at Kirin Brewing to where the woman came running to greet us. ***Middle:*** *Confusion in Tokyo transportation system. It's all in Japanese!* ***Bottom:*** *A hot beverage dispenser in Tokyo. Imagine getting a hot can of tea or coffee and trying to hold the hot metal in your bare hands.*

We sheepishly explained that there was no apology necessary as we were early and just wanted to know where we should go to wait.

She told us to come with her, and she started back up the road to what must have been the main building. As we entered the building, we could see that we were where the tour usually started because there were signs all around about the brewing process. The woman handed us a videotape, told us to watch it, said she'd be right back, then ran off again. Finally, we thought, we had found a place to cool our heels for the next couple of hours.

A couple of minutes later, the lady came running back, followed by a man in a hard hat, and they both apologized for keeping us waiting. Roger and I again said that no apologies were necessary, as we only wanted to hang out until the 3:00 P.M. tour. The man explained that his English was better, that he was an engineering manager at the brewery, and that he would give us a personal tour. We said thanks, but that wasn't necessary since it was now only about an hour and a half until the 3:00 P.M. tour. (Now you must understand, we were just two dressed-down guys on a Saturday waiting for a brewery tour. They had no idea that I had started a brewing company in the United States, although at this point, we made so little beer that no one was likely to have heard of us anyway.)

The manager gave us a complete tour of the brewery and explained that he was working the typical Saturday expected of most Japanese workers. He had left his job to give us a personal tour!

This manager seemed to enjoy my questions, which, I guess, were more specific than the ones he normally got from the public. Toward the end of the tour, I explained that I had started Pete's Brewing Company the year before and that I had a six-pack of Wicked Ale with me in a bag. His eyes widened when I showed him the six-pack. I asked if it would be possible to meet the plant manager and give him the sixer as a thank-you. Our tour guide said he'd check and ran off to see the plant manager. It seemed like nobody could walk in Japan when there was a guest around!

The senior executive was very gracious and took time to talk to us about beer in the United States. As we were talking, an assistant offered us several gifts: special Kirin beer glasses and a new test beer called Heartland that they were developing but hadn't released to the public yet. Kirin was experimenting with a new brew that was all barley malt-based, as compared to their regular products, which used other grains as adjuncts. The bottle made no reference to Kirin Brewing because they wanted to see if they could attract younger drinkers—who weren't going to identify themselves with the older generation that drank Kirin's traditional products. (It's funny to me now, because many of the bigger breweries in the United States did the same thing in the 1990s.) The new beer was a great, full-flavored golden lager-style beer. I don't know what happened to the product when they finally launched it, but it was a gas to get a preview. The plant manager loved getting a six-pack of Pete's Wicked Ale, and we talked for over half an hour. Then the plant manager had to get back to work, but he thanked us again before he left. (He *thanked* us!?)

Riding the train back to Tokyo, Roger and I looked at each other and wondered what the heck had just happened. We had arrived early, and yet we were treated like royalty. Now *that* was customer service! We talked about what would have happened if two Japanese-speaking tourists had arrived early for a beer tour at a brewery in St. Louis, Milwaukee, or Golden, Colorado. How would they have been treated? Having gone on those tours as an English-speaking person, I can guarantee that these two hypothetical Japanese tourists would not have gotten special treatment, let alone any general courtesies! This was one of many experiences that had led me to try to make every person's experience with Pete's Brewing Company a positive one.

One time I received a message that Steve Tomkins of Fox Television had called. We had recently announced a new ad agency, and my assumption was that he was calling about advertising on TV. I'm actually pretty good about returning phone calls, so even though I didn't want to talk to him about advertising, I made the call. Tomkins, it turns out, was a writer/producer for *The Simpsons* TV show. On a recent Continental Airlines flight, he had read an article in which I was interviewed.

During the interview, the reporter asked me if Homer Simpson would drink our beer. I had to laugh because we were not fans of *The Simpsons* until their second or third season. Amy and I never watched it, although *The Simpsons* were a staple of our kids' television diet. When Amy and I finally watched a few episodes of the show, we also became addicted. It has become must-see TV in our house. Anyway, Homer loves the cheap local Springfield beer, Duff's Beer. In the interview, I told a story about a recent trip I took to Springfield, Illinois. I spent some time in Chicago and then went downstate to Champaign–Urbana, Springfield, and other major metropolitan areas. In Springfield, I arranged to do a Brewmaster Dinner, where we use beer as an ingredient in and accompaniment to the food. The dinner was an outstanding success. Afterward, I met a lot of locals.

One woman was overjoyed that I had taken the time to come down to Springfield, and she asked me why I had come. I love to kid around with people, so I told her I had never had Duff's Beer and figured I could only get it in Springfield. I watched this strange look come over her face and realized that she didn't get my joke, so I told her about Duff's Beer on *The Simpsons*. She then said, with great confidence, that I was in the wrong place. The Simpsons weren't in Springfield, Illinois, but in Springfield, Missouri.

If you're not a *Simpsons* fan, then her statement won't mean anything to you. But, one of the longest running jokes on the show is that they never identify where Springfield is. Every time there might possibly be some clarification of which state Springfield is in, something

My autographed script from THE SIMPSONS.

clutters the screen so you never see it. I just had to crack up when this lady was so serious about Springfield being definitively in Missouri.

Back to Steve Tomkins. Steve loved that I had mentioned *The Simpsons* in the interview so much that he invited me down to Los Angeles to either a cast-reading of the script or to watch the recording of the actors. All the actors gather around a conference table for the cast reads, whereas when they do the actual recording, the actors usually come at different times. I opted to meet everyone and come to the cast read. When I told my family about this, our *Simpsons*-fanatical kids also wanted to go, as did Amy, my partner Mark, and our friend Ken Suyama.

On Halloween day, 1996, Steve took us to the conference room, where we got to meet all of the actors and Matt Groening, the creator of the show. My younger son and I were star struck. We were each given scripts, and we absolutely had to have all of the actors' autographs. It was such a kick in the pants to meet the actors and listen to them going back and forth between their regular voices and their character voices. Several of the actors did multiple voices. I even got Matt to draw me a Homer on my script!

The interplay among the actors reading in their characters' voices and the script itself had me in stitches. Amy elbowed me to quiet down, but it was too funny. When it was over, I was afraid that I had embarrassed Steve Tomkins. Fortunately, he told us the actors get great feedback when they can hear the audience laughing, so I helped their read go better. The show we sat in on was the 1997/1998 season premier. When it finally aired, I couldn't help but see the actors doing the script in my head, while the cartoon characters were on the screen.

In February 1997, I received a call from another Matt, Matt Barth our San Diego sales manager. Terry Bryant, a customer at a recent promotion, was a real fan of our beer and wanted to talk to me. It turned out that Terry, or "Turbo," was an air controller for TOPGUN (you know, of the Tom Cruise movie fame). He said that he and many others at TOPGUN were big fans of the beer, and that I was welcome to come out any time and meet them at their new base in Fallon, Nevada, about an hour east of Reno.

At my son's athletic event that evening, I told Amy about the call, and allowed as how I thought it would be neat to go visit the base. Did she know of anyone who had a private pilot's license? It turned out that the guy seated on the other side of Amy, who had worked with her on local educational projects, was a pilot, and he said he'd love to fly me out there. Jeff Miller, the pilot, took Mark and me to Fallon, and Terry picked us up. Nobody uses their real names out there; they go by their "handles." Terry was Turbo. I went as Wicked1, from my e-mail address. Jeff was Dr. Diesel. Mark told everyone to call him Rhino, and we all wondered where that came from. Mark, ever the comedian, said he was big, fat, and horny!

Me with an F-18 Hornet at TOPGUN in Fallon, Nevada.

The TOPGUN school was in its last day of a ten-week session, so the pilots would be going up on their final maneuvers. Unfortunately, the commanding officer wouldn't allow us to get into the cockpit of the fighter aircraft, let alone go up for a flight, but we were more than welcome to view the combat on computer screens and a huge video wall display. The action was incredible, the real-time information was immense, and it was very exciting to watch. Later we got to walk out on the tarmac and watch the planes return. The F-14s and F-18s do a low-level swing by the tower and expose their undersides so the tower controllers can make sure that each plane is in good condition to land. We were right under the planes as they swung by.

After the planes landed, we went out to do walk-arounds. The pilots, meanwhile, had to do debriefings on the exercise and, because of some of the information exchanged, it was a "classified" debriefing. We iced down the cases of beer we'd brought to share with the pilots while we were waiting for the debriefing to end.

We then gave a short talk, handed out the beers, and shot the bull for a while. I discovered that several of the instructors were also homebrewers, and they brought out their brews as well. I sleep better at night knowing that the best-of-the-best are into beer!

I've never been in the military, but I appreciate the time and effort our troops put in so I do try to meet their requests. Years ago I got a call from a local unit that had gotten our 800-number we put on the labels and asked to speak to Pete. These guys said they were having a party next week and wondered if I would come. I went, armed with a couple of cases of beer and Wicked t-shirts. They were wowed! It was an Army bomb disposal unit so they made me an official "Royal Defuzilier." I can now attend any party that any Army bomb disposal unit puts on, anywhere in the world. I think I have to bring the beer, though!

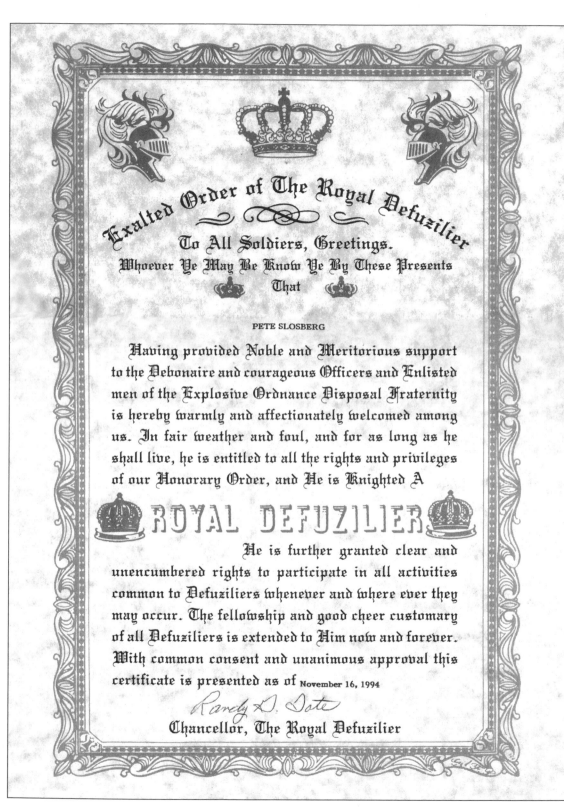

Exalted Order of The Royal Defuzilier

To All Soldiers, Greetings.
Whoever Ye May Be Know Ye By These Presents
That

PETE SLOSBERG

Having provided Noble and Meritorious support to the Debonaire and courageous Officers and Enlisted men of the Explosive Ordnance Disposal Fraternity is hereby warmly and affectionately welcomed among us. In fair weather and foul, and for as long as he shall live, he is entitled to all the rights and privileges of our Honorary Order, and He is Knighted A

ROYAL DEFUZILIER

He is further granted clear and unencumbered rights to participate in all activities common to Defuziliers whenever and where ever they may occur. The fellowship and good cheer customary of all Defuziliers is extended to Him now and forever. With common consent and unanimous approval this certificate is presented as of November 16, 1994

Randy D. Date
Chancellor, The Royal Defuzilier

Becoming an official defuzilier after a promotion with an Army bomb disposal unit at Moffet Field in Mountain View, California.

At our company-wide meetings, the sales staff gets together in one place to share ideas and learn about upcoming products. At one of these meetings, Dan Miron, our Los Angeles sales manager, told me a story about a bar on Sunset Boulevard called the Thunder Roadhouse. Dan had been trying to get our beer on draught there for some time. On his latest visit he was focused on getting our winter seasonal, Wicked Winter Brew, on tap. While he was there, Quentin Tarantino (of *Pulp Fiction* fame) went up to the bar to tell the manager that it was his favorite beer. The magic had happened again, and we were immediately put on tap.

I thought this story was neat, so I told Dan that when I came down to Los Angeles the next month I wanted to set aside some time for us to go thank the manager of Thunder Roadhouse for taking us on. When I got to L.A., we had some time to kill, so we went off to visit the Thunder Roadhouse. We met the manager and thanked him. Out of the corner of my eye, I also saw Tarantino sitting at a table eating lunch. I immediately went over to see him—I'm a huge fan of *Pulp Fiction*—and thanked him for helping us get our beer on tap there. He was eating with a friend and I felt weird interrupting his lunch, but I had to thank him for liking our beer and for his movie. I was so moved, I took the Pete's Brewing jacket I was wearing off my back and gave it to him! He was quite happy to have it and offered his thanks. Is this job cool, or what?!

For me, the only memorable thing about the first Greater New York Beer Festival in the fall of 1994 was arriving at Kennedy airport late from San Francisco and deciding to go straight to the festival to save time. The festival had already begun, so I put my suit bag under a table in the rear of our booth. The table was surrounded by a cloth skirt that hid anything underneath it. At the end of the evening, I went to get my bag and discovered it had been taken. Not that it couldn't happen anywhere, but it was the first thing I'd had stolen in a long, long time. Jackie the Jokeman (Jackie Martling), the writer for Howard Stern, was the emcee for the evening, and I told him of my plight, although, I wasn't expecting any action. It turned out many other items had been stolen that evening. The following July, I got a call from Jackie the Jokeman on my voicemail: "Hey Pete, this is Jackie the Jokeman from *The Howard Stern Show*, and I just wanted to let you know I found your bag! Just kidding! I'm having a party on the Fourth and could use some beer." I got a kick out of that message.

I knew it from the beginning, but Amy is an incredible lady. She's addicted to puzzles, mysteries, and nightly viewings of the TV game show *Jeopardy.* The kids always bugged her to try out for the show, and she constantly pooh-poohed the idea. In late 1995, *Jeopardy* announced that they were running a contestant search in San Francisco. Well, Amy finally broke down and went in to take the test. She was one of the few to pass the multiple-choice portion. Then she took a screen test to see how'd she react to being on camera. She passed again and was told that she'd be in a pool of possible contestants, but no guarantees. Several months passed and finally a letter came requesting her presence in Los Angeles at the studio, but still no guarantee that she'd get on.

The letter also contained pages of do's and don'ts. Amy discovered that contestants were not allowed to mention any commercial venture nor could they wear any clothing with logos on it. Mark,

Amy, and I took it as a personal challenge to figure out how we could get around the rules and sneak in a plug for Pete's Brewing Company. Unfortunately, when taping began we still hadn't been able to figure out a loophole in the rules. Amy went in a couple of hours early for preparations, and Mark and I went to the audience section of the studio, totally deflated by our failure to solve the dilemma.

With five tapings per day, we weren't sure which show Amy would get on, let alone if at all. Finally, she was selected for the third show of the day. Each show is broken up into different segments, and after the first commercial, the host, Alex Trebeck, comes back and does short interviews with the contestants, using notes about the contestants' backgrounds collected during the preliminary contestant searches.

All of a sudden, we heard Alex say to Amy, "I see from your background that you like to travel and that you like beer." Glory of glories, the door had opened. Amy said, "My husband *Pete* started a major *microbrewing* company, and *Pete* and I like to ..." Pure magic! Her answer flowed so smoothly, it fit within the rules, and it got us the plug after all. It couldn't have come out any better! The day after it actually aired, I received calls from people all over the country wondering if Amy was my wife. Today when I travel, people still ask me if that was Amy. Reruns of the show have made it as far as Canada, and I've been asked about Amy by someone up there who saw it. I knew Amy was smart, but this topped the cake. She came in second place on *Jeopardy,* but she's a winner in my mind.

According to the May 29, 1995, *San Jose Mercury News,* I was to blame for Governor Pete Wilson losing his bid for the presidency of the United States! Although I was not mentioned directly, the story pinpointed an event we held for the governor in Sacramento as the catalyst for his campaign's demise. It all began in 1990, when Senator Pete Wilson decided to run for governor of California. We discovered that many members of the campaign staff were fans of Pete's Wicked Ale. We agreed to supply the staffers with beer if we could be the "official inaugural ale" once Wilson was elected governor. When Wilson took office, I received an invitation to the inaugural ball in Sacramento. We made a special commemorative T-shirt that I wanted to hand-deliver to Governor Wilson and get a picture of him accepting it. Unfortunately, the Governor and Mrs. Wilson did not spend a lot of time at the main inaugural ball, and I didn't manage to get close enough to him for the photo.

Invitation to both inaugural balls for Governor Pete Wilson's two terms.

Later, while I was traveling on the east coast, I heard that there was going to be a second inaugural party in San Diego, where Wilson had once served as mayor. I diverted my return flight to San Diego so that I could attend the party. The governor spent a lot more time meeting with attendees, and I was able to introduce myself. Later on, I also got to meet Mrs. Wilson. When I introduced myself to her, she remarked, "Aren't you the guy that makes Pete's Wild Ale?" Although she didn't get the name of the beer correct, she was pretty damned close. I was pleasantly surprised, to say the least.

The next opportunity I had to meet the governor was in late 1993 at a dinner in Redwood Shores, California, where awards were handed out to the fastest growing California corporations. The governor was the keynote speaker, and he actually mentioned us in his speech. We had a six-pack of Pete's Wicked Ale stashed under the podium that the emcee was to give to the governor after his speech. When Wilson finished speaking, the emcee gave a plaque to the governor commemorating his speaking at this first annual awards dinner. The emcee then pulled out the six-pack, and the governor remarked that he already had some in his refrigerator! Not too bad for trying to get a little publicity.

In 1994, Pete Wilson ran again for the governorship and won. We decided to continue the tradition of giving him a commemorative piece of Wicked clothing. We had one of our company jackets customized for him and again I went off to the inaugural ball in Sacramento. This time the governor made a few opening remarks and then stepped into a roped-off area of the ballroom where only family and close friends could get in. I couldn't believe it. It looked like this would be a total wipeout, and there was no secondary event for me to fall back on. Then Wilson went over to the far side of his private area and started talking to members of the public standing nearby.

> **COCKTAIL**
> The first use of the term *cocktail* as a mixed drink is linked to the year of independence, 1776, and a barmaid named Betsy Flanagan at Halls Corners, in Elmsford, New York. Flanagan used cock feathers to decorate the back of the bar. When one of her customers requested a cocktail, she served the mixed drink with a feather in it.

Jacket in hand, I headed over toward the governor. As I made my way closer, I ran into a guy I had gone to high school with in Connecticut. What a time for a reunion! It turned out that his wife was a lawyer and wanted a judgeship, so they were also trying to get close enough to meet the governor. I was on a mission, so I excused myself and continued on my way. There were still six rows of people between me and the governor, and my fear was that he'd disappear before I could give him the jacket. Boy, was I nervous, but I had already come this far, so I yelled out, " Excuse me, governor, but I have something for you!" I held up the jacket and the six rows of people opened before me like the Red Sea had for Moses. The Governor first looked at me like, "Who the heck are you?" A moment later he recognized me, although I'm sure the Pete's Brewing logo on the jacket was the deciding factor. He motioned for me to come forward; I congratulated him on his victory and gave him the jacket.

He immediately put it on and went to show it to his wife and others. He came back and thanked me again, but he no longer had the jacket on. His wife had tried it on and had then passed it to others. Mrs. Wilson came over and thanked me, followed by some younger men and women who were big fans of our beer. Mission accomplished!

As the event went on, the jacket was no longer the key object of attention in the Governor's party. It was draped over the back of a chair. I simply had to make sure Governor Wilson didn't leave it behind. He and his entourage left before the ball was over, and most other folks left soon after they did. Not me though! I was staying until the end to see what would happen to the jacket. About a half hour after the Governor left, a man came up to the chair, grabbed the jacket, and walked briskly off. I dashed after him and introduced myself, explaining the connection between me and the jacket. He was very gracious and introduced himself as Bob White, the governor's chief of staff. Governor Wilson had given Bob explicit instructions not to bother

Lobbying at Capitol Hill with Beer Institute and National Association of Beer Wholesalers in 1994.

coming to work the next day if he didn't bring the jacket. What a great way to end the evening!

Months later, I was reflecting on some recent political activity in Washington, D.C. I'd gone to Capital Hill twice with the Beer Institute to lobby Congress on issues that might have negatively affected the brewing industry. It occurred to me that there were issues at the state level I ought to be looking into as well. Now believe me, I am pretty far removed from being politically active, but I wanted to do my share of educating people on beer issues.

My belief was that our legislators in Sacramento probably had good sources of information on the wine business, but most likely there was no reliable source for the beer business, even though there were well over 100 breweries operating in the state. I decided to hold a private beer-tasting for the governor and use that opportunity to talk about beer basics. I called Bob White, the governor's chief of staff, figuring I had nothing to lose.

White was on the road, so I left a message. The next morning, the phone rang, and it was Bob White returning my call—I repeat, returning my call. I was totally blown away that I'd gotten a return call! I explained about wanting to do a private tasting for the governor and his immediate staff. Bob said, "Hold on a second." He came back and suggested a beer blast for the Governor's entire staff instead. They had been working overtime since the inauguration and a party would do them good. Not what I was expecting, but an opportunity is an opportunity.

Approximately a week before the beer blast, I read in the local paper that the governor had just undergone throat surgery in San Diego and was recuperating in Los Angeles. This was bad news. I had really wanted to meet the governor again. The party was scheduled to begin at 5:00 P.M., so we arrived several hours early to get the lay of the land. Bob White was extremely appreciative of our efforts and kept repeating that no group had ever offered an event like this before. He also casually mentioned that the governor would probably show up for a short while. Yes! Dreams *do* come true!

When the beer blast started, we must have had about 150 staffers partying in the courtyard of the State Administrative building. Then Bob White and the governor came out. Unbelievably, Governor Wilson was wearing the jacket I'd given him at the inaugural ball. This was too cool!

Bob had told us that the governor probably couldn't speak because of his throat surgery. Sure enough, he was very social, but only nodded his head in response to questions. I gave the Governor a Wicked Ale and tried to have a short conversation before the activities started. Bob introduced me to the crowd and told the group that the governor had just approved a 25 percent raise for his staffers. The crowd went nuts and the governor grabbed the microphone and jokingly told Bob he was fired! The session lasted a couple of hours and then broke up.

After the beer blast, the governor spent a good deal of time on the campaign trail pursuing nomination as the Republican candidate for the presidency of the United States. His voice often failed, so his wife, Gayle, made some of his campaign speeches. Ultimately, Wilson backed out of the campaign and returned to his full-time post as governor of California. The *San Jose Mercury News* ran a post-mortem of the campaign and blamed its failure on Wilson having done three things his doctor had told him not to do at an event in Sacramento: drink cold liquids, drink alcoholic beverages, and talk. I'm not sure he actually drank any of the Wicked Ale I gave him, and telling Bob,

Please join Pete and Pete for a private Beer Tasting and Reception

Pete Wilson-Governor
Pete Slosberg-Founder of
Pete's Brewing Company

Tuesday, April 18

6:00 pm to 8:00 pm

Governor's Office
Council Room and Courtyard
Capitol Building
State Capitol

Pete's Wicked Ale, Pete's Wicked Lager, Pete's Wicked Red and Pete's Wicked Summer Brew

Invitation to the Governor's staff for the beer event we hosted in Sacramento in 1996.

"You're fired!" hardly constituted talking. However, I couldn't help feeling a small surge of professional pride to think that the *San Jose Mercury News* had blamed Pete's Wicked Ale for keeping Governor Wilson from becoming president of the United States.

There's a restaurant in Palo Alto, a couple of blocks from our beer company's headquarters, that we hadn't been able to crack. When our salesperson's best efforts didn't work, he asked me to go over and see what I could do. The owner looked at me funny when I walked in. "Say, aren't you the guy who used to trade me homebrews for empty bottles?" I was blown away that Chip Truett, who also owned Marvin Gardens restaurant where I got my bottles for homebrewing, remembered me, because to be honest, I didn't recognize him! He ended up carrying the beer. The message here is that you never know when homebrew gifts may come back as unexpected favors, even years later!

CHAPTER 7

WHAT'S IN A NAME?
(PETE'S SPECTRUM OF BEERS)

Ask ten brewers and get eleven opinions.
—OLD SWISS PROVERB

B eer books review hundreds or thousands of beers from around the world. I personally don't like these kinds of reviews because too often they reflect the author's personal biases rather than providing objective assessments. Sometimes the reviewers have gotten samples that aren't fresh and therefore aren't representative; they may review the beers against arbitrary criteria; and they simply can't keep up with all new beers entering the market and the old ones disappearing. Some books give backgrounds on the breweries themselves, with lots of pictures of brew kettles or fermentation tanks. Although such photos may be really interesting to beer enthusiasts, most of the people I talk to don't really care for them. They want to learn something about the various types of beers and how they relate to one another, but in a simple, easy way.

Having judged at homebrew and professional competitions locally, nationally, and internationally, it's very apparent that some are trying to make the definitions of beer styles too exact. In many competitions, styles are defined in terms of original gravity, color, bittering units, aromas, and so on. My question is, is a beer that falls just outside the strict lines by definition a bad beer? This really comes into play when there are a lot of entries in a competition, and a lot of those beers are very good. Some judges will throw a beer out just because the color is slightly off, even if everything else about the beer is great.

To further complicate matters, the American Homebrewers Association has one set of definitions, the professionals at the Great American Beer Festival another, and the British have yet a third set of style descriptions.

The fact is, beer styles have always evolved with time and as a result of brewing technology improvements. A porter from the mid-1700s, when that style was at its peak, was very different from today's version because the raw materials used to create it were different. For example, black patent malt didn't exist back then. In the 1700s, many of the porters were soured ("staled," in the terminology of the day) because they were stored in wooden vats where bacteria that lived in the wood ultimately soured the beer over its lengthy storage time.

It's also kind of funny how some styles have a broad set of criteria for their definitions—like amber ales—and other styles have extremely narrow criteria for their definition—like Belgian-style *tripels*. We had a huge debate at the Great American Beer Festival in 1994 over a *tripel* that was clearly the best beer for the style in terms of taste, but was slightly darker than "normal." Because of color, this terrific beer got a third-place medal instead of the first place it deserved.

A similar thing happened at the 1995 Great British Beer Festival when I was judging barley wines. The absolute best-tasting barley wine was called Norman Conquest, so named because its original gravity was 1066. The beer was fantastic, but some of the judges wanted it thrown out because it was too dark. Normally, barley wines are amber to brown. The brewer had decided to use some burnt malt

---

A STYLE DEFINITION

This example of a style definition comes from the guide to the Great American Beer Festival XIV:

Category: American Brown Ale
American brown ales look like their English-style brown ale subcategory counterparts but have an evident hop aroma and increased bitterness. They have medium body, and estery and fruity ester characters should be subdued; diacetyl should not be perceived. Chill haze is allowable at cold temperatures.

Original Gravity (degrees Plato): 1.040 to 1.055 (10 to 14 degrees Plato)
Apparent Extract/Final Gravity (degrees Plato): 1.010 to 1.018 (2.5 to 4.5 degrees Plato)
Alcohol by weight (volume): 3.3 to 4.7 percent (4 to 5.9 percent)
Bitterness (IBU): 25 to 60 IBU
Color SRM (EBC): 15 to 22 (35 to 90 EBC)

and the flavor was a beautiful blend of sweet, bitter, and alcohol, with a very pleasant burnt character. After much discussion, we voted this beer as best in its style. At the Great British Beer Festival, each best-of-style goes on to the finals for Best Beer of Britain. We weren't alone in our evaluation of Norman Conquest; the finals judges voted it the Best Beer in Britain! It was a hard-won award because some judges wanted it disqualified because it was slightly too dark. In my humble opinion, the beer-style bigots are going overboard, both in the strict definitions of styles and in judging beers too closely to style guide-lines. I know I'm going to take some heat for this opinion, but the fact remains that styles do evolve. Beer is not constant. It's a lot like the game of horseshoes: close does count.

As a believer in beer education, I've done my best to create a methodology for presenting information on beer styles in a visual way that makes it easily understandable. One of my jobs at ROLM involved developing sales materials for our products. It was clear that if we wanted the sales force to understand the technology, we had to create a picture that clearly described the technology. If we couldn't simplify the concept we'd lose the sales force and our customers as well. This inspired me to figure out how to simplify all there was to know about beer for the average person. At about 2 A.M. one morning I had a brainstorm. I went to my computer and roughed out a diagram that has served me well, for the last couple of years.

I've included in this book what we at Pete's Brewing Company call "Pete's Spectrum of Beers," an approach that positions beers and beer styles in relationship to each other. This shows how varieties of beer styles relate to one another.

The Spectrum of Beers is fundamentally divided into ales and lagers. The color bar places golden beers in the middle and darkens as the bar extends on either side through shades of amber, brown, and black. Sweetness comes from an emphasis on malt and increases as you go up the chart. Bitterness comes from an emphasis on hops and

THE ORIGIN OF LIGHT BEER

Light beer has come a long way from its initial invention. Having grown up on the east coast during the 1950s and 1960s, I was fortunate to have seen the original light beer, Gablinger's. It was invented by Dr. Joseph Owades for the Rheingold Brewing Company. Dr. Owades noted that calories come from the alcohol in beer as well as from the unfermentable sugars left in the beers. He invented a process that broke down the unfermentable sugars and allowed them to be converted to alcohol. Since this resulted in a higher alcohol content, the beer had to be diluted down to its original alcohol level. The light beer then had the same alcohol content as regular beer but with fewer calories and certainly a much lighter body. I distinctly remember the Gablinger's TV commercial where they showed a slice of bread being pulled out of the beer to demonstrate that there were fewer carbohydrates and therefore fewer calories.

This beer was *not* a commercial success. The rights to the beer were sold to Meisterbrau, a company in Chicago, that renamed it, Lite Beer. They also failed to make money off of it and sold the rights to the formula *and the name* to the Miller Brewing Company. The rest is history.

In order to save money and process time, other brewers have found another way to make light beer. Let's say that you were running a major brewery a couple of decades ago, and you'd just had a very successful year. Corporate headquarters calls and says, "Good work! We want you to do 50 percent more next year." You say, "No problem (gulp), just give me x millions of dollars to build more equipment and facilities." Corporate says, "No way. Just produce and sell that much more beer." Golly gee, what do you do?

The brewers of that era implemented an idea called high-gravity brewing. (Gravity, in this sense, doesn't mean serious, although I'm sure that the corporate czars were serious about increased production.) High gravity refers to specific gravity, the measure of the density of a liquid, with water as a reference point. Water has a specific gravity of 1.000. During the beermaking process, starches are converted into sugars in the mash tun and dissolve in the hot water. The dissolved sugars add density to the liquid. The higher the levels of dissolved solids, the higher the specific gravity. For example, Wicked Ale has a starting specific gravity of 1.052, which means it weighs 5.2 percent more than water. High-gravity brewing literally means that the brewer has added more material in the beginning of the process in order to get a higher-gravity wort. Think of this as making a beer concentrate.

If you make a beer concentrate, you can then add water at the end of the process to dilute the beer. In this manner, a brewery could produce 50 percent more beer without any increase in equipment or facilities. This process could very well lead some brewers to produce one concentrate, then add some water to get their regular beer, more water to get a light beer, and a little less water to get a super premium beer.

I wouldn't doubt that there are some light beers out there that are just diluted forms of their brewery's regular product. You can tell whether this is the case by putting the regular and light beers from the same brewery side by side. If they smell and taste different, then they are probably made using different processes. If one just comes across as a weaker form of the other, then the brewer probably just added water to dilute the high-gravity concentrate more than for the regular beer.

In one sense, this is literally a method of turning water into gold. If the price of the light beer is equal to or greater than the price of the regular beer, then the water used in a dilution process is pouring money straight into somebody's pocket!

increases as you go down. A quick look at the chart will tell you that both ales and lagers can be any color, sweetness, or bitterness. We haven't yet worked out a way to include the alcohol content or the body of the beer. We haven't dealt with aroma either, but I'm sure someone with enough time and money could develop scratch-and-sniffs for each beer or style!

With over 60 styles of beer available around the world, it would be very difficult to fit every style on this chart and still make sense of things. Styles are not easily defined—and many of them overlap. Also, although many brewers call their beers a certain style, the brews don't always conform to generally accepted standards of what that style is supposed to be. However, even with all of these caveats, we can still make progress in our charting approach.

The Spectrum chart shows 15 of the major styles of beer. The size of each style on the chart does not in any way, shape, or form represent the volume of the beer sold within the style. By far, the vast majority of beers sold in the United States are done in the American Lager style, which happens to be the smallest box on the chart. On the other hand, the Belgian Trappist or Abbey style is in one of the larger boxes but amounts to only a very tiny volume of the total market.

The Spectrum chart has helped us open the eyes of many beer retailers. In too many cases, they believe they are offering a wide variety of beers when they sell Bud, Bud Lite, Miller Genuine Draft, Miller Light, Coors Light, Stroh's Old Milwaukee, Pabst Blue Ribbon, and so on. That may be a wide choice of brand names, but when you plot the beers on the chart, they all fall near the center of the chart,

> **MYTH: LIGHT BEERS ARE SIGNIFICANTLY LOWER IN CALORIES THAN REGULAR BEERS**
>
> (This is a great one!) Light beers have taken a dramatic market share in the American beer market, so obviously this statement must be true, right? Well, the word "significantly," merits a closer look. In general, the typical 12-ounce beer has about 160 calories. The typical light beer has about 120 calories, although some have a little less. So let's be conservative and say the typical light beer has only 100 calories. So what's the difference in calories? About the equivalent of six potato chips! Very few of us drink beer alone, without any accompaniment. Personally, I'd rather have more flavor and eat six fewer chips per bottle.

just to the right on the lager side. The names may be different, but from a style perspective, they're all basically the same. Is this offering customers—meaning you—a choice?

When retailers see the chart, they gain a whole new perspective. We once designed a placemat version of the Wicked Spectrum for a restaurant chain. When we printed it for them, they said, "Stop! Wait! This will *not* work!" We wondered what we'd done wrong. It turned out they were upset because the mat showed that the beers they were offering their customers were all clustered in the middle. They wanted to change their beer portfolio before we did the final placemat, so that now it would display the "variety" of beers they were offering.

If the watering holes you go to don't carry a wide variety of beer styles, please find a way to show them the chart and make them realize how narrow their offerings really are. Seeing is believing, and hopefully they'll be open to offering a wider variety once they understand the truth.

If you want to fill out the chart with beers that are near and dear to you, here's how to do it. Accuracy is only relatively important. First, get a variety of beers. Maybe Bud for the lightest golden color available (all that rice lightens the color), Guinness Extra Stout for the darkest color and for maximum bitterness (in this case, a lot of hops plus burnt malt gives the beer a sharp bitterness), and one like Mackeson Cream Stout (which is black like Guinness but is one of the sweetest beers I've ever had). With three beers like these, you should be able to set the boundaries of your chart. For color, you have the lightest and the darkest of the beers available. For sweetness, you have Mackeson as the extreme. For bitterness, you have Guinness. For neutral flavor—that is, lack of sweetness or bitterness—you have Bud. Just about every other beer you come across will most likely fit within the boundaries set by these three.

To use the color scale, set out clear glasses of Bud and of Guinness. Place a glass of the beer you are interested in between the other two. Is the third glass closer to the golden Bud, or is it closer to the black Guiness? Is it somewhere near amber or brown? In many cases the label itself will say whether it's an ale or a lager. If it doesn't, then the Spectrum shows where several major styles appear on the ale or lager side.

To determine sweetness or bitterness, the process is only a little more difficult. The problem, if you can call it that, is that almost every beer has a sweet and a bitter component. How do you relate the two? My approach is to simplify. Since we can judge maximum sweet and bitter between Guinness and Mackeson, then you can guesstimate the sweet side of a beer you're interested in by comparing the sweet side to Mackeson. Is it barely sweet? Is it half as sweet? If Mackeson is a 10, then is the beer you're interested in a 2, 4, or 8? Employ the same process for the bitter side. If Guinness is a minus 10, then is the bitter component of the beer you're interested in a minus 2, minus 4, or minus 8? The positive and negative numbers indicate which half of the chart, upper (plus) or lower (minus), the beer falls in. To place a beer with a sweetness of plus 2 and a bitterness of minus 5, add the two numbers together to get minus 3. Therefore, you would place this beer about three-tenths of the way down the chart on the bitterness minus side. It's okay that the Spectrum of Beers is a little complicated and subject to individual tastes. We aren't trying to get absolute accuracy.

> **GROG**
>
> For hundreds of years, British sailors had daily rations of beer, and then rum, on their ships. At least they had one thing to look forward to in an otherwise tough environment. In 1740, the admiral of the fleet, Admiral Vernon, decided that the crews of Her Majesty's fleet should not be drinking straight rum, so he ordered that the rum be watered down. This innovation gave great offense to the sailors. Vernon was known for the cloaks he wore which were made from a course stiff wool known as grogram. The sailors called him Old Grog in retaliation. The term soon referred to the watered-down drinks Vernon had ordered for the fleet. From grog comes groggy, a term used to mean being drunk, but now is better known for being in a state of confusion and lack of coordination.

There is another way to evaluate beers without having to buy a bunch of them and taste them against Bud, Guinness, and Mackeson. Just use the version of the chart that we've already filled out. It has many of the common specialty beers and mass-marketed beers. Take a look at a new beer you're interested in and compare it to one already on the chart that has similar color and taste characteristics. For example, if an ale is relatively darker and more bitter than one we already have on the chart, then place the beer slightly left and down from the beer on the chart that you're comparing it with.

The Spectrum of Beers can be especially useful to bartenders and servers when trying to explain a beer to a customer, even if the server or bartender has never tasted the beer. If the customer knows one beer on the chart, every other beer on the chart can be described in terms of the one that the customer knows. For example, if a customer asks a server to describe Wicked Ale, the server can ask if the customer has ever had any of the other beers on the chart. Say the customer's had a Sierra Nevada Pale Ale. The server can point out on the chart that Sierra Nevada Pale Ale is on the left side, is amber in color, and is about halfway down because of its bitterness. Pete's Wicked Ale is to the left because it's darker, and it's up on the bitterness scale because it's less bitter. Thus, Pete's Wicked Ale is darker in color than Sierra Nevada Pale Ale and less bitter than Sierra. It's also more roasted in flavor because we use more roasted malt to get the darker color. We wouldn't say it's sweeter because it's still on the bitter side of the chart; a beer can be "less bitter" without being "more sweet."

The chart is simple and it works. You don't have to get into all of the technical gobbledygook of the beer-style bigots in order to describe a beer. If you're really into beers, you'll probably see a beer on the chart that looks like it's on the wrong side. I'll admit that I took some liberties, but not without good justification.

The purpose of beer education is to bring down the fear factor. The reason servers and bartenders don't talk about specialty beers is that they don't know how to describe them. The reason people don't want to try them is that they're afraid to try something they may not like. When beer education is made simple, they can, based on their own experience, try a new light-colored or roasted, sweet or bitter beer. Using the spectrum as a visual, they can see where the brands fall and help others choose what they might like, rather than randomly picking something new. In general, most people are afraid to experiment. Making beer more accessible through its history, the fun of it, and some simplified technical background is the best way I know to encourage more people to try different styles.

CHAPTER 8

THE EVOLUTION OF BEER

The mouth of a perfectly happy man is filled with beer.

—Ancient Egyptian wisdom, 2200 B.C.

A s you can see, you don't have to be a rocket scientist to make beer, although perhaps my degree in space mechanics and jet propulsion has helped from time to time. The brewing processes have remained fundamentally the same for thousands of years, though technology has obviously allowed us to improve in the process and make beers that are more consistant from batch to batch.

You may find this hard to believe, but up until about 300 years ago, all beers made from barley were dark ales. Let me repeat—*all beers were dark ales up until 300 years ago!*

For most of the twentieth century, it's been hard to find dark beers in the United States, so how come things have changed so dramatically in the past 300 years? Well, it all comes down to heat. Heat is what makes beer more interesting, creates uniqueness, and is the fundamental origin of the wide variety of beer styles. When brewers would dry the wet sprouted grain, they would usually put the wet grain on a grate over a fire. Inevitably, the fire would increase or decrease whenever the fuel source burned hotter or less intensely. At peak times, the flames would reach up and burn some of the kernels, turning them from brown to black. When the beer was made from the dried grain, only a few burned kernels would be enough to darken the beer. No matter what the brewers did during this malting (drying) process, some of the grain would burn. Typical fuel sources included wood, straw, or coal, all of which burn inconsistently and give off a lot of smoke. Thus, not only were all beers dark ales, they were also like *rauchbier* (*rauch* being German for smoke), since the grain absorbed the smoke and released that flavor into the beer.

All styles haven't been around forever. The fact is that as technology has changed, so has what people are used to drinking. It stopped me dead in the street the day I finally understood that until 1700 all beers were dark, murky ales. I had never "gotten" that. Since I didn't know smokey beers existed, the first time I ever tried one I thought it was kind of interesting. Folks 300 years ago would have been so tired of dark, smokey beer, they'd have been intrigued by something else. All of their beers had this smokiness to them because brewers then didn't have any other way of drying the grain.

My advice to you is never to take beer for granted: it's still evolving. Many styles have come about because of local constraints on materials or water supplies. Styles also evolve because of technology. Even government regulation has affected the evolution of beer. We don't live in a static environment, so strict style guidelines are almost by definition, too definitive. As I mentioned in the last chapter, a brewer's artistry in developing a fantastic product almost got panned by the beer-style bigots because it was a little bit darker than the prescribed style. The 1995 Best Beer of Britain was almost a throwaway!

Why is history important? It's the history *around* beer that's important. The fact is, beer has been a part of civilization since the days we were civilized. Everyone knows that the pilgrims landed on Plymouth Rock, but did you know that the Pilgrims were going to Virginia. The only reason they landed at Plymouth Rock was because the crew was running low on beer. There are lots of similar stories about beer embedded in our history that we don't know. Today we use phrases that come from beer without even realizing it.

I've become a real fan of beer terms, but I've also collected the stories behind other terms that have been killing me for years until I find out where them come from. For example, take the phrase, "the

MYTH: THE PILGRIMS LANDED AT PLYMOUTH ROCK IN SEARCH OF RELIGIOUS FREEDOM

Everybody knows that the Pilgrims landed at Plymouth Rock, Massachusetts, in 1620 in search of a place to live where they might have religious freedom forevermore. What most history books do not tell you is why the Pilgrims landed at Plymouth Rock when it was not their destination when they left England.

During this period in Europe, many of the water supplies were polluted, and water in general was not fit to drink. Beer, on the other hand, was sterilized during boiling and was thus safe to drink, as well as healthy, because of the vitamins from the grains and yeast. On ships, beer was the beverage of choice—it wouldn't kill you and it might even keep you healthier.

When the Pilgrims booked passage on the Mayflower to the Virginia colonies, they weren't the owners of the ship. They were just paying passengers. Due to the vagaries of navigation, the Mayflower hit land further north than planned. Attempts to navigate south were abandoned because of dangerous shoals and roaring breakers. The ship's log tells us that the ship's master and mariners were eager to get back to their home port in England: "We could not now take time to further search or consider, our victuals being much spent, especially our beer." The final decision to land in Plymouth was driven by something perhaps even more fundamental than faith. The ship's log speaks of how the passengers "were hasted ashore and made to drink water that the seamen might have the more beer." I love it! They kicked the passengers off so they could have enough beer to get back to England with!

MYTH: DOUBLEBOCKS ARE *TWICE AS STRONG AS* BOCKS

About 300 years ago, bock beers were consumed during the spring to celebrate the end of winter. During lent, when people had to fast, the brewers of Munich, who at the time were mostly Italian Catholic monks, petitioned the Pope to be allowed to brew an even stronger version of bock beer so that they could consume it during Lent for nourishment. After all, Germans viewed beer as liquid bread. The Pope approved. This special brew became known as *doppelbock* or doublebock. Technically, this brew has to have an original gravity of 18 degrees Plato, as compared to regular bock beer, which has to have an original gravity of at least 16 degrees Plato. Therefore, this brew is not double the strength of bock beer, but only slightly higher.

The Paulist monks running Paulaner Brewery in Munich started a naming convention for his style. They first gave this strong brew a religious name, Salvator, after the savior. It then became the norm to name doublebock with a word that ended with the four-letter "ator" combination. Soon there were doublebocks with names like Celebrator, Optimator, and so on. If you are in a store and see a beer with a name ending in "ator," it will probably be a high-strength doublebock, even if the word doublebock doesn't appear on the label. The most interesting name I've seen for a commercial doublebock is one from California that plays off on the inherent strength of the beer. It's name is SeeYouLator!

whole nine yards." A proper English suit requires nine yards of material. That's also the origin of the phrase, "dressed to the nines." That's one of my favorites. I had always assumed it came from sports. How the hell did I find out it was tied to English suits? I call this the "A-ha" factor, that all-of-sudden realization that pops into your head when you learn something you never knew before, and suddenly things fall into place.

When I was trying to understand beer, people threw a lot of information at me, and I could only retain a very small percentage of it. But when you embrace the A-ha! factor, it's easier to remember things. For example, if I tell you that ales have a fruity aroma and lagers don't, and that in ancient Greek, *Briton* meant beer, I'll bet dollars to doughnuts that you will remember Briton means beer a lot longer than the fruity aroma. But if you go into a restaurant and see an ale and a lager on the menu, the Briton thing will pop back into your mind and with it will come the primary difference between ale and lager. When I tell people that ales are fruity and lagers aren't, I'd guess that at least 80 percent of them would forget it by the next time they go into a bar. But by associating them with *"Briton* is ancient Greek for beer," the information will probably come right back for them.

The following sections will take you through the color descriptors for beers and tell you how the colors developed, as well as how some of the styles originated. Remember, brewing is mechanical. History is where the romance is!

BROWN BEERS

As I said at the beginning of this chapter, all beers were brown ales up until about 300 years ago. It's hard to pinpoint the origin of a particular brown beer because they've always been around. Even in medieval Europe, at least from the Alps up to the North Sea, beers from barley were made at so-called "brown" or "red breweries," named after the color of the beers they made. Places that brewed wheat malt beers were called "white breweries" because the beers were lighter in color and had a thick, white head.

Look again at the Spectrum of Beers. The primary beer styles of this color are *doublebocks* on the lager side, and English and American brown ales on the ale side. Doublebocks are very brown because of the amount of malt used. The ingredients are the same as regular *bocks,* but because brewers use more malt, doublebocks get a higher alcohol strength. The extra amber-colored malt darkens the beer.

Now let's go back in time to the turn of the 1700s. Some beers were still being made without hops, and they were called ales. Beers that were made with hops were called beers. Other ingredients were also used in making beer, including molasses, another source of sugar. In fact, there was a so-called "two-penny beer" that was made from treacle, a form of burnt molasses.

It's important for you to know that these beers weren't necessarily good. Brewing techniques were still a mystery, even to brewers; sometimes things worked out nicely and sometimes they didn't. Beer went bad, sometimes on purpose because of the vats it was stored in. One form of beer back then was called "stale" beer. This beer wasn't stale but aged for a long time in wooden casks where it would develop a tartness from bacteria living in the wood of the casks. There were many types of beers available back then, but this cast of characters is enough to continue with the story of brown ales.

In 1722, a brewer by the name of Ralph Harwood owned a pub in London where he sold ale, beer, and two-penny. His customers were typically porters, the heavy workers of London. The porters wanted a mixture of beers: one-third ale, one-third beer, and one-third two-penny. He called the collection of three thirds, or three threads, an Entire or Entire Butt (the name for a cask). The taste of this mixture was in high demand. In the course of serving all of his customers, Harwood didn't have time to individually mix each of the three. Instead, he brewed a beer from scratch that he had hoped would taste like the mixture of his three beers. He named this new beer porter, after his customers. This beer has come to be a slightly darker beer than English and American brown ales.

Personally, I think there is a little more to this story. First and foremost, most beers of the time were not reproducible. The science of brewing had not advanced enough for us to believe that any of Harwood's beers tasted alike, batch after batch. Additionally, a good number of batches would have turned sour; it is likely that the original porter tasted differently from batch to batch. The brewing books of the 1700s suggested that brewers ought to blend bad beer with good beer so they could sell it all. Another suggestion was that they make beer with strong flavorings, such as those from spices, which would help mask the taste of beer gone bad. In many respects, adding

Sir John Barleycorn, Miss Hop, and their only child, Master Porter. This engraving, illustrating the close relationship between agriculture and beer, was published by Thomas Tegg, circa 1800.

more roasted grain adds significant burnt flavor, and that helps mask "off" flavors.

The most likely scenario, in my humble opinion, was that Harwood was mixing two of his "lighter" style beers, the ale and the beer, with two-penny, which was a black beer made from treacle (burnt molasses). The two-penny would have covered up any mistakes in the ale or beer. Therefore, this enterprising businessman would not have lost any money on his bad batches. I give Harwood credit because this new beer, porter, took England by storm. It became the most popular beer in England at the time.

Another version of porter was one that was served extremely young; that is, without aging or staling. This version was called a "mild." Mild it wasn't, because young beers are very rough in taste. Mild also wasn't mild in alcohol, since it was a strong beer like porter. What it was, was cheap! Without aging, the price could be kept low. Therefore, milds were the beers of the common people. They could even be made during the summer, since there was no real aging and bacteria wouldn't have sufficient time to dominate the taste of the beer.

Milds continued to be the cheap, everyday drink of the working population. Let's move on to 1915 and the Defence of the Realm Act. As a result of this act, beer was now to be taxed according to its alcoholic strength. To keep the beers of the common workers affordable, breweries actually started to make milds that were also mild in alcoholic strength. The alcohol content of a mild today is in the 2-percent to 3-percent range. This is yet another fine example of how styles evolve over time.

In England, beer has traditionally been consumed in pubs on draught. Back in the 1920s, people began to accept the idea of buying bottled beers. Newcastle Brewing decided to come up with a new formula to take advantage of bottles. They created Newcastle Brown, which was effectively a bottled mild. A-ha! We've finally made it to this century. English brown ales like Newcastle Brown, are indeed brown. They tend to emphasize the malt in the beer rather than the hops. Therefore, as you can see on the Spectrum of Beers, English brown ales are on the sweet side.

American brown ales have a slightly different story. First of all, this wasn't an "official" style until about 1992. My theory on how this style got started is directly related to the progress of American homebrewing of the 1970s and early 1980s. Homebrewers in the United States were never limited to brewing only ales or only lagers. They have been fortunate in the increase of generally available sources for raw materials, as well as an ever-expanding library of homebrewing books. In many cases, experimentation by American homebrewers has created new styles. For example, American pale ale is much more hoppy and bitter than its English pale ale cousin.

So where did the American brown ale style come from? One of the biggest beer competitions is the Great American Beer Festival held in Denver, Colorado. We first entered Wicked Ale in the competition in 1987, where we won a silver medal in the ale category. Back then, on the ale side of the competition there were categories for porter, stout, cream ale, and the all-encompassing ale. We were judged the second best in the ale category. In 1988, they added more categories, including brown ale, and we got a silver medal again. In 1992, they added another category called American brown ale, and we got the gold medal. I've been told that it was because of the creation of Wicked Ale, with its maltiness and balancing hop bitterness, that this new style got recognized. Not bad for playing around with ingredients for the fun and creativity of it!

> **PORTERHOUSE STEAK**
>
> After the introduction of porters in 1722, the style found wide acceptance. Alehouses that sold mostly porter soon became known as porterhouses. The actual origin of the term "porterhouse steak" is in question, but the obvious answer is that specialty steaks served at porterhouses became known as porterhouse steaks. In 1814, Martin Harrison opened an eating house in New York City that became renowned for its wonderful beef and porter. Some believe that this restaurant was actually the first to use the term porterhouse steak.

BLACK BEERS

Black beers are typified by stouts on the ale side, and *Schwartzbiers* (*schwartz* means black in German) on the lager side. As you can see from the Spectrum of Beers, there are stouts that are sweet and bitter and also types of schwartzbiers that are sweet and bitter. The key characteristic of black beers is the burnt flavor of fully roasted barley malt. The real revolution in black beers came in 1817, with the invention of the drum roaster by Daniel Wheeler. Wheeler patented his process, and the malt made in his machine is therefore called "black patent" malt.

Before Wheeler's invention, the darkest the traditional malting process could deliver was a brown malt. It was also known as "blown malt" because the kernels of grain would begin to spontaneously combust from the high heat when left over the fire a little longer to blacken. Wheeler's invention was a rotating drum with a water spray. As the malt dried over the high heat, the drum's rotation and the water spray kept the malt from combusting. Brewers fianlly had a black malt.

It was this malt that revolutionized the brewing of dark beers. Porters were the dominant style in England for about 50 years after the first porters were brewed. But beer drinkers there wanted an even stronger version of porter. Brewers responded by adding more brown malt, which made the beer a bit more dark, as well as more burnt and bitter in taste. These beers were called "stout-porters." Over time, stout-porters became known as just stouts.

With the invention of black patent malt, brewers gained a more efficient process. The production of brown malt had been risky because of the likelihood of the roasting malt combusting, and that had made such beers more expensive. Black patent took away those risks, and because it was black, brewers needed less of it (as compared to brown malt) to darken and flavor the beer. This saved money, so within five years, just about every brewer of any size in England changed over to the new process. The new porters became very dark, and stouts became absolutely black. These beers also became much more consistent.

MILK OR CREAM STOUTS

The original stouts were very dark and had a burnt and bitter taste. After several decades, brewers came up with alternatives by adding lactose, a non-fermentable sugar to the beer. Lactose, when added to the brewing process, is not fermented by yeast and stays sweet. This sweetness overpowers the burnt, bitter flavor of the original stout. These beers became known as milk or cream stouts because lactose was known as milk sugar. Mackeson Stout is a good example of this style.

AMBER BEERS

The next advancement in beermaking was the use of coke as a fuel source. It burned more evenly and imparted no unappealing aromas; brewers could control temperatures better, although some grain still burned. With coke, you could brew an amber-colored beer instead of what had been, almost universally, a dark beer. Another improvement was the use of a tile oven to dry the grain. Tiny holes were drilled into the tiles to allow the heat to rise up while keeping the flames below. The combination of coke and improvements in the ovens led to the rapid rise of pale ales (amber in color) in the early 1700s.

The only other significant change came in the design of a metallic bell that was put above the fire, just below the grain. This kept the flames under the the bell, but allowed the heat to rise up around the side of the bell to dry the wet grain. Beers could now be made slightly lighter in color, and they weren't smokey. The beers became more amber in color without the burned grain. (Light golden-colored beers were still not available.) It wasn't until the invention of indirect heating of the grain in 1842 that it became possible to brew golden beers. Indirect heating meant that outside air was drawn in and heated, but it was kept separate from the fire. The warmed air was blown through the wet grain to dry it, but at a much lower temperature than air heated directly by a fire.

It's hard to talk about pale ales without mentioning Burton-upon-Trent, which became the dominant brewing center in Britain next to London. The water of London, like that of Munich, is high in mineral content, which makes it hard to brew lighter-colored beers. Because the starting water wasn't acidic enough, in London and Munich they could only use roasted barley malt to make their beers. The roasted barley malt added enough acidity to the water to get the biochemical processes going. Nobody understood the chemistry of beermaking then, so they made the only thing they could — dark beers.

When folks started using coke as fuel, Burton-upon-Trent
really came into its own. The mineral content of the town's water
was such that it had a natural acidity perfect for making beers with
the new, lighter barley malt. Thus
were pale ales born, and so began
the dominance of Burton brewers.

Now, when Burton-upon-
Trent, far from the coasts of England,

FIRST TRADEMARK
One of the many Burton brewing companies that grew
in prominence was Bass. Bass Pale Ale became world-
famous. As a matter of fact, the triangle symbol of Bass
was the first recognized trademark in the world.

was trying to become a brewing power, the brewers had to figure
out how to get raw materials and how to send finished beer off to
consumers. At the time, no transportation infrastructure existed.
Although I can't be so bold as to say that it was only because of
brewing, but the emergence of Burton as a center in the brewing
trade brought with it the development of roads, canals, and eventually train networks that moved supplies into Burton and finished
product out. As far as I'm concerned, it was one more example of
how brewing influenced society in very fundamental ways.

Amber beers, whether ales or lagers, come in a fairly wide
variety of styles, but the light roasted or nutty flavor that comes from
the lightly roasted malt is common to all of them. From there, the
styles diverge. If you look at the Spectrum of Beers, you'll see that on
the ale side, the dominant style in this color is pale or amber ales. In
general, these beers emphasize some malt character, but also hop bitterness. American pale ales emphasize hops even more—that is, they
have more bitterness.

It's worth noting another amber-colored beer style. It is a
variant of pale ale called India pale ale. As England colonized the
Indian subcontinent in the late 1700s and early 1800s, military and
civil servants living there missed the English styles of beers they had
had at home, but importing beer required a three-month ocean voyage
that crossed the equator twice. The time as well as the heat ruined the
beer in transit. Imagine seeing a ship coming into port and anticipating

having beer at last, only to find out it had spoiled. And the beer didn't spoil on just this ship or that ship; it spoiled on *every* ship. Before the invention of pasteurization, beer spoiled very quickly. So, for thousands of years, it was made and consumed locally before it could go bad.

Naturally the British tried to make their home-style beers in India. It didn't work, partly because of India's warmer temperatures, and partly because the raw materials available for making beer weren't the same. What they were able to make tasted nothing like what they were used to, and they wanted something better! Sounds like a business opportunity for somebody with a solution, doesn't it.

Mark Hodgson, a London brewer in the 1820s, certainly thought so. What Hodgson recognized was that the trade business between England and India was mostly one way. Trading companies paid big fees to transport the unique products of India on ships back to England. There was not as much demand for English goods to be shipped to India. Thus, there was a pricing differential in freight between goods going to India (lower) and goods coming back to England (higher). An astute businessman, Hodgson negotiated good rates for shipping his newly invented beer to India.

And just what was this new beverage? It took advantage of two attributes of beer. First, alcohol is a preservative. If some alcohol will help stabilize a beer, then a lot of alcohol ought to give it a lot more stability. Hodgson brewed a beer with a greater barley malt content, much more than normal. More malt meant more sugars in the

---

CHANGING BEER RECIPES

Dr. Joseph Owades, the inventor of light beer, has analyzed commercial beers for decades. What's extremely interesting is to see how commercial brewers have modified their beer formulas to meet changing taste patterns. Anheuser Busch, for example, has modified Budweiser several times since World War II. The measurement for bitterness is called a bitterness unit (BU). In 1946, Bud had a BU of 20. By 1970, it had dropped to 17, and in 1980 it fell to 14, where it's been ever since. Most specialty beers have BUs of 20 and higher. For example, Heineken has a BU of 19, Bass 23, and Pete's Wicked Ale 28.

The body of many large commercial beers has decreased as well in this time frame. The body of beer, which really means how thick or thin it feels on the tongue, can be measured by something called apparent extract that is a measure of solids dissolved in the liquid.

mash tun. More sugars meant that the yeast converted this extra
sugar into more alcohol. Second, stability can also come from hops.
Hops had become the dominant spice in beer because it had a natural
preservative in it. If some hops helped stabilize a beer, then a lot of
hops ought to really stabilize it. Enough, Hodgson hoped, to survive
a three-month voyage. His India pale ales were malty, alcoholic, and
bitter, but they arrived in drinkable shape. So, did Hodgson win enor-
mous fame? Not quite. His volume was low because he was a relatively
small brewer, and he never gained the visibility his work deserved.

By the 1820s, Burton-upon-Trent had fallen on hard times.
Besides supplying lots of beer to England, the brewers of Burton had
developed a huge market for high-strength beers in the Baltic Sea area,
including the Russian Imperial court in St. Petersburg. In the early 1800s,
Napoleon stationed his fleet in parts of the Baltic to disrupt the trade
carried on English ships. This limitation on sales couldn't have come
at a worse time, because the Russian government had also slapped a very
high excise tax on English beers coming into Russia. Facing severe losses
in what had been a large market, Burton brewers jumped on board (no
pun intended) the India pale ale business. They already had the capacity
to brew a lot of beer and experience in shipping it overseas. The Burton
brewers looked to the India pale ale business to bring themselves back
to prominance and dominance. Hodgson had his day in the sun, but
the Burton brewers ultimately took over the colonial trade in beer.

On the lager side of amber beers there is the major style known as
Märzen Oktoberfest. The Märzen style and Oktoberfest styles are
basically the same. A slight variant of Märzen is called Vienna. The
styles span slightly sweet to slightly bitter. The Märzen style is named
after the month of March.

These beers were made toward the end of the brewing season. It was too hot to brew during the summer months, since bacteria became more active in warmer temperatures. In summer, the bacteria became just too numerous and competed with yeast during fermentation—and the bacteria generally won. Any beers made at this time of the year had to be consumed quickly, before the bacteria made them go bad. Sometimes these beers were stored in ice caves during the summer—where they aged (lagered)—and were consumed at the end of the summer in celebration of the harvest, as well as to commemorate the original Oktoberfest celebration.

Another type of amber-colored lager is bock beer. There are many theories on the origin of bock beer, some more believable than others. The generally accepted story places its roots in the town of Einbeck, Lower Saxony, in northern Germany. This style, as originally brewed in Einbeck, was made with barley and wheat malts. Wheat made the beer a lighter color. When the style reached Munich, the brewers faced an immediate problem: the water supply of Munich. It was similar to the problem of producing amber beers in London; that is, they had to contend with water that wasn't acidic enough. Munich's brewers had to use darker malts to acidify the water for brewing. As the success of Munich's bock beers grew, the style changed from the lighter color of Einbeck to the darker color of the Munich brews.

OKTOBERFEST

The first Oktoberfest was held in 1810 to celebrate the marriage of King Ludwig I to Princess Therese von Sachsen-Hildburghausen in October. The first festival took place in a field in Munich, and the Oktoberfest celebrations have been held in Munich ever since.

During my sabbatical, Amy and I visited Germany. We arrived on October 10, 1985, and were eager to attend Oktoberfest. But alas, we soon found out that Oktoberfest is held mostly in September. The festival is 16 days long and ends on the first Sunday in October.

Einbeck was one of several Baltic cities that were members of the Hanseatic League. At the height of the league in the fourteenth and fifteenth centuries, Einbeck was Germany's top beer-producing town. These brewers also took advantage of alcohol's ability to act as a natural preservative, making their brew from more grain, which extracted more sugar and yielded a higher alcohol content. The alcohol stabilized the beer for travel. Current German definitions of bock beer say that it has to have an original gravity of 16 degrees Plato. Most beers have a starting gravity of 12 degrees to 13 degrees Plato, which means that bock beer is about a quarter to a third stronger than regular beer.

> **WORD/PHRASE: BOOTLEGGER**
> Prohibition prompted the invention of many methods for handling illegal liquor. Gentlemen of the era were known to wear high boots. Some individuals had the tops of their boots modified with custom-made compartments where they could hide their spirits and thus be assured of a drink when one was desired or smuggle them into speakeasies and other distribution centers.

The pronunciation of "beck" was *bock* in many German dialects, so Ein**beck** became Ein**bock**. This style became well-known throughout the Hanseatic trading area. In 1614, the brewers of Munich attempted to replicate this style and did such a good job that they put Munich on the beer map of the world. They helped their cause by bringing the head brewer of Einbeck down to Munich to show them how it was done. In fact, the historical record tells us that they kept the Einbeck brewer under house-arrest at the Hofbrau Haus in Munich. This style, with it's Munich twist, became very popular.

Bob Brown, in the book, *Let There be Beer*, traces the name *bock* back to the Roman Emperor Julian. Julian insisted that beer could never be an offspring of Zeus, like wine, because of its foul smell. Beers of the time, like lambic, that spontaneously fermented with wild yeast and bacteria in the air developed rather distinctive aromas. Julian thought the smell of beer was more like the odor of a goat than the bouquet of wine!

Some people believe that bock beers were to be consumed under the zodiacal sign of the goat, Capricorn (December 23 to January 20). Others think that bock beers were made under the sign of Capricorn for consumption during springtime. Another animal of the zodiac, Aries the Ram, is the sign for the mid-year Equinox, but it most likely wasn't associated with bock, even though "ram" is another translation of the German word bock. The brewers of Einbeck made bock beers year-round. Personally, I like to think of this higher-strength, beefier brew being merrily consumed at the close of winter and the rebirth of spring.

Another story of the origin of bock centers on an argument between a personage from Lower Saxony (area where Einbeck is located) and a Duke in Bavaria (where Munich is) about whose beer was better. They finally decided to have a contest. Each had to drink beer from the other's area, chugging it out of very large vessels. After half an hour, they had to stand on one leg and thread a needle. A maid was sent to get the needles and thread, and she mistakenly left the gate to the courtyard open. The Bavarian was able to thread his needle on the first try. The guest from Lower Saxony dropped his needle and thread three times, drunkenly rolled on the ground, and proclaiming that a goat had entered the courtyard and knocked him over. The Bavarian laughingly said that the bock that had knocked the guest over was actually the beer brewed in Munich. In commemoration of this event, the court brewery in Munich brewed the strong, sweet bock we have today.

GOLDEN BEERS

We've seen that beer gets its color from the drying and roasting of the barley at the end of the malting process. The longer and

> **FACT: BOCK MEANS BILLY GOAT**
> Bock beers traditionally use a billy goat on the label because the German word *ziegenbock* (or just bock) means "billy goat." It's true folks!

hotter the drying process, the darker the malt becomes and the darker the resulting beer. The remarkable thing about golden beers, which represent the vast majority of all beers consumed around the world today, is that they are a fairly recent arrival to the brewing world. Pilseners are the most common kind of golden beer.

I get a kick out of asking my audiences whether they've heard of the beer style called Pilsener. Usually 90 percent of the hands go up. Then I ask who can describe what the heck a Pilsener is, and all the hands go down. Actually, some people keep their hands up and

MYTH: BOCK BEERS ARE MADE FROM SCRAPPINGS TAKEN FROM BREWING KETTLES EACH SPRING

When I lived in Rochester, New York, I still wasn't a beer drinker, although socially an occasional beer crossed my lips. Genessee Cream Ale was the local beer of choice. Each spring for only a couple of weeks, people would literally jump at the chance to get the long-anticipated seasonal beer that Genessee Brewing called Genny Bock.

I was truly amazed at how many people talked about this seasonal beer. They'd go out and buy large stacks of cases before it disappeared for another year. Not knowing anything about beer, I asked these Genny Bock fanatics what was so great about it and, by the way, what was a bock beer? To a person, they gave me the same answer: Once a year, the brewery would go in and scrape down the brewing tanks to get rid of the crud that had accumulated during the course of the past year. This crud was darker and added a unique flavor to the beer. It would accumulate at the bottom of the brewing tank with the lighter beer at the top of the tank. Thus the bock beer was only brewed during this "spring cleaning" of the tanks. Hey, it sounded good enough for me. When I first tried it, it was a darker color and did have more flavor, so that must have been how they made it, right?

Now I know better. First of all, in a brewery, cleanliness is paramount. After each batch, everything is cleaned and disinfected so crud does not accumulate in the tanks. Second, when you make beer in brewing vessels, the beer is the same from top to bottom. Dark beer isn't at the bottom and light beer isn't at the top. The beer does not separate. Last, bock beer is it's own style brewed separately to celebrate spring.

PITCHER

When I first heard of leather cups, I found the idea intriguing: How the heck did they sew the leather to make a cup and still keep it from leaking? (Sorry; I'm too much of an engineer sometimes. A couple of hundred years ago in Britain, leather drinking vessels were called Black Jacks because they were made from black leather. They were also fairly large, sometimes holding as much as a gallon of beer. To make these big drinking vessels waterproof, the insides were lined with tar, also known as pitch. It's because of the pitch lining that we now call other large containers for liquids "pitchers."

I was once given a small Black Jack by a Scottish brewer. I was happy to note that the pitch used in Black Jacks is the same as the pitch brewers have used to line wooden barrels. It didn't make the beer smell or taste like you'd expect road pitch to—that stuff crews spray on the roads during the summer to fill in the cracks. So, next time you're in a bar ordering a pitcher of beer, think about drinking from the pitch-lined Black Jacks of a couple hundred years ago.

say that Pilsener is a beer that originated in some town in the Czech Republic. That is correct, but it doesn't describe what a Pilsener is.

Up until 1842, all beers were fairly dark, and they were usually unfiltered or murky. Nobody seemed to mind because nobody could see what they were drinking. Over the millennia, people have drunk beer out of shells, horns, and skulls, and used containers made from wood, pewter, ceramics, leather, and even glass. The glass that was available in past centuries wasn't what we're used to today: it was not transparent. Thus, none of these drinking vessels let you see what you were drinking. If you couldn't see the beer, it didn't really matter what it looked like.

History usually shows change coming in steps, rather than quantum leaps. In 1842, the glassmakers of Pilsen, a city in the Bohemian part of the Czech Republic, invented a new process that allowed for the making of relatively cheap, affordable clear glass.

MAZERS

Between the thirteenth and sixteenth centuries, the most common drinking vessels were called "mazers." These drinking vessels were made from wood, with the most preferred made from maple. The most sought-after type of maple was the spotted or speckled variety, commonly known as bird's-eye maple. It comes from the part of the trunk where several branches meet. The origin of the word mazer is from the middle German *mase*, meaning "a spot." Hence a cup or bowl made of spotted maple became known as a mazer. Interestingly, mase is also the origin of the word "measles."

Although transparent glass had been around for some time, it had been really expensive, so only those at the very top of society could afford it. With the advent of cheap clear glass, a new common drinking vessel became available. Guess what happened when people could finally see the dark, murky liquid that had been hidden from them for thousands of years? Their typical reaction appears to have been, *"Yuck!"*

This led brewers to devise new ways of making beer so it would look great in these clear drinking glasses. In order to brew a beer that was lighter in color, the brewers of Pilsen devised a new way of drying the grain so that it wouldn't burn at all. They constructed baffles that allowed the cooler outside air to enter and be warmed in a space above the fire chamber. This heated air was cooler than air heated directly by the fire, and no smokiness or off odors got into the brew because the hot, smokey air from the fire never mixed with the fresh hot air that had been heated in the baffles.

Now brewers could control the heated air and moderate the temperatures as they wished. The wet grain could be dried without being burned. This resulted in a type of grain called pale malt, which could be used to make a golden beer. The final step was filtering the beer. After filtering, a golden beer would actually sparkle in the clear glass when held up to the light. This new beer caused a revolution, and the Pilsener style soon took over the world. Today, any beer that is a lager, that's golden, and that's clear can be called a Pilsener!

For the record, golden ales didn't really start to appear in England until about 1845. Why did acceptance there lag behind? The people of England weren't slow to want the new golden beers; their government slowed the inevitable spread of golden beers to England. For whatever reason, the government put high taxes on the newly created clear glass so it remained relatively unaffordable. Not until 1845, did the government relax that tax. At that point, brewers and beer drinkers in England went through the same process as the residents of Pilsen. They didn't like the dark, cloudy beers they could now see, and British brewers quickly got on the bandwagon and started brewing golden beers.

Within the Pilsener category, there are a variety of sub-styles. The most popular, in terms of sheer volume consumed, is American lager or, as it's sometimes known, American light lager, which is very light in color, taste, and aroma. This style occupies a small space just to the right of the center on the Pete's Spectrum of Beers. It can be just slightly sweet or bitter. Since the style by definition minimizes flavor, any flavor would be a lot within these sub-styles.

The more flavorful versions of the Pilsener style are the Bohemian Pilseners and the German Pilseners. Bohemia is the part of the Czech Republic where Pilsen is located. The most notable characteristic of Bohemian Pilseners is the emphasis on the hops. A Bohemian Pilsener will start out with a slight sweetness from the malt at the front tip of your tongue, but that's soon followed by a delightful lingering bitterness on the back of the tongue. The taste sensations are accompanied by the fragrant aroma of the hops when you smell a Bohemian Pilsener. Truly a classic! Hold one up to the light and see it sparkle through the clear glass, smell the wonderful hop aroma, and then taste this slightly sweet and delectably bitter liquid of the gods.

I have to admit that when I tried the original Pilsner, Pilsner Urquell, at the brewery in Pilsen, it was not only true to the style, but also absolutely one of the best beers in the world. On this particular trip, a weekend excursion into the Czech Republic during a business trip to Munich, my friend Joan Gurasich and I traveled through Pilsen to Prague and back, all in a weekend. Finding the brewery was one of the strangest experiences I've come across in my brewery searches. We left Munich very early on Saturday morning and got to Pilsen about 10:30 A.M. This city of over 100,000 people was deserted; there were no cars moving, no people walking outside, nobody anywhere. We followed signs to the city centrum and the tourist information center. At the information center, we saw four other people, and that was it. We got directions to the brewery but found out that it was closed on Saturdays. All was not lost, however, because the pub at the brewery was open, and we were able to get fresh beer. A liter of Pilsner Urquell cost about forty cents in 1989. I splurged and had two!

On the way back the next day, our path crossed through Pilsen, so of course we had to stop at the brewery. This time it was Sunday, and the city that had been deserted the day before was totally back to normal. People were everywhere. My friend and I thought we had passed through the *Twilight Zone*. I still don't know what caused the Saturday disappearance of the population of this mid-sized city.

By this time, our Czech money was dwindling. We had converted just enough to get us through the weekend. We discovered that to use the bathrooms at the pub at the brewery, you have to pay an attendant. Our Czech money supply was only enough for beer and one person going to the bathroom. Fortunately, Joan let me go.

The other flavorful version of Pilsener is the German Pilsener, sometimes called a Pils. The German version is also incredible. In a nutshell, the German Pilseners put more emphasis on the malt flavor and sweetness. These beers are still bitter, but they don't have the lingering bitterness of the Bohemian Pilseners. Their malt flavor is more pronounced than their Bohemian counterparts. Both are great beers. An interesting experiment is to taste a German and Bohemian Pilsener side-by-side to see for yourself how the malt and hop emphasis changes slightly between the two sub-styles.

I do have to laugh about one thing connected to Pilsener Urquell. They bill themselves as the original Pilsener, dating back to the 1300s. While I don't doubt that they were the original Pilsener, I do think specifying the 1300s is a bit of a stretch, especially since the Pilsener style wasn't developed until 1842. They may be the original Pilsener, and the brewery may date back to the 1300s, but it's funny when they try to combine these two facts.

THE EFFECT OF GOVERNMENT ON BEER

Over the ages, there were a lot of laws passed in what we now know as Germany regarding beer. One of the first of these laws was an ordinance issued in Nürnberg in 1290 prohibiting the use of oats, wheat, and rye in brewing. Within the state of Bavaria, local beer laws were also passed from time to time. In 1487, a Munich ordinance stipulated that only barley, hops, and water could be used in the making of beer. The "beer laws" often went beyond the control of ingredients, to limit the price of beer as well.

In 1516, Bavaria instituted the Purity Law, the Reinheitsgebot, which decreed that beer could only be made from barley, hops, and water. Later on, the list was expanded to include wheat, but barley was definately the dominant beer grain. What's funny about all these regulations, is that no one knew about the function of yeast until the 1800s or so, and the Germans didn't include it in any of those early edicts.

The English also limited the ingredients that could be used in making beer. Those early brewers got a little out of hand, using bittering herbs and spices that were cheaper than hops and substituting hallucinogens for barley malt because they were cheaper. If you could make a beer that gave you a buzz but saved scads of money, some brewers were definitely going to do it. The British finally came up with their own laws to regulate ingredients, though they weren't as limiting as the Germans' Reinheitsgebot.

Was Reinheitsgebot a good thing? The answer depends on your point of view. I believe it served a purpose for keeping bad things out of beer. But, there are some incredible styles of beer from Belgium and England that would have been ruled out because they contain additives like spices, fruit, candy sugar (rock candy), and so on. Even styles like oatmeal stouts or honey beers would have been outlawed. In fact, Reinheitsgebot has now been deemed illegal in Germany because of its membership in the European Community (EC). Reinheitsgebot prohibited beers made by other member countries from being sold in Germany, and that barrier had to fall when Germany joined the EC.

When you go to a store in the United States and buy a bottle of Bass, look at the label. At the bottom are three letters, IPA. Taste this beer. Not bad for an amber or pale ale, but India pale ale, I don't think so. So why does Bass put IPA on the label? I understand it's meant to be a historical note, not a reflection on the current beer. I will say this: The

REINHEITSGEBOT: THE GERMAN BEER PURITY LAW OF 1516

Here's a translation of the law by Karl Eden, published in *Zymurgy,* vol. 16, no. 4 (Special Issue, 1993)

We hereby proclaim and decree, by Authority of our Province, that henceforth in the Duchy of Bavaria, in the country as well as in the cities and marketplaces, the following rules apply to the sale of beer:

From Michaelmas to Georgi, the price of one Mass [a Bavarian liter 1,069] or one Kopf [a bowl-shaped container for fluids, not quite one mass] is not to exceed one Pfennig Munich value, &

From Georgi to Michaelmas, the Mass shall not be sold for more than two Pfennig of the same value, the Kopf not more than three Heller [a Heller is usually one-half Pfennig].

If this not be adhered to, the punishment stated below shall be administered.

Should any person brew, or otherwise have, other beers than March beer, it is not to be sold any higher than one Pfennig, per Mass.

Furthermore, we wish to emphasize that in [the] future in all cities, markets, and in the country, the only ingredients used for the brewing of beer must be Barley, Hops, and Water. Whosoever knowingly disregards or transgresses upon this ordinance, shall be punished by the Court authorities' confiscating such barrels of beer, without fail.

Should, however, an innkeeper in the country, city, or markets buy two or three pails of beer [containing 60 mass] and sell it again to the common peasantry, he alone shall be permitted to charge one Heller more for the Mass or the Kopf, than mentioned above. Furthermore, should there arise a scarcity and subsequent price increase of the barley [also considering that the times of the harvest differ, due to location], We, the Bavarian Duchy, shall have the right to order curtailments for the good of all concerned.

government of England has done a lot to affect beer styles. Taxes on coke, taxes on clear glass, taxes on malt, taxes on beer, taxes on … Well, you get the point.

One of the most damaging government regulations (aside from Prohibition, which affected beer styles by making *all* of them illegal) was England's 1915 Defence of the Realm Act. It affected beer manufacturing and consumption in many ways, but the most critical, in my mind, was that it shifted taxes on beer to a sliding scale. The higher the alcoholic content of a beer, the higher the taxes on it. The higher the taxes, the more limited the consumption would be. During the course of the twentieth century, the brewers of England have responded to this act by lowering the alcoholic strength of their beers. The actual measure used for taxation is the original gravity of the beer, which represents the amount of dissolved sugar in the liquid before fermentation. The higher the original gravity, the higher the potential alcohol in the beer. Between 1915 and now, the average original gravity in British beers has gone down about 40 percent.

That means most English beers are now about half the strength of our beers. As a matter of fact, they call these beers "session beers" because you can drink a lot of them without getting wasted.

POSH

The word "posh," which we know as meaning something really nice, is not really a word, per se, but an acronym. It comes from Port Outbound, Starboard Homebound. The association to beer may be a bit loose, but it's still pretty cool. In order for beer to last the three-month voyage from Britain to the Indian sub-continent, brewers had to develop a special style of beer that was hearty enough and stable enough not to turn sour and spoil while at sea. India pale ale (IPA) was developed so that the British civil servants and the military could have home-style beers in Asia. Because of the prevailing winds on the long journey, one side of the ship tended to be more comfortable (less hot) than the other side. Ship owners charged more for the comfortable or posh side: portside outbound, starboard homebound.

Once, after judging beers at the Great British Beer Festival, I traveled with my wife to Belgium for several days. I asked Michael Jackson, the famous beer writer, to recommend a bar in Ostend (the ferry stop in Belgium) with a good selection of Belgian beers. He directed us to an affordable hotel with a pub that had a fantastic beer selection—over 400 Belgian beers to choose from. We sampled several beers and talked to the owner about how great these beers were and how they could best be appreciated when sipped out of big Belgian goblets.

The owner listened to my comments and said he was pleased that I understood Belgian beers. He said that most of the British who came over didn't. Why? Because they assumed they would still be drinking the English session beers with 2- to 3-percent alcohol instead of 6- to 8-percent alcohol. If you drink a half a dozen beers, that difference in alcohol content adds up quickly. It suddenly dawned on me that the 1990 soccer riots in Belgium could have been caused by the British drinking their normal quantities, but now drinking the higher strength Belgian beers. The owner of the bar smiled when I said that, and my theory may have been confirmed that evening. Michael had said the hotel was adequate, and we found out that adequate meant it had paper-thin walls. While trying to sleep at 3:00 A.M. Two Brits started arguing next door and soon escalated into exchanging blows as well. It sounded as if they were *in* our room. I could only think about how much Belgian beer they had probably consumed.

Unfortunately, the lower strength of British beers means that a lot of the classic styles from Britain no longer resemble their former selves. If they did, the price for the beer would be a lot higher because those beers originally had a much higher alcohol content. In any case, Bass and other British brewers put IPA on their current beer because that is the prevailing style in England today. And even then, it's certainly not the IPA of England of the 1820s nor of America today!

Did you ever imagine that beer covered such a wide-ranging landscape? There is certainly a lot more to beer than Bud, Miller, and Coors. These three brewers dominate the U.S. markets, producing almost 80 percent of the beer sold here. Specialty brewing has brought diversity, choice, color, flavor, aroma, and a greater sense of beer history to the public, and I hope that you've gotten enough of a sense of the wonders beer can hold to experiment on your own.

Looking back, you can see that brown beers were the original beers, and that improvements in malting due to the drum roaster, the use of coke as fuel, and figuring out how to supply indirect hot air for drying helped create black, amber, and golden beers respectively. The chemistry of water, technology improvements, government regulation, and to some extent, human greed have led to the creation and modification of many styles. For example, golden beer couldn't have been invented in London or Munich. A brewer's art and technique can also lead to different results and new styles. And let's not forget that sometimes even accidents or failures can lead to new styles altogether, as was the case for my first commerical beer, Pete's Wicked Ale.

May beer-style bigots be damned! They lack the historical perspective to realize that their edicts on beers styles are altogether too static and too contraining. Unfortunately, they often rule over competitions and define styles so narrowly that independent judges are forced to pass over truly amazing beers and give awards to "cookie-cutter" brews. This is the part of judging competitions that I don't enjoy.

Beer has as much diversity, if not more, than wine. Beer has had an intimate impact on human history. When all is said and done, though, it really boils down to grabbing a frothy one with friends and just enjoying it. You don't have to be a beer geek to get satisfaction, but I hope you've learned enough to increase your appreciation for beer. I hope we never go overboard and develop as snobby an attitude as some wine drinkers have. Maybe one day you'll be able to detect the difference between Saaz hops and Cascade hops, but as long as you can grab a beer and think, this looks great, smells great, and tastes great, then I've done my job.

CHAPTER 9

Attack of the King:
Millie v. Spuds MacKenzie

You can only drink thirty or forty glasses of beer a day, no matter how rich you are.

—Adolphus A. Busch

Competition in business is a given. It takes real determination for small businesses to weather the competition and survive, especially when the competition is a multibillion-dollar-a-year business. Pete's Brewing Company has had the distinct honor of twice being directly attacked by Anheuser Busch (AB), the makers of Budweiser, the "king of beers."

The first conflict centered around using my dog Millie on our initial label. About six months after we launched the beer, my partner, Mark, was over at my house watching the David Letterman show, and during the program, out struts another English bull terrier, Spuds MacKenzie, the designated party animal from AB. We couldn't believe it—two breweries using English bull terriers at the same time? We were pissed. It wasn't long before we received a letter from AB stating that it had come to their attention through the federal label approval process that we were using a bull terrier and that was causing confusion in the marketplace, so we were to stop using our dog. Now they had gone too far!

We had our lawyer send a letter specifying the details and time frame of our use of Millie on the label. It took almost a year to get a response to our letter. By then, AB relented and stated that they had no problem with our using Millie on the label. Of course they

Top: *Me holding the original Millie six-pack and bottle with the Latin motto* Cave canum nidentum, *"Beware of the Shining White Dog."* **Middle:** *Me, Mark Bronder, Audrey MacLean (another investor), and Millie.* **Bottom:** *Millie.*

wouldn't have a problem with our using Millie: We were first!
Maybe they didn't have a problem, but we did. We checked with several lawyers and got the same basic response. We only sold our beer in California, so the absolute best we could hope for would be to prohibit the use of Spuds MacKenzie in California. There were no guarantees that this would be the ultimate result. If anything, we could lose our company in legal fees. Did we want to be in the legal business or in the beer business? We were first, but what mattered was who had the most financial resources.

We watched Spuds age as a marketing tool and then there came the public outcry that Spuds, the party animal, had the potential to induce underage drinkers to start drinking. So, in 1989, Millie disappeared along with Spuds, her well-to-do imitator, and we went forward with a new label. We never forgot Millie, however. She did come back for a short stint on our tenth-anniversary label.

Round two with Anheuser Busch took place in 1994. We had teamed with the advertising agency of Goodby, Silverstein in San Francisco to produce some TV ads. Our budget did not allow us to go national with the ad campaign, but we planned to hit eight metropolitan areas where there was a high incidence of specialty beer drinking, including Seattle, San Francisco, Boston, and Denver. The ads were to show me at a table on the street in San Francisco trying to give away my autograph or a "picture with Pete" to passers-by. Of course, no one would want them, and we would finish with the tag line, "Not Yet World Famous." It was brilliant! We were treating our beers very seriously, but having fun with ourselves. The three resulting spots had a great sense of humor; I, of course, was the butt of the jokes.

It was a lot of fun to make the spots, but I was nervous as hell. Not having done anything like this before, I was real curious about what I'd have to do. When the initial filming day arrived, I had no idea what was going to happen. I was to show up at a certain address in San Francisco at 7:00 A.M. and Jeff Goodby, one of the agency principals, would take me through the activities of the next several days. Well, I showed up at the appropriate time and place. All Jeff told me was to put the radio piece in my ear, attach a hidden microphone to my shirt, and take a seat behind the actual table where I'd be sitting for the filming. That was it. That was the only instruction. I can usually go with the flow, but I was real nervous at this point.

The first location was in the financial district, and people were on their way to work. The cameras were hidden; we wanted to get unrehearsed, "real" responses from the folks walking by. It was exciting to see the crew do all of the setups and watch the agency people stationed at the ends of the block to get people to sign waivers after they were "on-camera." We had bottles and signage indicating that I was "the Pete" of Pete's Brewing Company. The only problem was that I didn't know what the hell I was supposed to be doing! Jeff came through over my ear-piece—he was in a van across the street—and told me to try to get people to stop, sometimes for autographs, sometimes for pictures, or even just to talk about sports. The whole point was to have people blow me off.

It was in the high 40s for most of the day, and I only had a short-sleeved polo shirt on, so I was nervous *and* freezing, but what the hell, why fight it, let's just go on with the show. I started encouraging people to stop. Jeff was great! He always suggested things for me to say, some of which were so off-the-wall that they'd get a reaction out of people. Most people ignored me, but I was amazed at how many people actually stopped. Many of them knew of me, and at least a dozen turned out to be people I actually knew. Sometimes crowds would form, and Jeff would scream through the ear piece to get rid of these people. What he wanted was the reaction of those who blew me off. It got to be a lot of fun.

Jeff didn't always help me out. He wanted to throw me some curve balls and get my reaction recorded on film. The best one he did was send a cop up to my table to grill me about what was going on. At the beginning of the day, Jeff introduced me to a San Francisco motorcycle sergeant who would be with us for the shoot to control traffic when we needed it. He stationed himself off to the side, but stayed within sight.

Lo and behold, this other cop comes up to me and starts shaking me down with questions about what I'm doing on the street with beer and where is my permit. The motorcycle cop had suddenly vanished, so I whispered into my hidden microphone for Jeff to bring out the permit. No response. I'm desperately trying to explain things. The cop ultimately breaks into a smile and tells me he's an actor, and that they just wanted to put me on the spot. It worked. On the final ad, if you look carefully, you can see me essentially crapping in my pants as I try to talk my way out of the situation.

The ads were a hit. People remembered them and to this day, they come up to me and tell me now much they liked the ads. After the TV ads, we tried some radio spots, but they were never as popular. Folks just loved those 1994 TV ads. Even the venerable *New York Times* rated those TV spots among the top ten campaigns of the year! Now *that* was a real endorsement. Unfortunately, someone else took notice as well.

Almost immediately after we won those accolades from *The New York Times*, Anheuser Busch, our friends from St. Louis, approached Goodby, Silverstein with a business proposition. Wouldn't Goody, Silverstein rather have a reported $31 million account with Bud Ice Beer instead of the tiny little $1 million account with Pete's Brewing Company? Well, business is business. Goodby, Silverstein made the decision to drop us and go with AB. Generally, ad agencies will only work with one client in a given industry, so we were left high and dry—"iced" by AB.

Los Altos

Town Crier

| Wednesday, Sept. 7, 1994 | Serving the residents of Los Altos, Los Altos Hills and Mountain View | Vol. 47, No. 36 • 50 cents |

Fun ads, fine ale, big bucks

Los Altos Hills resident hits the big time with beer advertising campaign.
Page 7

ST. LOUIS POST-DISPATCH

BUSINESS

• SATURDAY, OCTOBER 19, 1996

Wicked Drive

Microbrewer Isn't Afraid Of The Big Boys

We didn't take this lying down. We staged a protest out-side of Goodby, Silverstein's office in San Francisco to at least get some press coverage of what had happened. The protest attracted modest support of passers-by on the street, and some people called AB's headquarters in St. Louis to protest. Best of all, a reporter/photographer from the Associated Press came by at almost the exact time that an ad agency across the street unfurled a two-story banner out their window exclaiming, "Will work for beer." Timing is everything. We got coverage in about 30 newspapers around the country with the picture of the other agency's banner. The protest also helped us develop a new agency relationship. We soon received requests from over 300 agencies around the country to be our new partner.

Left: *During the Goodby, Silverstein protest, another ad agency down the street wanted our business.* **Right:** *Me protesting Goodby, Silverstein.*

Our latest round with AB involves their use of muscle to tell their wholesalers (mostly independent business people) to drop any products that they carry that aren't AB products. This "request" is followed up with financial incentives for the wholesalers who dropped other products (such as ours). Most consumers don't hear a lot about what competitive actions go on, but trust me, the big guys have the resources to make the competitive arena favorable for themselves through covert as well as overt actions.

Anheuser Busch has also gone after contract brewers. They ran a campaign that asked where these beers are made. AB was trying to imply that beers like ours are the same as the beers of the brewery where we rent time and space to create our special offerings. This couldn't be further from the truth. I did, however, come across some interesting material in my historical research. It just so happens that Budweiser, AB's flagship product, was somebody else's contract brew AB took over!

Aldolphus Busch traveled around Europe with this friend of his, Carl Conrad. In 1873, Conrad, who was a wine merchant, contracted with Busch to brew a beer for him called Budweiser. Busch didn't bottle the beer for Conrad but shipped it to him in bulk for his company to bottle and sell. In January 1883, C. Conrad and Company went into bankruptcy. AB, Conrad's largest creditor, took over the bottling and selling of Budweiser. A court case eight years later confirmed the transfer of the Budweiser title to AB. I think it's just a little funny to see the big guy going after the little guy on the contract beer issue when their flagship beer was originally somebody else's contract brew!

Competition comes in all shapes and sizes. Sometimes it's hard to just hold your own and make enough money to keep the doors open, without having to worry about fighting off giants. Such are the challenges of doing business in the twentieth century.

Part Three

BEER IS PROOF THAT GOD LOVES US

—BENJAMIN FRANKLIN

CHAPTER 10

THE INDIANA JONES OF BEER

Mike Hammer drinks beer because I can't spell cognac.

—MICKEY SPILLANE

T here are times when you hear things that are just too hard to believe. There are, however, beer stories—true stories—for almost anything.

One starts back in the summer of 1993. At the time, we were launching a new product called Pete's Wicked Red, an amber ale. Red beers were the rage, and many of the large brewers were coming out with "red" products. We wanted to see if we could separate Wicked Red from the others by saying that red beers weren't a marketing gimmick, that there was actually a historical perspective to red beers.

When we introduced our product, I called Alan Eames whom I had met the year before at the KQED beer festival. Alan is so animated that the stories he tells come to life—usually beer stories. Alan's nom-de-plume is "The Beer King" or "The Indiana Jones of Beer." Why? Because he's spent so many years researching the history of beer and its role in indigenous cultures around the world. Alan holds a Ph.D. in cultural anthroplogy, and is author of *The Secret Life of Beer, A Beer Drinker's Companion,* and *The Oldenberg Beer Drinker's Bible.* He also reads and translates ancient hieroglyphics!

Alan has been prolific in writing stories about beer in magazines and newspapers as well and is an active speaker at industry events. He was even on the *Today Show* on NBC talking about beer history, and was so animated that Bryant Gumbel wasn't able to get a word in edgewise. Alan has a good sense of humor. For example, he had previously run a pub in Portland, Maine, by the name of Three Dollar Dewey's. After I met him, I was curious about where this name came from. "Oh," he said, "you never heard the phrase one dollar lookee, two dollar touchee, and three dollar dewey?"

When I asked Alan about Egyptian beer, the beer stories literally flowed off his tongue. I was stoked, but also skeptical about the authenticity of many of the things I heard. With Alan, you never know what's real. So much sounded like cock-and-bull stories; in many cases, they often sounded completely unbelievable. In any case, I was in awe of Alan, almost intimidated by his vast knowledge. I'd ask a question about a beer style or an ancient culture, and he'd rattle off stories until I asked him another question. He was fast too.

Regarding red beers, he told me that black beers from Sumeria

Wicked Red label and six-pack with Hathor on the lower right side.

were the first recorded beers and red beers from Egypt were the second recorded beers. Well, that knocked me back. Should I believe him? If we were going to integrate this type of information into the launch of the Wicked Red product, I had to make sure there was some element of truth to it. (Who am I to know the truth?) I requested more information and Alan responded with the story of Hathor and how "red" beers were said to have come to Earth in ancient Egypt.

This story was pretty wild, but I thanked Alan for his help anyway. We decided to work the Egyptian theme into the introduction of the beer, so we used an actual glyph of Hathor on the label. The labels and six-packs for Wicked Red went into production, even though I was not convinced that the story had any validity. I was just

COCK AND BULL

Cock-and-bull stories are basically bullshit stories. Over the centuries, pubs in Britain have had elaborate pub signs. Initially, many signs used representations of animals and birds found out in the countryside and on farms. In a town called Stony Stratford, which was on the main road from London to the French coast, there were two pubs. One was called The Cock and the other was called The Bull. Both were staging inns, where stagecoaches would change teams of horses. While the tired horses were being exchanged for fresh ones, the travelers would retire to the pub for a refreshing drink of ale or beer. Back then, the British distinguished between ale and beer because hops, a flavoring spice in beer, was a relatively recent introduction to Britain. Ales contained no hops, whereas beer had them.

During the middle of the 1700s, Britain and France were continually fighting. The owners of these two inns were invenerate rumor mongerers and loved to tell outrageous tales of what was happening at the war front. When these tales were brought back to London, they were believed at first, but after a while, it became clear that these tales were nonsense, especially if they were heard at either The Cock or The Bull. "Just another cock-and-bull story" became synonymous with any tall tale.

betting that the Indiana Jones of Beer had to be correct, no matter how far-fetched his stories sounded to me.

Each August since 1993, with my family accompanying me several times, I've been a beer judge at the Great British Beer Festival, one of the most incredible beer festivals in the world. Just imagine hundreds of cask-conditioned real ales from Britain, as well as several hundred of the best beers from the rest of the world all in one place! We started shipping beer to the U.K. in early 1994, so part of the trip included spending time with our importer, handsome, charismatic, and personable Conor Brennan, in the market trying to sell our products. Between the festival and working with Conor, the days were pretty full, and the only time I saw my family was for a few hours at night, since I left for work before they got up in the morning.

Hathor is the glyph that looks like the body of a woman with the head of a cow. In ancient Egypt, the cow represented nourishment. Thus Hathor, as goddess of beer, was good for mankind.

On one of the few days we had together as a family, we ventured out to the British Museum. I had never been there on my earlier trips to London, so it was a great opportunity, especially since I had an interest in Egyptian antiquities—my roommate in graduate school was an Egyptologist! It was when we entered the Egyptian section of the British Museum that my heart started pounding. There, among the countless rooms housing all these antiquities, I might find some confirmation on Hathor and red beers.

The first exhibit that caught my eye was a black rock. Everything else in the room was some shade of grey, but this rock was an eye-arresting black. Approaching the rock and getting through all the people admiring it still didn't allow me to see exactly what it was. I got closer, I saw that it was only a flat rock with three sets of writing on it. What was the big attraction?

THE STORY OF HATHOR AND RED BEER

Ra, the sun-god, discovered that mankind had not been praying nor even paying attention to the gods. He grew very upset and decided to get even with mankind for ignoring the deities. Ra called forth his daughter Hathor, the divine mother figure who had suckled the pharaoh with her milk.

Ra gave Hathor three days in which she was to teach mankind a lesson. Hathor was incensed when she learned of mankind's lack of respect for the gods and took on the shape of a raging lioness. By the end of the first day, Hathor was so tired from killing people that she curled up under a tree and fell asleep.

That night, Ra looked down upon the Earth and saw the carnage that Hathor had wrought. He had a change of heart. Acting quickly, Ra sent his helpers to Aswan to bring back large quantities of red clay. Ra mixed the clay with seven thousand jars of beer to make the beer look like blood. This beer mixture was then sent to Earth and formed into a lake around where Hathor lay sleeping. The lake was flooded to a height of three hands or 22.5 cm. (I love how these myths are so "accurate.")

In the morning, Hathor awoke to a wonderful aroma. She looked around and saw herself surrounded by a lake of blood. She rose and walked to the lake's edge. The smell was so wonderful that she started to lick the liquid. Licks became gulps, and soon Hathor was so bloated with the blood-red beer that she collapsed in a stupor.

When Hathor awoke two days later, she discovered that her three days were up, and she had to return to the heavens. Mankind was saved because red beer was sent to Earth, thousands of years ago!

A cold chill went up my spine as I read the description plaque. I was standing within a couple of feet of one of the most incredible pieces of history, the holy grail of deciphering hieroglyphics: the Rosetta Stone. My goodness, I thought, the darn thing actually exists. This stone was the key that allowed scholars to finally decipher what all these Egyptian symbols actually meant, because the hieroglyphic text was translated into ancient Greek and Demotic. Wow! This discovery had opened the door to mysteries about Egypt that hadn't been answered for thousands of years.

I spent the next several hours looking around for references to Hathor and beer. No luck. All I found were small-scale scenes of life in ancient Egypt that included several breweries. That was neat,

Me at the 1993 Great British Beer Festival.

but they didn't confirm any part of the story of Hathor and red beer. Amy and the kids were getting antsy, so minus the confirmation I'd sought, I dejectedly started to leave the building.

On the way out, we decided to stop by the museum bookstore for some souvenirs. While the kids looked at stuff, I ambled over to the book section and scanned titles. One title, *Egyptian Myths,* immediately caught my eye. With a rising pulse rate, I pulled the book out and leafed to the end to see if there was any mention of Hathor in the index. Yes, there was! Whirling through the pages to the right one, I splayed the book open and read the story of Hathor and how red beers were brought to Earth. Alan was right; it wasn't just a cock-and-bull story! Alan and *Egyptian Myths* unlocked a desire inside of me to pursue the fabulous history of beer I had only suspected the existance of. Alan Eames had started me down the path of the rich history of beer, and a book had cemented my newfound interest.

I was so impressed with Alan, that I later asked him to become my mentor. We worked out an arrangement whereby he sent books or copies of articles in a monthly care package; later, we would talk about the stuff by phone. I also began to do some of my own research to see what historical resources were available and where such treasures actually existed. It was amazing. The serendipity of meeting Alan and finding a book kindled a passion for kowledge in me that is strong even today.

On this same trip to England, I met a charming woman at the Great British Beer Festival. Dr. Fiona Wood was the archivist at the Brewers and Retailers Trade Association at Portman Square in London. I asked her if it was possible for me to come over and check out the archive. She was happy to oblige.

At the appointed time, Dr. Wood walked me into the archive. It was really nothing more than a conference room with floor-to-ceiling shelves on three walls packed with books, periodicals, and industry statistics. The section of the archive dedicated to historical books about beer was only about a quarter of the total collection, but, boy, did it have some good stuff! The first time I laid my eyes on the books, I saw classics like *Curiosities of Ale and Beer* by John Bickerdyke, circa 1880, and *London and Country Brewer* by an unknown author, circa 1730. Besides the classic beer books, there were contemporary books that also contained very interesting stories.

The archive may not have had everything, but it was a great place to start. I only had about four hours to devote to the collection, and, reading just a few of the books, I realized that this wasn't going to be enough time. I asked Fiona if I could copy some of the books. She led me to a small copier, where I felt like a field mouse hiding in the corner of a grainery! I tried my utmost to copy as much as possible before I either ran out of time or got kicked off the machine by the workers who sat in the room.

OPERATION XXX DEPTH CHARGE FITMENT

Beer has been a staple of the British military for a very long time. Daily rations of beer for soldiers and sailors is a centuries-old custom. During World War II, one of most incredible military operations centered around beer. Operation XXX Depth Charge Fitment was scheduled to be carried out after D-Day. During the Normandy campaign, the invading troops had plenty of supplies of guns and ammunition, but not much beer.

This deficiency was soon remedied by the Strong and Company Brewery of Romsey, England, working in close cooperation with engineers of the Royal Air Force. Fittings were developed so that barrels of beer could be set under the wings of Hurricane and Spitfire fighter bombers. The idea was that the planes would land at the forward airfields and drop off the beer for the arriving troops before returning to pick up the real bombs. Nothing like having the foresight to make sure the beer arrives before the troops!

I chose the titles that were familiar to me at the time. There was a small window next to the copier that looked out on an alley so I could either look at the bare wall in front of me or into the alley. Copying is pretty mind numbing work. Some of them were 500 to 700 pages long! I eventually got a rhythm going. Time went by quickly, and just as I was approaching my time limit, horror of horrors, the machine broke down.

Having worked for Xerox for several years, I didn't panic. Good thing—it was just out of paper, and even I can fix that problem. Soon I was back in business, and managed to finish copying six classics before I had to leave. I figured that there was a chance that I'd be back as a judge again at the Great British Beer Festival, and I'd be able to sneak away to make more copies at Fiona's archive.

Sure enough, I've been a judge at the festival five times now, and I've gone back to visit Fiona's archive each time. Nothing changed: I would go to my corner with the small copier and have at it for as long as they'd let me. Sometimes I'd get kicked off the machine for short runs by workers, and I also had my fill of error messages. One time, the machine failed. Even though I was only a financial analyst for Xerox, I kept telling myself that I could fix the copier. I *had* to, because if I broke the machine, I figured my welcome, which wasn't exactly warm anyway by the end of one of my sessions, would get real thin.

After my fourth marathon copying session, Dr. Wood told me I'd have to stop. I guess that there had been too many complaints about my hogging the machine. I hadn't acquired all the copies I wanted, but she had been so good to me that I could only be very appreciative of what she had already allowed me to do.

Since my momentous visit to the British Museum, I've been to the Scottish Brewing Archives, the Whitbread Archives, and the Guinness Archives, as well as archives at the Siebel Institute in Chicago (America's oldest brewing school), at The Stroh's Brewing Company, and at Anheuser Busch. There's a lot of great information and history out there, but it takes a driven beer nut to go review those historical records!

The visit to AB was very, very unusual. On an plane trip a couple of years ago, I sat next to an AB sales executive and struck up a conversation with him about beer and some of the history I had gleaned from my readings. He mentioned that they had a great archive in St. Louis and that I should call the archivist to arrange a visit. In 1996, I finally had the opportunity to visit St. Louis on business. About a month beforehand, I called up the archivist to make an appointment. He wasn't there, but I left a message on his machine. I never got a call back. Two weeks before the trip, I left another message and got the same response. He may have been out sick or on vacation or even traveling, but I was a little offended that no one ever bothered to call.

In my messages, I had indicated that I would come over at 8:30 A.M. on a given day. I figured that I had nothing to lose by trying one last time. The man actually answered his phone! Again I explained who I was and what I wanted to do. He was somewhat abrupt with me and said that the AB archives were for internal use only. The information I was looking for was in the AB library, not the archives. He gave me the name and number of the librarian. I had to laugh to myself. By this time, AB had been hounding several specialty brewers, including us, primarily through some hatchet-job journalism on NBC's *Dateline* program. So here I was, trying to get into their library, but being interpreted as trying to get a look at their internal documents!

The librarian, Ann Launstein, was amenable to my visit and allowed me in. Initially, she was very leery, but after I related some of the cool beer stories I had come across and told her about some of the books that I had copied, she became more relaxed.

I told her about my search for historical beer information, and she walked me through the library into her private office. She unlocked some bookshelves, and revealed a gold mine of information.

When I looked at what was on her shelves, I was astounded to see multiple copies of some key titles, some of which had never been opened. She was amazed that I knew about so many of the books. Nobody had ever expressed an interest in them, so they'd stayed hidden away in her office. A kindred soul had been found. My time was too limited to really go through what she had available, but I knew the connection had been made. As I flipped through some of the books, she kept bringing me others to look at. It was fantastic! She now copies me on new additions to her library.

This past August, I again served as a judge at the Great Britian Beer Festival and decided to call Dr. Wood just to say hello. I found out that she had had a baby and was no longer working at the archive. The receptionist asked me if I wanted to see her replacement. Don't tell anybody, but I was able to make more copies this past summer!

CHAPTER 11

ADD A LITTLE SPICE TO YOUR LIFE

It is gratifying in these days of hop and malt substitutes and
other abominations, to know that the princes of the trade
still adhere to genuine malt and hops. ... For those who sell
adulterated beer ... no punishment can be too great.

—*W. T. MARCHANT, 1888*

When I ask people what beer is made from, many say it is made from hops. That's wrong. As I explained earlier, beer is made from grain, and hops is one of the spices used to improve the flavor. Fundamentally, through the mashing process and the creation of sugars, beer made only from grain will come out sweet. The closest example of that flavor available today is a beverage called Malta. Generally dark, Malta is popular in the Caribbean and South America. In most cases, it's just unfermented wort, the sweet result of mashing. It's an acquired taste, even for those of us who are sugar-holics. Since the earliest recorded history of beer, people have generally not liked the taste of beer made only with grain. For most that kind of beer is just too sweet. Through the centuries, brewers have added other flavorings to offset the sweetness of the grain, using just about every spice, herb, flower, bark, or twig you can imagine.

The dominant additives to grain beer have been things that are bitter. On your tongue, taste buds that detect sweet are on the front tip and taste buds that detect bitter are on the back of the tongue in the throat area. Sour and salty taste buds are on the side of the tongue. Front-to-back taste sensations have come to dominate beer.

HOPS

A great quote about hops in beer comes from an old English book dated to 1578, about 50 years after hops became cultivated in England:

> The hoppes shall be wholesome for the body and pleasenter of verdure or taste than such as be disorderly handled. You can not make above 8 or 9 gallons of indifferent ale out of one bushel of mault, yet you may, with the assitance of hoppe, draw 18 to 20 gallons of very good beere; neither is the hoppe more profitable to enlarge the quantity of your drincke, than necessary to prolong the continuance thereof; *for if your ale may endure a fortnight, your beere, through the benefit of the hoppe, shall continue a month;* and what grace it yieldeth to the taste, all men may judge that have sense in their mouths; and if the controversie be betwixt beere and ale, which of them two, shall we place in preheminence, it sufficeth, for the glory and commendation of the beere, that here in our countreye ale giveth place to it; and that most of our countrymen doe abhorre and abandon ale as lothsome drincke; in other nations beere is of great estimacion; and strayngers entertayned as their most choyce and delicate drincke; without hoppe it wanteth its chiefe grace and best verdure.

Contrasting tastes of bitter and sweet appear to be the most appealing across time, location, and culture. There is, however, one major exception —most contemporary mass-marketed beers, in which most taste has been minimized, whether sweet, bitter, or both. Lack of flavor sells!

How hops became the most common flavoring in beer makes for an interesting story. Other bitter additives have certainly come and gone. Central Europe first used hops around the eighth century. England didn't use hops until about the year 1500, and even then, they weren't accepted with open arms.

HOPS

The botanical name for hops is *Humulus lupulus*, within the family *Cannabinaceae*. Yes, you may know of another part of this family, Cannabis/Mary Jane/Marijuana. Although hops contain some con-

centration of the same active ingredient— tetra-hydra-cannabinol (THC)—the concentration is so low that you'd get sick before you'd get high by smoking it. (And just because I live in northern California doesn't mean I've tried it.) The *Lupulus* part comes from the Latin word for wolf. One could wonder why a strong word like wolf would be applied to hops, which need poles

Stringing frames for growing hops.

and wires to support the vines in their growth. Romans called hops *Lupus salictarius* because it grew on willows, much like a wolf amongst sheep. The Romans used willows as a source of medicine and as a means of protecting river banks, so to them hops were nothing but a weed that caused destruction.

Early historical references to hops in beer include those made by Pliny in his *Natural History*. Pliny states that the Germans preserved their beer with hops. Hop gardens, or humuloria, were known to exist during the eighth and ninth centuries in France and Germany.

A hop harvest.

Although hops were known in England prior to the Norman Conquest, they weren't generally used in making ales. Beer historians generally accept that hops as a beer ingredient were introduced to the English around the year 1500. Flemish immigrants, fleeing from persecution in the low countries, crossed the English Channel and arrived on the southeast coast, near Kent. Many brought hop plants with them, and the first records of the English actually growing hops date back to 1524. The first written mention of the use of hops in beer in England was in the manuscript, *Promptuarium Parvulum*, written in 1440. In it, ale is described as being consumed new, whereas beer, made with hops, was for keeping because of the preservative quality of the hops. Ale (beer without hops) had been king in England. The introduction of hops was slow to achieve recognition, but a new common name soon emerged that differentiated it from ale. That name was "beer."

Hops contain an acid that ultimately makes beer bitter. Known as alpha acid or humulone (remember, the scientific name for hops is *humulus* lupulus). Unfortunately for the brewer, this acid is not dissolvable or soluble in beer. Its normal form is a crystalline solid. However, if hops are added to the brewing process when the liquid is boiling, the alpha acid forms an isomer—a closely related chemical form. The isomer of alpha acid is iso-alpha-acid, or iso-humulone, and it is soluble in hot liquid. When hops are added during the brew kettle boiling, the isomer acid imparts bitterness to the beer.

One might expect the brewer to add all of the hops at the beginning of the boil, but that's not how it's done. Why? Because hops also have an oil that gives the flower a terrific aroma. (The flower itself also gives a unique flavor to beer.) If all of the hops are added at the beginning of the boil, the brewer would maximize the bitterness in the beer, but the boiling would drive off the volatile aroma molecules from the oil. The flavor from the hops would also be muted after a long boil.

> ### HEBREWS AND BEER
> Rabbinical tradition says that Hebrews were free from leprosy during their captivity in Babylon because they drank *"siceram veprium id est, ex lupulis confectam,"* that is, sicera made with hops, which I think could be none other than bitter beer.

Brewers typically add hops in three stages during the boil. Hops for bittering are added at the beginning of the boil. Hops for flavoring are added during the middle of the boil. Hops for aroma are added at the end of the boil. The timing of these hop additions allow brewers to adjust the bitterness, flavor, and aroma produced by the hops.

Human ingenuity led to adjustments that achieved other results as well. Since one of the main reasons hops were used was their ability to stabilize or delay spoiling of beer, brewers soon made hops their spice of choice. But hops are bitter. Some brewers, primarily in Belgium, discovered that hops also deteriorate over time. That is, the oils for aroma and the acids for bittering deteriorate over time, but *not* the chemicals that give beer stability. These brewers discovered that if they stored hops for about three years, they didn't get any flavor or aroma from the hops, but the spice still helped preserve the beer.

So it was that hops became the spice of choice in beer. Because of this, or maybe because of the lobbying efforts of hop growers, U.S. regulations now mandate that there must be hops in the brew for the product to be called beer. Now, this doesn't mean that hops are the only spice in beer. Many brewers go beyond hops, using them as a base but adding other flavors. Throughout history a wide variety of spices, herbs, flowers, and such have been used, and even today many beers include alternatives to hops for flavor and aroma. Nutmeg, coriander, and cinnamon are examples of spices that are used, particularly in winter holiday beers. A number of brewers are going back to the historical record to brew beers with alternative flavorings, adding fruit flavors, honey flavors, nut flavors, and so on.

PUNCH

The word "punch" is derived from the Hindustani word *paunch,* meaning "five." Paunch was a beverage that was a mixture of five main ingredients: spirits, water, sugar, lemon, and spices. East India traders introduced the drink to England in the 1600s. In India, they even added toasted biscuits to the drink. The English adopted the drink and beefed it up:

Whene'er a bowl of punch we make
Four striking opposites we take—
The strong, the weak, the sour, the sweet,
Together mixed, most kindly meet.
And when they happily unite
The bowl is pregnant with delight.

ALTERNATIVE SPICES

Hops only grow in a fairly narrow band of latitude around the Earth. In the United States, most hops are grown in the Pacific Northwest. If you traveled around the world at that approximate latitude, you'd hit other major hop growing areas in southern England, southern Germany, and the Czech Republic. As you travel south from the equator, you'll find major hop growing areas like the Nelson region of New Zealand. You may be able to grow hops outside this region, but it isn't easy. As you go to lower latitudes, it gets too hot, and as you go to more northern latitudes, it gets too cold.

Hops weren't grown in Scotland because it was too cold, so local brewers utilized other flavorings and spices in their beers. Heather and bog myrtle were common ingredients way back when.

SPICES

The following is an interesting list of beer additives that were common in 1822:

Sugar. This can hardly be called a drug; but as it is a great assistant from its saccharine qualities, it may be used as before directed, in private families, when malt is very dear. Indeed, the legislature has at times permitted the use in public breweries.

Spanish Juice *(licorice).* This is of two sorts, the one grown in this country and the other imported from Spain and Italy. There is no comparison between them, the foreign juice being so eminently superior; it gives flavour and colour to porter; and in the absence of the extract, I would, if brewing privately for my family, a brown beer, or for table beer, always use a portion of juice; say a pound to a quarter of malt, and so in proportion.

Coriander Seed. This is an excellent flavour; not to be used too freely. The seed should be ground or pounded. It is a very excellent stomachic, and one of the stimulants I would use in private brewing, both for flavor and real excellence.

Caraway Seed. This is a fine aromatic—warm and stomachic—gives a beautiful flavour to ale. At the moment you are about to cleanse, take half an ounce, finely powered, in proportion to one quarter of malt—mix it up with your flour and salt, and rouse it well in your tun. This quantity, however small, will give a most delightful flavour to your ale.

Orange Pea. This is ground orange peel, dried. A small quantity used in the copper before turning out, gives a very fine flavour to the gyle [wort]. There can be nothing pernicious in its use.

Ginger. This common and useful stimulant is used either in the copper or the tun. It is said, when used in the copper, to cause a flatness in the gyle. However, as a stomachic, its well-known qualities stand no need of my recommendation.

Liquorice Root. This is the root grown in this country, and known by the name of stick liquorice. It is dried and ground to a powder, and is used in ale brewings to give a sweet flavor. After all, it is useless.

Salt of Tarter. This is used in many families when beer grows too forward or stale. You put a small quantity at the bottom of your jug and draw your beer into it. This serves in a measure to correct the acidity.

Calcined Oyster Shells. A very powerful alkali, and is sometimes used to recover beer that has got too stale. You will procure the powder at the chemists. Mix it up in balls with treacle and flour, well-dried, and put two or three of these balls as large as the bung hole will admit; after a day, bung down your beer. I have heard this is highly extolled, but I confess I know little of it.

Cocculus Indicus. One of the class of drugs said to be used in the brewery, and certainly highly deleterious; its qualities are narcotic, and create a false stimulus, by which drunkenness is produced without any real strength from the beer—it creates the most violent headaches, and other diseases. Indeed, it deserves the reprobation of the public, and the just punishment of the legislature, whenever discovered in the brewery.

Opiates. Have been made up by certain drug people, in various shapes, and recommended by them as substitutes for malt; they are justly prohibited, and cannot be too much condemned.

Grains of Paradise. Are a warm and stimulating nature, creating an unnatural heat in the mouth and throat; giving a false strength to your drink, and causing a continual drought.

SPICES (continued)

Capsicum. Another stimulative, very hot, and pungent; much better left out.

Tobacco. I have heard this much extolled, but never tried it; it is of course hot and pungent, giving colour to your gyle, though, I should presume, a very unpleasant flavour. This is one of the stimulants I should avoid.

Quassia. A most excellent bitter. It is said by Quincey, in his Dispensatory, to have been discovered by a Negro slave, in the island of Surinam, during the time of a malignant fever. The decoction of this wood proved almost a specific, and brought it into universal practice. When used in the brewery it can only serve for beers to be immediately used. However wholesome the bitter, yet that oily glutinous flavour, so well known in the quality of the hops, is entirely wanting in this wood, and no dependence can be placed in the keeping of the beer.

Gentian Root. Another fine aromatic bitter; and when necessity drives the private brewer to find a substitute for hops, these two [quassia and gentian root], properly mixed and ground, are excellent succedaneum.

Ginsing. A root imported from the East—a most powerful tonic, and excellent bitter—may always be used to advantage.

Calomus Aramaticua. It is also another excellent bitter, very wholesome, and stomachic. These are the bitters that private brewers may resort to when hops become six shillings per pound.

Hatshorn Shavings. About a quarter of a pound to a quarter of malt, thrown into the copper when full boiling, serves to make the beer very fine; or ivory dust will answer the same, and is cheaper.

The Triumph of Quassia, published by H. Humphrey in 1806, depicts the main brewers of the time carrying Quassi, a negro who, in 1730, discovered medicinal properties in a South American tree now named after him. Bitter in taste, quassia was used by brewers during the Napoleonic wars as a substitute for high-priced hops. Sam II is at the front of the barrel, Combe at the back, followed by Barclay in the blue coat. On the horse are Lord W. Pelty, Lord Grenville, and Charles James Fox.

Salt. Every experienced brewer knows the value of salt. It is cleansing, detergent, and assists to soften hard liquor; if brewing with spring water, throw into the copper a handful or more of salt, according to the quantity.

Colouring. Formerly the essentia binae, or burnt sugar, was used in most porter breweries; afterwards colour was allowed by the excise; but the act was repealed in 1817. Colouring is made from boiling sugar in an iron pot to a certain consistence, and is certainly desirable in brewing brown beers, and gives both colour and flavour. Private persons may still use colour. About a pint to a quarter of malt, thrown into the copper in full ebullition just before you turn out. Elderberry juice, boiled down with strong course sugar, makes excellent colouring.

Don't be afraid to try beers with spices other than hops. They may not be familiar, but they're not totally weird! Sample them when you have the chance. The character will be different, but you may find some combinations you like even better than having hops as the only spice. Remember, beer has been around for 10,000 years, and it's only in the last few hundred that hops has dominated.

All kinds of ingredients, equipment, and training materials are readily available today. Brewing at home has never been easier. Back in 1979, I was a little bit ahead of the curve and had to sort out a lot of questions; there weren't many books or homebrew clubs to turn to. It's totally different today. With some luck and skill, you can make fantastic, world-class beers. I've judged the finals at the American Homebrewers Association's national competition, and these beers will knock your socks off! Many of them are better than most commercial beers, including beers from microbreweries and brewpubs. Of course, homebrewers don't have to be able to make two batches taste the same, but some do and have gone on to be great professional brewers. You don't have to go that far to make beer as a hobby and have some fun.

> **TIP**
>
> In taverns some time ago, publicans would place a hat or a bowl near the front entry to the establishment. If you wanted to be served—or more importantly, served quickly—you dropped money into the container as you came in. That drew the attention of the server and you would be waited on in a timely fashion. Tip is an acronym for To Insure Promptness or To Insure Prompt service.

CHAPTER 12

ENJOYING BEER
(THAT'S WHAT IT'S ALL ABOUT, ISN'T IT?)

I'll be willing to take a lesser salary. How much do beer, cigars,
and peanuts cost anyway? I don't need much to have fun.

—BRIAN KILREA, winningest coach in Ottawa 67's history

(minor league hockey), on his retirement in 1994

Beer has been the center of my life for many years now, but not the only focus. I enjoy life, everything from my beer to my job. While enjoyment of one's work isn't something every person is lucky enough to arrange, I think everyone should be able to enjoy his or her leisure, whether it's through beer or through something else.

If there's a down side to the beer business, it's not seeing my family very much. Fortunately, they seem to understand and know how much I love them. Because I travel so much, I've developed interests over the years to sustain me on the road. Trying new beers and catching up with old beer favorites that aren't available in California is one outlet; good barbecue and good cigars also catch my attention as I travel.

When I started to travel as part of my "real job" at ROLM, I got frustrated with spending evenings in endless hotels. Hotel concierges usually recommended expensive places where the food wasn't very good. As I traveled more, the cities all seemed to look the same. I love what

*Under the
arch in Saint Louis
eating barbecue.*

I call local color, those things that are unique to each city: the catfish and hush puppies of Atlanta; the fried ravioli in Saint Louis; the blue crabs of Baltimore. Now, these are the neat things that catch my fancy when I travel. There's always barbecue available too: Texas-style, Memphis-style, Kansas City–style, Carolina-style, West Coast–style, you name it. I can usually find a unique gastronomic adventure in any city. The search for the best barbecue has added immense pleasure to my traveling, as well as immense proportions to my waistline.

When Amy and I moved to the west coast, we lived in Pasadena for a while before moving to the Bay Area. Not far from where we lived was a barbecue place called Robbie's Rib Cage. With a name like that, we had to try it. Their barbecue was heavenly! We learned that they would smoke any meat you cared to bring in for a small price per pound. Parties at our home usually included a turkey that Robbie had smoked for us. We were hooked.

When we moved to the Bay Area in 1979, we wondered whether we'd be able to find 'cue that was anywhere near as good as Robbie's. Before we had kids, Amy and I used to spend weekends going around the whole Bay Area searching out great ribs. Sometimes it was just the two of us and other times it was with friends, usually homebrewing buddies who were barbecue lovers. The best methodology for sampling, especially when we hit half a dozen places in an afternoon, was to get a multiple meat sampler to share for the whole table. Everyone got enough to taste everything without getting too full. It's the only way to graze on barbecue.

We didn't hit pay dirt until my initial winemaking endeavors took us to Wine and the People in Berkeley. Fortuitously, as I mentioned in chapter 2, about two blocks from Wine and the People we came across Everett and Jones Barbecue. They serve unbelievable ribs, links, and chicken with choices of mild, medium, and WOW sauce. If Robbie's was a BBQ home run, Everett and Jones was a grand slam. Their sauce is outstanding and puts every other sauce I've tried in my travels to shame. At home I use it on everything, including baked potatoes. When I ran a marathon (and yes, I completed all 26 miles) I ran in a Super Q T-shirt from Everett and Jones.

Crossing the finish line in my Everett and Jones Super Q T-shirt with my son on my shoulders when I ran a marathon.

Amy and I must have hit a hundred barbecue places in the Bay Area. Some were good and some were not so good. Some have lasted and many have long since shut their doors. It's hard to generalize anything about barbecue in the Bay Area, let alone the whole country, but I think I've discovered what I believe to be a fundamental Law of Nature concerning barbecue:

SLOSBERG'S LAW OF RIBS:
The Quality of the Ribs Is Inversely Proportional to
The Quality of the Neighborhood.

The Law of Ribs has served me well for almost two decades. I follow it in just about all of my domestic travels. Armadillo Willie's in my home town of Los Altos, California, is the biggest exception, but people have shot holes in parts of Einstein's work, too.

I learned how to apply the Law of Ribs from author and food critic Calvin Trillin during President Jimmy Carter's administration. (Trillin had made Arthur Bryant's BBQ in Kansas City world-famous by calling it his favorite restaurant. Supposedly Carter would stop in Kansas City on his cross-country travels just to get fresh 'cue from Arthur Bryant's. For my taste, LC's in Kansas City has it all over Arthur Bryant's, although Arthur Bryant's is very, very good.) I heard an interview with Trillin on the radio, in which he told how he found these great hole-in-the-wall restaurants around the country to review. Instead of asking hotel concierges where to eat, he turned to the bell-hops. In the early 1970s, Trillin would find out from the bell-hops whether any of them had just come home from Vietnam. If so, he'd ask the vet where he planned to go for his first dinner home. These weren't the most expensive places—they were the places that these guys had been dreaming about as their tours of duty drew to an end. An absolutely astute way to find the best in local cuisine, if you ask me!

Using part of Calvin's methodology, I started looking for local workers in the hotels and asking them where they went for the best 'cue in town. Of course I'd get some strange looks, but I also got some pretty fine recommendations. Not all recommendations are equal though. Sometimes hotel people send me to decent neighborhoods, and sometimes they send me to places like the northern tip of Washington, D.C., where the surroundings are extremely questionable. One barbecue place I was sent to had no tables, but it did have floor-to-ceiling bullet-proof glass. Food and money were exchanged using a bin that could open in only one direction at a time. Even so, Slosberg's Law of Ribs has held up well over the years!

This love of smoked meat led me to also fall in love with an obscure style of beer that has died out just about everywhere except for a small town in Franconia, northern Bavaria, called Bamberg. Here they dry their barley over beechwood fires. The grain absorbs the smoke from the burning wood and imparts that flavor and aroma into the beer, which is called *rauchbier* in German or "smoke beer" in English. I love the smoke aroma that comes through in the beer, and you can taste it as well. However, my wife calls it salami beer and isn't a big fan of it. This surprises me because Amy likes Scotch whiskey, which is basically distilled smoke beer. The major difference is that in Bamberg they use beechwood to smoke the grain and in Scotland they use peat.

If you work hard at something and have a little luck besides, many wonderful things can happen. One of my crowning achievements was being invited to be a judge at the largest barbecue competition in the country, the American Royal Barbecue Competition in Kansas City. You have to have won at the state level to be in the national competition, so what makes it there is the best of the best. Entrants range from backyard buddies to commercial ventures. Only the excellence of the 'cue matters. I was among about 60 judges, including some that were certified barbecue judges—now, there's a qualification I'd like to gain in the coming year! The barbecue competition is broken up into four categories: ribs, chicken, brisket, and links. The foods are judged on appearance, texture, and taste. This was very serious work.

Between judging rounds, we got to do a lot of socializing. I felt as though I was amongst friends. When I'd mention some of the top joints I'd discovered through of Slosberg's Law of Ribs, several others at my table would nod—they'd been to these places! I wasn't the only crazy rib fanatic in the world; there were other crazies just like me. I was home!

Cigars, which now are a huge fad, have interested me from my childhood days. My grandfather, Sam Slosberg, was a cigar-chomping kind of guy. One of my fondest memories is hanging around my grandfather as a kid, especially being in his car. There was always either a live cigar smoking up his car or a pile of dead butts in the ashtray. I have always associated him with the aroma of cigars, and I loved to drive with him. It's funny, because my parents always refused to ride in his car due to the "fragrant aromas." When I first heard people complain about the foul smell of cigars, I couldn't understand what they were talking about. To me, the aroma of a cigar is a beautiful and desirous thing.

Sam's business was grain, as was his father's and also my father's. Yantic Grain supplied feed grain to farmers in eastern Connecticut. My father once asked me what I was paying for barley as a homebrewer and was blown away because I was paying between five to ten times the price of feed grain. Even though I took a different career path than my forefathers, it's kind of interesting that I wound up affiliated with the grain business after all.

Anyway, getting back to cigars. In college, there was a good cigar store across the street from the main entrance to Columbia

My great-grandfather Charles and grand-father Sam's grain business.

University. I finally got into the stogie habit, but I couldn't afford to pay very much, so I got into some low-priced cigars manufactured in Connecticut and Pennsylvania. It was just such a damn fine way to sit back and relax! I didn't smoke that often, maybe a couple per month, but I enjoyed them enormously. My habit has increased to at most one per week, and my preference is to smoke the best that I can get.

So what are the best cigars available? A lot of people will say Cuban. I don't think the answer is so simple. A good analogy is when people ask me my favorite beer. The fact is that with beer and cigars, as well as with many other consumables that come in a variety of flavors and aromas, different styles will seem best for different times of the day or times of the year. For example, I tend to like lighter-flavored, golden beers during the day and heavier-bodied darker beers in the evening, or when the temperature gets colder. The same is true for cigars. Cigars range from light to full-bodied, and I prefer a lighter cigar during the day and a heavier-bodied stogie in the evening. A great cigar, though, is good any time of day or year.

If I had to name only one cigar as my favorite, as of this writing I would pick a work of art from Miami, Florida. I actually discovered this manna from heaven in Boston, where I'd gone for the Boston Brewers' Festival. This was a super event back then, and I used the trip to visit my folks in Norwich, Connecticut, about 100 miles away. For the 1994 Boston Festival, I happened to stop at a well-respected cigar store in downtown Boston called Ehrlichs. Paul MacDonald is the owner, and he knows a lot about specialty beers and cigars. I recommend that you visit his store if you ever get the chance.

Me and Kristin Seuell enjoying a stogie.

MOORE & BODE CIGARS
"Tobacco Blenders since 1990"
We fully guarantee the quality of these cigars.
Handmade in Miami using only exceptionally fine tobaccos.
Available through these Factory Authorized Retailers

David P. Ehrlich Co., Boston, MA • Leavitt & Pierce, Cambridge, MA • Bombay Cigar Society, Redondo Beach, CA • Bennington Tobacconist, Sarasota, FL • Bennington Tobacconist, Boca Raton, FL • Cousin's Cigar Co., Cleveland, OH • Royal Cigar Co., Atlanta, GA • Iwan Ries & Co., Chicago, IL • Barclay-Rex Pipe Shops, New York, NY • Sherlock's Haven, San Francisco, CA • Art's Premium Cigars, Orlando, FL • Tinder Box, Charlotte, NC

MOORE & BODE CIGARS, Inc.
810 Southwest 16th Avenue
Miami, FL 33135 U.S.A.

At Ehrlichs, I inquired about a cigar to smoke on the way to my folks' house. The trip would take about an hour and a half, and I wanted something relatively mild with a lot of flavor. Mildness to me is indicated by how much a cigar fouls my tongue. Having to brush my teeth and tongue after a stogie is a cost of enjoying a cigar. One brushing usually takes care of a mild cigar. A medium cigar may take two brushings, and it might take three brushings for a really strong cigar.

Paul recommended a new cigar he had just started to carry, a Moore and Bode, Miami-blend stogie named a "Brass." The Brass was shaped strangely, in that it was about 6 inches long, tapered to a point at one end, and had about a 52 ring at the other end. (In cigar speak, the "ring size" is the diameter of the cigar in 64ths of an inch.)

As I turned onto Interstate 93 south, I lit this little beauty up. It gave off a great aroma. A couple of puffs and I knew the draw was almost perfect, tight without having to really pull the smoke through.

On the tongue the smoke tasted good without the sourness that's typical of many cigars. I slipped a Grateful Dead tape into the stereo system, set the car on cruise control, and savored my trip down the highway. The flavor and aroma stayed constant all the way down the burn. Unbelievable! This just doesn't happen with the vast majority of cigars. As I pulled into my parents' driveway, I was on the last quarter-inch of the Brass and about to burn my finger tips. The cigar was still a pleasure to smoke. I knew then that I had to meet the people who made these cigars. Fortunately, I'd had the foresight to write down the address of Moore and Bode when I bought this one.

It was at least six months before I had an opportunity to go to Miami. I remembered to bring the address with me and told our salespeople in south Florida that I wanted our first stop to be Moore and Bode in Little Havana on Calle Ocho (Eighth Street). I planned on bringing along some of our beer for a present to the best cigars makers I had come across. Moore and Bode was actually located on Sixteenth Avenue, just off Calle Ocho. It was just a couple of small rooms with five people at cigar-rolling stations. It reminded me, in a way, of the cramped quarters of many small microbreweries when they're just starting up.

Sharon Moore and her husband, Robert Bode, started the factory in 1991. Sharon runs the factory and designs the cigars. I prostrated myself before her! I was in the presence of an artist. After relating my story about my first Brass, I gave her the beers we'd brought along. She told me her company's story and explained that she named the tapered cigars after brass horn instruments, which are also tapered. She explained that they made a bigger stogie called a Full Brass, as well as a full complement of other, more standard sizes. Am I selling her cigars? You bet! They've told me I'm their number one salesperson!

I did a Brewmaster Dinner one of the evenings that I was in Miami at a nice restaurant in Coconut Grove. At these events, I take the time to share some background about beer and beer history. I thought that Sharon and Robert might enjoy learning about beer. They came and loved it. We each recognized in the other the true love of what we did for a living.

Later, back at their factory, Sharon demonstrated the artistry of cigarmaking for me. Her cigars are a blend of about seven different tobaccos. She took me into the back room and let me smell each of the tobaccos, in the as-is state as well as after each was lit with fire. In this way, I was able to smell the components and see how they all fit together. The artistry of cigarmaking is unmistakable when one watches the maestro, the most experienced rollers, roll a Brass. I never understood the complexity of rolling until I saw it done at Moore and Bode. It's no small challenge to roll a variable diameter cigar with seven different tobaccos to create a product that tastes the same from top to bottom. This just doesn't happen by accident; it is truly artistry. I learned that only the maestros are able to make these odd-shaped cigars because of the skill required. If you're undecided about buying a cigar, go for the tapered ones, such as a torpedo or pyramid. You may pay more, but you're going to get a better-quality cigar.

At one point I foolishly asked Sharon what tobacco she used in her cigars. I saw a twinkle in her eye as she asked, "what yeast do you use in making your beer?" I got her point! Brewers never reveal the type of yeast they use. Each strain of yeast works in different ways and gives off unique characteristics in the resulting beer. Likewise, Sharon was protecting the sources of her ingredients. I respected that; and now I go out of my way to meet with Sharon and Robert whenever I'm in south Florida. Visiting Calle Ocho for Cafe Cubano or Cafe con Leche and stopping for a stogie at Moore and Bode is not just another shopping trip. It absolutely makes a hectic travel schedule

LUNCHEON

During the middle ages, breakfast and dinner were the biggest meals. Between the two came a light noon repast called "nunchion," which was a combination of noon and *schenken* (noon drinking). If you were drinking your lunch or nunchion with some bread, then it was a luncheon (from "lunch," which was the word for a large chunk of bread). Luncheons were typically a tankard of ale and some bread.

slow down for a drink of strong, sweet coffee served in thimble-sized cups and the aroma of the best cigars I know of.

In the past year or so, we've done several events with Moore and Bode, with them sending cigar rollers to our beer events, including their maestro. Watching the rollers and tasting the cigars along with our beers has made a lot of friends for both of us. If you meet me on my travels and want to shoot the breeze with me, make sure you have a Miami blend Brass

> **WHEN IS A WAGON A GOOD CIGAR?**
> In the 1800s, the town of Conestoga, Pennsylvania, was famous not only for building the wagons that the pioneers took across the country but also for making fine cigars of the day. Stogie is just a shortened form of Conestoga.

cigar. There's nothing better than kicking back with a great beer and great cigar.

By now I'm sure you've detected a subtle theme to my favorite things—smoked beer, barbecue, and cigars.

In my raving about beer and my other favorite things, I can't neglect to mention the cooking of Candy Schermerhorn, the author of *The Great American Beer Cookbook* (Boulder: Brewers Publications, 1993) and owner of the Globe Brewery and Barbecue Company in Globe, Arizona. Candy isn't just a talented cook; she's an artist when it comes to cooking with beer. In 1995, we had Candy design a menu for our company meeting. Entertaining almost 150 people in a hotel ballroom is certainly not the best venue for a world-class dinner. What Candy came up with was not only the best beer dinner I've ever had, but one of the top three dinners I've ever had in my life.

Each course was spectacular, highlighting what could be done with beer and food, but most incredible of all were the soup and dessert courses. The soup mixed a Southwestern-spiced, roasted corn and crab chowder with our Wicked Summer Brew, a filtered wheat

SUMMER'S ROASTED CORN AND CRAB CHOWDER

by Candy Schermerhorn

This sublime chowder is a real show-stopper, combining three favorite summer foods: grilled corn, fresh crab meat, and beer! Serves eight.

5 ears grilled corn, cut off cob
  (corn should be cooked over high heat to sear
  the outside without overcooking the kernels)
2 tablespoons unsalted butter
1 large onion, finely chopped
1 large shallot, finely chopped
1 teaspoon half-sharp paprika
1 teaspoon finely crushed French thyme
1 each small red, yellow, and green pepper, finely chopped
  (or 1/2 large of each type of pepper)
1 1/2 cups Pete's Wicked Summer Brew
6 tablespoons butter
1 cup all-purpose flour
3 cups hot half-n-half or milk
1 cup cleaned, shredded crab meat
1 cup sour cream (regular or lite)
4 strips honey-cured bacon, cooked crisp and crumbled
50/50 mixture of finely minced scallions
  and Italian parsley for garnish

1. Heat butter in a heavy pan over medium heat. Toss in onion and saute until translucent. Add shallot, paprika, thyme, and peppers. Cook until fragrant and peppers are lightly wilted. Pour in beer and simmer over low heat for 10 minutes.

2. While vegetables are simmering, melt butter in a separate pan. Sprinkle in flour and cook over medium-low heat until bubbly and cooked but not browned. Slowly pour in hot milk, whisking constantly until smooth. Pour into vegetable mixture, add corn, and cook over medium-low heat until thickened.

3. When ready to serve, stir in crab meat and sour cream. Serve garnished with scallion/parsley mixture and a sprinkling of crumbled bacon.

If desired, roast an additional ear of corn and use corn cut from this ear as garnish, along with the bacon.

beer with a hint of lemon in it. Candy paired the chowder with our Wicked Honey Wheat, an unfiltered American-style wheat beer brewed with honey. The wide variety of flavors were all perceptible, including the Wicked Summer Brew, but they also blended incredibly well. The Honey Wheat beer flavors complimented the soup and acted as an enhancement. The result was a gastronomic masterpiece. We later served this soup at our booth at the 1997 Aspen Food and Wine Festival and were the hit of the show. I had a ton of fun walking around the booths sipping on a cup of the soup instead of beer or wine. Even Julia Child came by and gave the soup-and-beer combination high praise!

That said, the dessert had to be the most astounding pairing I've ever tasted. Candy made a chocolate almond torte with Wicked Ale as an ingredient, accompanied by our Wicked Winter Brew, an amber ale made with raspberry and a hint of nutmeg. The extraordinary part was how perfectly the flavors contrasted. The idea had turned me off when I saw it on her list, but I kept an open mind and stood by my faith in Candy's abilities as a cook.

The torte was incredibly rich and chocolaty. Each forkful exploded with rich flavors in your mouth. The intensity of the flavor came close to hurting and overwhelming my tastebuds but never got that far. The Wicked Winter Brew cut right through the intense flavor of the torte. The explosion of taste from the torte literally melted away when the Winter Brew went across the tongue. The flavor of the beer was very agreeable, and it brought your tastebuds back down to normal, only to have the next bite of torte explode in your mouth again. Explosion, calmness, explosion, calmness; the contrasting flavors worked spectacularly well together.

Hell, the dessert course was almost sexual in nature! Beer is wonderful, but extraordinary beer and excellent food working together is at the pinnacle of world achievements.

Recently, I suffered through almost two years of Sharon being out of the Miami blend. Then I received a bundle of Miami-blend Brass cigars in the mail and let out a whoop of complete joy. Moore and Bode's other blend is very, very good, but to my taste, the Miami-blend cigars are the gift of the tobacco gods. Rumor has it that there may be more blends in the near future, and I'm looking forward to them with great anticipation.

CHAPTER 13

BAD BEER CAN'T HURT YOU

*If you drink beer, you die. If you don't drink beer, you die
anyway. So you might as well drink it.*

—Old German Proverb

S
o maybe you're thinking about going out and paying some
good bucks to try a new beer you've never had before. How
do you know if you're going to like it? Even better, how will you know
whether you don't like it because you don't like it or because it has
gone bad? As a consumer, you should be armed with enough information to not only make wise choices in the beers you want to sample
but also be able to know whether the particular beer you're sampling
is still in good shape. Since there are many new brews available, you
may not know what these beers should taste like. Is a particular taste
or aroma that you detect a pleasing attribute of the beer or is it a by-
product of something that's damaging the beer?

With no point of reference, it's difficult to develop your
palate to detect when a beer has spoiled. Until now, without a chemistry lab to simulate beer problems, there has been no way for people
to get a quick education on beer problems. Now, even you can
become an expert in a very short time and without any equipment.
We've tried these experiments with many of our wholesalers, retailers,
and customers. We call this training, "The Good, the Bad, and the
Ugly." It will empower you to reject bad beer with confidence. Learn
how to say no and send it back when it's bad. It's better for you and
for the brewer, since no brewer wants a customer to be drinking a bad
version of a good beer. No one wants to look foolish around friends,

especially when they're experimenting with new beers. With our training, you not only won't look foolish; you'll also impress your friends—and bartenders—with your new-found knowledge.

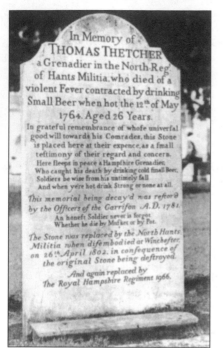

IMPORTANT: When it comes to bad beer and how to detect it, start with this invaluable fact. *Bad beer cannot hurt you!* The magic and mystery of the brewing process creates an environment that is acidic. In fact, the pH of beer is acidic to the point of preventing any bacteria that could hurt humans from surviving. Not only is beer good for you, but even bad beer won't make you sick (as long as you don't overindulge, of course).

Here's a case of a "small beer" killing Thomas Thetcher.

Beer is a perishable product that is generally at its best at the time of its packaging. From then on, a number of things can destroy beer. Heat and light are the two most common enemies. Where kegs are concerned, unclean beer lines and age can also kill a beer. Beers that are high in alcohol and hops and that still have living yeast in them are more resilent. Bear in mind, however, that few beers fall into this category anymore.

How do light, heat, age, or bad beer lines kill beer? Let's take a look at each foe in turn.

OXIDATION: HEAT, AGE, AND WET CARDBOARD

Whenever beer is packaged in bottles, cans, or kegs, some air, however minute an amount, is trapped inside the package. The oxygen in that air is highly reactive, and it combines with chemicals in the beer to form by-products and age the beer. These by-products damage the beer's taste and aroma.

A fourteenth-century tavern and cellar.

Chemicals can form that have the "delightful" aroma and taste of wet cardboard. The longer the aging or oxidation process goes on, the stronger the aroma and taste of wet cardboard. Chemical reactions also take away some of the high notes of aroma and taste. Try thinking of it this way: The highest notes on a piano keyboard are on the right side; the lowest notes are on the left. Imagine, over time, that the keys on the right side get stuck and cannot move; therefore, those high notes disappear. Over time, more and more of the keys on the right side stick and cannot be played. Eventually the stuck keys affect the playing. This is similar to what oxidation does to beer.

The first sign that a beer is going bad is the loss of the high notes of aroma and flavor. Before long, the wet cardboard aroma and flavor will dominate everything. Heat accelerates the oxidation process. Beers stored cold will eventually have oxidation problems, but they will stay good much longer than beers that are stored in a warm environment. Storing beer next to a furnace or near a window in direct sunlight are probably the two worst things you can do; all that heat and light are really going to accelerate the aging process.

To educate your palette, you have to taste some bad beer, on purpose! First, go to the store and get three bottles of the same beer. Try a golden, an amber, and a dark beer, for a total of nine bottles, so that you can learn the effect of oxidation on a variety of beer styles. Take a bottle of each of the styles you've purchased, unscrew the bottle cap, and blow air in the bottles. That's all it will take to accelerate the oxidation process. By blowing air in, you dramatically increase the amount of oxygen in the bottle. Reseal the bottle caps and let the beer sit for seven days. Next, take the second bottle of each style, blow air inside, close them up, and wait another week. After two weeks, for each style you'll have a "fresh" bottle, second bottle that's been in accelerated oxidation for one week, and another that's been in accelerated oxidation for two weeks. Now you're ready to do your own side-by-side aroma and taste test.

Pour each of the nine beers into a wide-mouthed glass, so there's room for you to stick your nose in the glass and smell the beer. For each style, smell the fresh version first, then the week-old version, and last the two-week-old version. Can you tell the difference? The high notes of the malt and hop aroma of each fresh beer should be significantly diminished in the week-old version. The two-week-old version should treat you to the distinct aroma of wet cardboard.

Performing this experiment across the three different beer styles should give you a good idea of what happens when beer goes bad. The oxidation is more noticeable in the lighter style of beer than in the darker styles because the roasted malt in the darker style has a stronger aroma and flavor that better mask defects.

Once you've become familiar with the give-away aroma effects of oxidation, don't accept beers that are oxidized. You cannot appreciate all of the creativity the brewers put into their work if you drink damaged beer. Date coding is a partial solution, but be conscious of how the beer has been handled at the retail store where you bought it. Also be careful of how you store beer at home. I have seen beers with a normal life of six months become overly oxidized within just one month! Exposure to hot temperatures can destroy fresh, young beer within days. Don't leave beer in the backseat of your car all day when it's hot out. You'll only accelerate the downward spiral of the beer's quality. Drink beer as soon as you can after buying it; don't tempt fate by storing it at home for any length of time.

SKUNKING: BEWARE THE GREEN-BOTTLE EFFECT

People are often aware that you shouldn't leave beer in sunlight, but they don't necessarily know why. The problems light can cause don't just come from sunlight—light from regular light bulbs or florescent light bulbs will destroy beer just as effectively. So what's the problem with light? A specific wavelength of ultraviolet light actually reacts with the hops in beer and changes it. It's yet another scientific chemical reaction that can damage beer, but you can remember it by a very unscientific name. Light turns beer "skunky." You know, that wonderful aroma from that cute black animal with the big white stripe down its back?

Unless the container is totally opaque or metallic, some light will get into your beer. Black bottles are best but brown bottles are generally more available and do an adequate job of filtering the light. Unfortunately, green and clear bottles allow the dangerous ultraviolet light into the beer.

Green bottles—may they live in marketing infamy! If you go to a beer store, you'll see that most imported beer comes in green bottles. The marketing departments of these companies must have determined that Americans like green bottles, and given the volume they sell here, I guess they're right. I have to laugh, though. In their native countries, many of these beers come in brown bottles, not green ones. The brewers are making sure that the hometown people have fresh beer. If you ask these companies whether selling their beer in green bottles in the United States damages the beer, they say they "never" receive complaints, so there must not be a problem!

I guess Americans have become used to the flavor of green-bottle beers. In fact, I've been to many bars around the country and have seen fellow Americans try Heineken on tap out of kegs and not like it. What they are tasting is fresher product! Since kegs are made out of metal, no light can get in, and the beer doesn't get skunky. People here are so used to the odd odor that they think the fresher version is actually worse. Once, I gave a talk to my Columbia Business School alumni association and described the green-bottle effect. Afterward, several people came up with questions. One gentleman handed me his card and walked off with a scowl. I looked down and saw that he was a vice president at Heineken. Oh well, if the truth hurts ...

I lead lots of beer education seminars around the country and in our offices in California. I get most of the beers for the sessions at the local Safeway and have gotten to know the head of the liquor department there. He wondered why I came in so often to buy a variety of beers, and I told him about the educational seminars. His interest was piqued, and he asked if he could attend one. When he came, we sampled two green-bottle European beers. These two beers had obviously been exposed to too much light, since they were really skunked. After tasting them, the liquor manager got a strange look on his face, and he asked me if I'd bought the two beers at his store. Yep. His next comment was very profound: "You mean I'm selling *these* beers to my customers?" You bet! Not only aren't most beer drinkers aware of the problem,

> ### TAKING SOMEONE DOWN A PEG
>
> This saying comes from one of the many attempts made over the centuries to limit drinking. In old-time Britain, King Edgar, influenced by the Archbishop of Canterbury, closed a number of alehouses by limiting each village or small town to only one such alehouse. He also ordered the use of cups with pins (pegs) or nicks in them, and decreed that "what person drank passed the pins in one draught should forfeit a penny."
>
> Later, in 1102, Bishop Anselm issued a canon in another effort to control drinking: "Let no priest go to drinking bouts nor drink to pegs." Drinking bowls in the taverns were often used communally. As the bowl was passed from customer to customer, each was only supposed to drink from one mark or peg to the next. These drinking vessels typically held two quarts and had eight pegs marking the inside of the cup. This practice of sharing a container continued until the end of the nineteenth century.
>
> Instead of limiting consumption, such laws actually led to provocative drinking challenges. Initially an occasional sport, the practice developed into a full-fledged custom called "pin drinking" or "pin-nicking." The person who could take his opponent "down a peg" quickest would win.

but most retailers are unaware of it as well. If you purchase green-bottle beer, make sure you look for enclosed six-packs, twelve-packs, or cases. Individual bottles or open six-pack containers are very likely to be skunked.

If you want to test this at home, buy an individual green-bottle beer that's been standing exposed on a shelf. (Chances are it's already skunked.) Buy another bottle of that beer that's been in an enclosed package or buy the same beer in a can; this will be used as the baseline for comparison, providing the fresh taste of that particular beer. When you get home, keep the "baseline" beer away from heat and light, but put the exposed bottle near a window. Direct sunlight is the biggest accelerator of skunking, but you don't want too much heat because that will cause oxidation, and for this test you're trying to isolate the effects of skunking. A week's exposure to indirect light ought to do the trick. Side-by-side tasting of the protected and exposed beer should give you a memorable lesson in what light can do to a brew that's sold in green bottles. What an apt term "skunking" is!

Clear bottles are not all the same. Some clear-bottled beers get real skunked, real fast. Others don't get skunked at all. How can that be? As I mentioned earlier, the skunkiness comes from the interaction between ultraviolet light and a component of the hop cone. Since it's difficult to control all light sources, some brewers change the properties of the hop itself. Brewers that want to use clear bottles for their beers without the risk of skunking special-order a hop extract that has been chemically treated to take out the component that turns the beer when exposed to light. That's okay, except that treating the hops this way affects the flavor and aroma of the hop extract so much that it's hard to tell the brewer has used hops at all. This isn't a problem, I guess, if you're brewing a beer for minimal flavor and aroma.

Bad Beer from Kegs?

When you go to a bar or restaurant and ask for a beer on draught, the bartender takes a glass, goes to the tap, and pours you an ice-cold brew. What could be finer or simpler than this? Actually, there is still room for things to go wrong, ranging from the beer itself going bad to a dirty beer line or tap handle, all of which can result in sour beer. A sour beer, like a nice tart lemonade, will scream at you from the sides of your tongue.

In general, kegged beer is not pasteurized. It was Louis Pasteur, in the mid- to late-1800s who did research on both wine and beer and produced the definitive work on what yeast actually is. He discovered that if you heated the finished product to certain temperatures for certain times, any bacteria that remained in the beer would be killed. The most common of these bacteria, if left to grow uncontrolled, would turn the beer sour. Pasteurization allowed beer to be stabilized for longer shelf life (about six months). Of course, the heating required for pasteurization does age the beer slightly.

Brewers have found that for an unpasteurized beer kept ice-cold, bacteria will not have an adverse affect for about two months. The American distribution network, from the brewery to distributor to the bar or restaurant, has been designed to keep the kegs ice-cold. Since keg beer is "fresher" tasting and the distribution network has been set up to keep the kegs ice-cold, the beer in them is generally not pasteurized. If, for some reason, kegs are allowed to warm or to go beyond the age limits, the bacteria in the beer grow and turn the beer sour.

Beer lines from the keg to the tap handle are generally made of plastic. If the lines are not regularly cleaned and disinfected, bacteria can survive and begin to propagate. If a particular beer hasn't sold much, then the bacteria in the line may have time to swim upstream into the keg itself and sour the beer in the keg. Not cleaning the plumbing in the tap handle can also allow the bacteria to grow, and if the beer on that line has not sold much, the bacteria in the handle plumbing can also go upstream and sour the beer in the keg.

CLEANLINESS IS NEXT TO GODLINESS!

How do you know when beer is turning or has turned sour? Get three bottles of three different styles of beer, like you did when we experimented with the effects of oxidation. Instead of blowing air in to the bottles, put in a teaspoon of plain yogurt, and then screw the top back on. If you are close to a health food store, you can buy a container of live lactobacillus culture and a half-dozen drops of that will do the trick as well. Actually, the drops are better because then you won't have the solids of the yogurt floating in the beer.

Leave the yogurt or drops in for a week, then put some in the second bottle of each style. At the end of another week you'll have a fresh bottle, a week-old sour beer, and a two-week-old sour beer. Try tasting these side-by-side and notice how the sourness increases. Taste them across the three styles and see how the sourness is affected by the base flavors of the three beers. Sour beer is not easily forgotten!

SEND IT BACK!

I hope you'll try the tests I've suggested. When you put that kind of firsthand experience together with the historical truths, you should be able to appreciate the breadth of what brewers are actually producing. You'll understand the wide variety of raw materials that are used and the creative artistry that brewers employ in manipulating the process to create wonderful brews. This is the best part of learning about beer.

The bad part is that you'll know when you're getting a beer that's not right. Most, if not all, beers are in good shape when they leave the brewery, but there is no guarantee that they'll still be in good shape by the time they reach you. Lots of things can and do go wrong. After all the effort the brewer has put into making great beer, once it leaves the brewery, there's not much a brewer can do, and most retailers don't know enough about beer to handle it correctly.

I get a sad but satisfied sense of pleasure when I hear a beer retailer exclaim after tasting bad beer, "I sell beers that taste like this?" I guess you can't solve all of the world's problems easily or quickly. The first step in any long-term process is to get people to admit that something's wrong. If they can do that, they might find they can actually do something about it.

If you buy a beer, and it's not good, complain! Don't put up with it. If there aren't any complaints, then nobody will know that they are selling bad beer. We in the brewing industry go to great lengths to keep beer fresh all the way to you, the consumer, but there are just too many factors that are beyond our control. If more con-sumers complained, you can bet that store and bar practices would change, and you'd be drinking fresher-tasting beer. So, try these experiments. They'll make it possible for you to detect problems, to put a name to them, and to have the confidence to return a bad beer.

What can you do in a bar to assure yourself that you're getting a good version of a beer? Ask the bartender when they tapped the keg. If it's been two weeks, you're running a risk. If it was a week ago, you're probably okay. Tapped today? Go for it, and you'll probably enjoy a second one!

CHAPTER 14

BEER MYTHS AND OLD WIVES' TALES

My grandmother is over eighty and still doesn't need glasses.
Drinks right out of the bottle.

—HENNY YOUNGMAN

I give a lot of beer education classes around the country, and one of the things I love to do is to walk in with a bottle of Wicked Ale that has a straw sticking out of it. I do this for several reasons. The first is to see how long it takes to get a reaction from the crowd because, frankly, who the hell drinks beer with a straw? Don't ask me why, but some audiences take about thirty seconds to ask me about it, and other audiences will take thirty minutes. I get a sense of whether the audience is paying attention by how long it takes for the question to surface. In any case, the question itself makes a perfect lead-in to an important part of my talk. I point out that there are a lot of stories about how you'll get higher quicker if you drink beer through a straw. That's just an old wives' tale. I point out that straws were, in fact, invented for drinking beer. Few people know that! It gets their attention and sets everyone up for the rest of the presentation.

In my historical research, I've encountered a good number of stories, words, and phrases that come from beer. You've already seen a number of them throughout the text. Some may seem made up or untrue, but believe me, they aren't cock-and-bull stories. These bits of history bring beer to life and show how intertwined the world of beer and human history really are.

In my talks I also take on some of the hype folks hear about beer. So, much of what you hear about beer is garbage. All too often,

Me demonstrating drinking with a straw.

INVENTION OF THE STRAW

Whether the ancients were using grain for making beer, bread, or gruel, the grains were first crushed for processing. In the case of beer, the husk of the barley sank to the bottom, and pieces of the crushed kernel and yeast rose to the top. Imagine drinking a beer thousands of years ago. Filtering was limited at best, so a lot of grain particles would accumulate at the top of the drinking container, usually some type of bowl back then. When you put the bowl to your mouth, in addition to swallowing some interesting beer, you'd also get a lip full of crud. That must have taken away some of the pleasure of the experience.

The ancient peoples were pretty smart, though. Historical records from Egypt and other areas up to northern Europe indicate that people had found a common solution for the lip-crud problem. They would go down to the local river and pick hollow reeds growing in the water. Once they'd broken off the top and the bottom of the reed, they'd insert this hollow tube through the floaters at the top and have crud-free access to the good beer underneath. Yes, straws were invented for drinking beer!

we're told only what the big companies want us to believe. When a large beer company hasn't much to offer, they'll take a term and play it up, trying to make it sound like a positive attribute of their product. They put a spin on the truth or play off of common misconceptions that have been passed down for ages.

In this chapter, I'll try to cut through some of the marketing bull-shit, and shed some light on why you ought to have an open mind about beer. You'll also find historical beer anecdotes ranging from myths and religious tie-ins to words or phrases

Woodcut of women using drinking straws.

and other neat facts that I've discovered. And it's only a fraction of the wealth of interesting material that's out there. I hope you'll be as fasci-nated as I am by the amazing amount of human life and culture that is intertwined with the history and lore of beer.

Enjoy!

MYTH: ONLY BEERS LABELED "COLD FILTERED" ARE COLD FILTERED

Go to the liquor store and look at the beers for sale there. Some of the packaging will prominently say that the beer inside is cold-filtered, implying that this somehow sets it apart from the rest of beerdom and, of course, makes it better beer. Well, that's just plain WRONG! In fact, *all* beers are cold filtered. Chances are the specially labeled "cold-filtered" beers are actually "sterile filtered."

Most American like clear, filtered beer. At the brewery, the wort and beer go through several stages of filtering. As explained in chapter 3, the husk layer in the lauter tun screens out some of the crushed grain solids. The whirlpool spins the beer, separating hop particles and other solid matter (like proteins) from the wort. The only problem is that the whirlpool is very hot—the wort stays close to the boiling temperature of the brew kettle. The temperature prevents some of the proteins from coalescing because the heat makes the molecules move around a lot. As a result, there are still going to be proteins in the beer when you filter it through the diatomaceous earth (DE). These proteins are too small for even the DE to catch.

If the temperature of the beer is then allowed to get close to freezing, the remaining proteins in the beer will slow down and begin to stick to each other, forming what's called a "chill haze." When a brewer filters beer at warmer temperatures, the proteins slip through and stay in the beer. If a customer then orders that beer after it has been chilled for delivery, he or she will get a cloudy beer due to the chill haze. As the beer warms up, the proteins will break up and the beer will clarify.

Most Americans don't like cloudy beer. If they get a hazy beer, they think something is wrong with it. They also don't like beer served at warmer temperatures, so something has to be done to minimize the chill haze. The answer? Cold-filtering the beer. All breweries chill their beer close to the freezing point so that the chill haze forms. Then they put the beer through the DE and the stuck-together proteins are filtered out. Result? Clear beer.

But if all breweries cold-filter their beers, then why do only some of them use "cold-filtered" on their packaging? They are probably referring to what is know as sterile filtration. It is extremely difficult to keep bottles and cans ice-cold throughout the distribution network because of the sheer magnitude of the business and the investment required for adequate refrigeration.

In order to have their beers taste "fresher," some breweries don't pasteurize their beer. Instead they put the beer through a different

EARLY MORNING ON THE GUINNESS FARM.

An interesting new machine for harvesting our choice barley.

INDUSTRY IN THE GUINNESS MALTINGS.
A magnetic solution to the age-old problem of ensuring an even application of water to the barley.

ROASTING THE GUINNESS BARLEY.

A delicate moment during this somewhat hazardous operation.

HOP PICKING TIME IN THE GUINNESS FIELDS.

A creditable effort to secure an errant hop.

MIXING THE GUINNESS MASH.

An efficient plant for successfully combining the essential Guinness ingredients.

FILTERING THE GUINNESS WORT.

Guinness experts ensuring that all the hops are successfully filtered from the brew.

FERMENTING THE GUINNESS.

Some simple precautions prior to the addition of the Guinness super-active yeast.

JOHN
IRELAND

BOTTLING THE GUINNESS.

Our modern plant which includes an interesting contrivance for adding the unique creamy head.

type of filter. Sterile filters have holes so small (0.45 micron—that's a mere 45 hundred-millionths of an inch!) that bacteria in the beer cannot get through. Pretty ingenious! You get the same result as you would with pasteurization—no bacteria—without heating the beer. (I love great ideas like this.)

So, is sterile filtering the ultimate solution? There's no such thing as a free lunch. Sterile filtering does such a great job at getting rid of any potential bacteria, but it also filters out any microscopic pieces of barley malt in the beer. In other words, in removing the bacteria, this process filters out flavor (less malt, less flavor). So, sterile filtering works well, but it's only a good solution for those styles of beer where you *don't* want much flavor in the beer.

MYTH: ICE BEERS ARE FROZEN AND THE ICY WATER SLUSH IS FILTERED OUT

The recent popularity of ice beers has brought great success to several breweries. Even though sales have tapered off, ice beers are still around. What, you may ask, is an ice beer? If you believe the hype (and by now you have surely realized that there's a *lot* of hype in the beer business!), you'd be thinking that breweries must have put in new equipment to freeze beer. When you chill beer down to about 29 °F, the water in the beer starts to solidify but the alcohol stays liquid (because water freezes at 32 °F, and alcohol freezes at a lower temperature). The hype would have you believe that the brewers filter out the watery slush and what is left behind has a higher concentration of alcohol—the strength of the beer has been increased.

At least this imagined process has its roots in reality. Earlier, I told you how bock beer came to be, and talked about the origin of doublebocks (doppelbocks). The Germans, seeking to create an even stronger beer, met with some technical problems. Beer yeast, can actually be killed by the alcohol it creates during fermentation. Depending on the yeast strain, when the alcohol concentration gets to about 8 to 10 percent, the yeast dies and fermentation stops.

The Germans came up with the idea of making a double-bock, freezing it, and then filtering off some of the water ice. And indeed this did raise the alcohol concentration of the beer. The German name for this style is *eisbock* (*eis* in German means and is pronounced as "ice"). An example of this this style of beer is Kulmbacher Reichlebrau Eisbock. The alcohol content of this style can be in excess of 10 percent alcohol by volume.

So are the ice beers made in the United States directly associated with the eisbock style? If you think so, excuse me while I get my deed to the Golden Gate Bridge so that I can sell it to you! I can't speak to how any particular brewery makes its own ice beers, but here are a couple of common scenarios.

The first is the path of least resistance, one that requires no extra investment on the part of the brewer. Since ice beers generally have a higher alcohol level than regular beer, it's possible that breweries, when making their high-gravity beer concentrate, simply add less water at the end of the process to end up with a higher-strength product. Another likely approach is for a brewery to invest in the equipment to freeze the beer and to filter out the water ice. They would be able to do what the marketers say they're doing, but guess what? It's illegal to do that in the United States. The government has determined that by taking water (that is water ice) out of beer, you are performing a type of distillation. Brewers aren't licensed to distill, only distillers can distill. That tells me that either the brewers aren't really making true ice beers or they are adding the water back to the beer at the end of the process to bring it back to it's normal, lower strength. One thing that's obviously certain is that none of these brewers are brewing doublebocks first.

MYTH: LIGHT ICE BEER

And then there's the concept of "light" ice beer. An oxymoron is a combination of contradictory or incongruous words, opposites like "jumbo shrimp" or "military intelligence." "Light ice" is another fine example. The whole idea of ice beer is that it has greater strength and thus, contains more calories. How you can have a "light ice" is beyond me!

In general, most U.S. ice beers are the same strength as regular beer, so I really don't know what the brewers are trying to accomplish. Several years ago, another style of beer called "dry beers" came out, but quickly disappeared. Dry beers have an extended fermentation, which allows any residual sugars to be fermented out. "Dry" in this instance means the opposite of sweet, as in dry and sweet wines. The term "dry" was confusing for the public because most people didn't know what it meant. How beer, which is wet, could be dry? Maybe, just maybe, the brewers were looking for a "sales handle" that would be more meaningful. Most people drink their beers ice cold, so perhaps the marketing types thought the idea of "ice beer" might attract more buyers.

MYTH: HEART OF THE HOP

I love the phrase "Heart of the Hop" because it implies that the goodness of the hop comes from its heart or center. The actual source of the goodness of hops comes from little yellow sacs within the hop petals. These sacs contain the acids that make beer bitter, the oils that give it aroma, and the chemicals that preserve it. The rest of the flower is secondary. Truth be known, the "heart" of the hop is the stem at the center of the flower.

MYTH: DOUBLE-HOPPED

"Double-hopped" is a great term because it implies that hops have either been used twice or maybe that twice the amount of hops have been used in making the beer. In the first case, that's not saying much—most beers have hops put in three and in some cases four times during the brewing process. In order to get the right amount of bitterness, flavor, and aroma, hops have to be added during three different parts of the process. To make the beer bitter, the hops are put in the brew kettle and boiled for at least an hour. (The acids in the hops can only be chemically modified and thus dissolved in the wort at boiling temperatures.) The problem is that the flavor and aroma of the hops are driven off in the steam. To capture the hops flavor, you have to add more halfway through the boil. That allows some flavor to get in because those hops aren't boiled long enough for all the acids modified. Aroma hops are added at the end of the boil, so that the more delicate aroma does not get driven off by the heat.

Some do a fourth addition of hops as well, in a process known as "dry hopping." In this process, hops are added to the finished beer while it is resting at cold temperature. At the cold temperature, only the hop oils that provide aroma go into the beer. We use dry hopping for Wicked Ale to give it an enhanced aroma.

If most brewers use three hop additions, and some use four, then what the heck does double-hopping mean? If it means that twice the amount of hops have been added during brewing, then those beers should be bitter—a lot more bitter than other beers. But when I taste beers that have been double-hopped, I have a hard time finding any difference. In fact, if you compare a double-hopped beer to a specialty beer, you might wonder whether the double-hopped beer has any hops in it at all!

MYTH: DARK BEERS ARE STRONGER IN ALCOHOL THAN LIGHTER BEERS

One experiment I have fun with at seminars is to put eight beers in front of each person. Two of these beers mark the extremes: a Budweiser and a Guinness Pub Draught. That is, a light golden and a black beer. The other six beers vary, but demonstrate the fact that between these two extremes you'll find beers that range in color from dark golden to amber and brown in color.

After identifying all of the beers, I'll ask the group to tell me which is the lightest and which is the heaviest in alcohol. The answers often reflect what people have heard from friends—most often usually old wives' tales. Most people believe that the beer with the lowest alcohol is the lightest in color and the one with the highest alcohol is the darkest beer.

The reality is that Budweiser usually has the highest alcohol content amongst the eight beers, and Guinness Pub Draught has the lowest. In fact, Guinness Pub Draught has less alcohol than light beers! Budweiser has about 3.95 percent alcohol by weight and Guinness Pub Draught about 3.1 percent. Most American beers, including specialty beers, have 3.5 to 4.0 percent alcohol by weight. Guinness is interesting because they make about 20 versions of Guinness Stout for various markets around the world. My understanding is that these 20 versions range from 3 to 7 percent alcohol by weight.

MYTH: BEER GETS BETTER WITH AGE

Beer is best consumed soon after it is packaged. The longer you hold on to beer, the greater the chance of the beer oxidizing and going bad. The rare exceptions are those beers that are high in alcohol, high in hops content, and full of living yeast. The few beers that have these attributes benefit first from the fact that alcohol itself is a preservative; the more alcohol there is, the longer the beer will be stable. Second, hops have a natural preservative in them, so more hops means more preservative. Last, although live yeast will make the beer cloudy, it will also absorb any residual oxygen that gets into the beer during the packaging phase.

MYTH: BEER THAT'S CLOUDY HAS GONE BAD

Americans love clear, ice-cold, light-colored beers. Is this because there was some historical problem, a time when Americans were bothered by cloudy beer? No, it's just that despite the 60-odd styles of beer available around the world, we in America were given no choice by the large industrial breweries. We got minor variations of a minor (but large volume) style, American light lager, typically a clear filtered beer. Deprived of other choice, we simply got used to clear beer and came to believe that cloudy beer had to be bad—why else hadn't the big guys produced it for us?

Believe me, there are plenty of wonderful styles of beer that are unfiltered, including *hefeweizens, wits,* Abbeys, and barley wines. Those and others are now becoming available to Americans. Cloudiness in beer comes from yeast, which has done the fermentation.

MYTH: BEER SHOULD BE SERVED ICE COLD, AND THE COROLLARY, BRITISH BEERS ARE SERVED WARM

The serving temperature of beer is a controversial issue. Frankly, there *is* no proper answer. It all comes down to personal choice. However, it's worth talking about how temperature affects beer's flavor and aroma.

Simply put, coldness numbs the tongue and minimizes the aromas of the beer. As the temperature goes up, the taste buds become more attuned to flavors and the warmer beer gets, the more active the volatile gasses in the beer become. Therefore, aromas become more evident in warmer beer.

Personally, I don't like my beer served ice cold. I've gotten some strange looks when I've asked servers in some bars to de-ice my glass in hot water, before they pour my beer. That will raise the temperature of the ice cold beer that pours out of the tap a couple of degrees and allow a little more of the flavor and aroma to come through. A frozen glass only chills the beer further and reduces the pleasure I get from really tasting the beer I've ordered.

Having spent a good deal of time drinking beers in pubs in England, as well as judging beers professionally there, I can state without equivocation that British beers are not served warm. The standard

manner of pouring beers in Britain is to serve the beer from a keg
kept in the cellar of the pub, where the temperature is typically in
the 50s. While this is warmer than the standard of serving temperature in the United States the (mid- to low-30s), beer in the 50s is certainly not warm. I prefer the English temperature, but I do like the
American level of carbonation better than the much lower level typical
of most British beers. (Americans like to call British beers flat, but
they're not. They just have a much lower level of carbonation.) If
I had my druthers, I'd put my beers in a fridge about half an hour
before I was going to drink. The beer would get cool, but not ice cold.

I think the Belgians have taken the art of drinking beer at
higher temperatures to new levels. Belgian brewers usually have a
unique glass for each of their beers that accentuates the particular
attributes of each one. It's incredible to go into a Belgian bar and see
racks of glassware hanging from the ceiling. When you order a beer,
the bartender puts it in the appropriate glass. Most of these glasses
have wide mouths and stems with a foot, sort of like a wine glass on
steroids. When you hold the glass with the stem between your fingers,
the bowl of the glass rests in your palm. In this way, the heat from
your hand can warm up the beer and intensify the aroma and taste.
I must admit, however, that there is a time and place for everything.
When I'm water skiing, a nice ice-cold Mickey's Big Mouth does
indeed hit the spot!

MYTH: SAUERKRAUT IS A CURE FOR HANGOVERS

Lots of people have folk medicines to cure a hangover, but do any
of them work? I think it's interesting that even the ancients sought
a cure.

The Egyptians had a great term for hangovers, "the pulling
of the hair." Their cure was a very popular and simple remedy—
cabbage! Athenaeus, a Greek, wrote a verse about this particular cure:

Last evening you were drinking deep,

So now your head aches, go to sleep,

Take some boiled cabbage, when you wake,

And there's an end of your headache.

Another Greek, Eubulus, also wrote of this cure:

Wife, quick! some cabbage boil of virtues healing,

That I may rid me of this seedy feeling.

Is it a coincidence that the Germans, the largest per-capita beer drinkers in the world, also consume vast amounts of cabbage, often in the form of sauerkraut? All kidding aside, in the 1970s German scientists announced that they had isolated chemicals called chelators in cabbage and sauerkraut. Hangovers are primarily caused by acetaldehydes created during fermentation, and chelators are known to offset the effect of the acetaldehydes. So next time you drink a brew too many eat some cabbage!

MYTH: CANADIAN BEER IS STRONGER THAN AMERICAN BEER

Early in my beer-drinking career, I returned from a trip to Canada with a number of additions to my beer can collection. When I looked closely at the beer cans, I saw that most of them had an alcohol content of about 5 percent. I thought I remembered that most American beers were in the 3.5 to 4 percent range and that some states made a big deal over 3.2 percent beers. So, Canadian beers are significantly higher in alcohol than American beers, right?

It turns out that there are two methods for measuring the alcoholic content of liquids. One is to measure the alcoholic content by the *weight* of the liquid as is done in the United States. The other is to measure the alcohol by the *volume* of the liquid that the alcohol represents as is done in Canada. You'll get a different answer, depending on which approach you take.

Why? Because alcohol is lighter than water (beer is about 95 percent water). If you have a gallon of water and a gallon of alcohol, the volume of both is the same—a gallon. But if you weigh them, the gallon of alcohol will weigh only 80 percent of what the gallon of water weighs. Conversely, the gallon of water will weigh 125 percent of (or 1.25 times) as much as the gallon of alcohol. If you measure the alcoholic content as alcohol by weight, you'll get a lower number than if you measure the alcohol by volume. For example, a beer might have an alcoholic content of 4 percent by weight, but 5 percent by volume.

So, are Canadian beers that much higher in alcohol? Since most American beers are just slightly under 4 percent by weight, and most Canadian beers are about 5 percent by volume, they are roughly equivalent in alcohol content. Well, maybe the Canadian beers are just slightly higher, not by a significant amount.

Up until 1995, the alcohol content of American beers was measured as alcohol by weight (ABW). Beers from the rest of the world have been measured as alcohol by volume (ABV). In 1995, the Supreme Court of the United States ruled that the Bureau of Alcohol, Tobacco, and Firearms' (BATF) statute that prohibited listing the alcoholic content on beer labels was illegal. Although there are a few issues that still have to be resolved, U.S. companies can now list the alcoholic content of their beers. Personally I think we should all move to listing it by volume; that would put us in step with the rest of the world.

MYTH: MOVING BEER BACK AND FORTH FROM HOT TO COLD WILL DESTROY IT

Some people have asked me if buying beer that's been kept cold in the store, taking it home in a hot car, putting it in a cold fridge, and then taking it out on a hot day will ruin it. The issue isn't how often it goes from cold to hot, or vice versa, but how hot the beer actually gets and for how long. In general, in the time it takes to get your beer from the store to your fridge shouldn't noticeably affect it. The time frame is probably too short and the amount of heat the beer is exposed to is too little to do any real damage. However, if the beer is kept at 100 degrees for a full day, it loses some freshness. It's also a function of how old and oxidized the beer was when you bought it.

MYTH: BEER SHOULD BE POURED DOWN THE SIDE OF A GLASS

I love answering this question! Even though it turns out to be a matter of personal preference, there are a few good reasons why you don't want to gently pour a beer down the side of a glass that has been tipped at an angle. Pouring gently into a glass avoids creating a big head and the beer doesn't spill over the side of the glass.

First of all, you want to pour a beer straight down into the glass because it *will* create a big head. Most beers, especially American beers, have a high degree of carbonation—that is, they contain a lot of dissolved carbon dioxide gas. This gas is going to escape from the liquid one way or another, but you have a choice and some control over how that happens. If you pour the beer straight down and let it form a big head, you're letting the gas escape into the atmosphere faster. If you gently pour the beer down the side of a tipped glass and only get a small head, most of the gas stays in the beer. When you drink it, the agitation of the liquid going down your esophagus and into your stomach will release that gas. The way this gas escapes from the human body is through a big BURP!

A second, but related problem caused by drinking beer that still contains a lot of gas is that as it builds up in your stomach it will make you feel more full.

The third, and perhaps the best reason for pouring a big head on beer is that the escaping gas carries with it the aromatic compounds of the hops and malted barley. Beer smells a lot better when you release the gas in a big pour.

Myth: Batch Numbers on Beer Labels Mean Something

This one's fun as well. Batch numbers are meaningless, especially for big brewers. For small brewers, there may be some ego boost that comes from achieving a sizeable number of batches. But I'd worry if they thought their batches were so wildly different in taste or aroma that each one was a special edition! I'd say that would point to significant problems in their process.

It's true that the brewing process is complex and magical, and it can be very difficult to get each batch to taste the same. Nonetheless, most brewers reach a level of sophistication that allows them to keep their batch-to-batch flavor profiles so close that only an expert would be able to detect the variances. For the vast majority of beers, there are no readily perceived differences among batches. It's not like vintage years for wine.

You should know that there is no uniform brew size for the big brewers, although most brew in the 400- to 1,000-barrel range. A barrel is 31 U.S. gallons, or about 14 cases of beer. Assuming a 500-barrel batch size and minimal beer losses in the packaging process, each batch results in approximately 7,000 cases. That doesn't go very far for a big brand, so they probably make lots and lots of batches each year. A brand that sells a million barrels a year—as Sam Adams—would have to make 2,000 batches to meet demand if they made 500-barrel batches (which they don't). One could jokingly argue that the batch numbers on the labels are more indicative of how often labels are ordered than of how many batches of beer a company has produced.

HOW THE OCEAN TIDES ORIGINATED

According to Norse legend, the great god Thor was traveling with his goats on his chariot in the company of another god, Loki. They arrived in the land of the giant Skrymir, who challenged Thor and Loki to a number of games and races, all of which they lost. Thor's great strength was well-known, so Skrymir asked Thor what feats he could perform to show that the stories about him were true. Thor offered to challenge anyone to a drinking match.

Skrymir took Thor into his great hall and asked one of his assistants to bring Thor an ale drinking horn. He told Thor that a man was a great drinker if he could finish the ale horn in one draught. Most men could finish it in two draughts. One had to be very weak if he could not finish the horn in three draughts. Thor took the horn, which, although it wasn't all that big, was fairly long.

To prove himself worthy of his reputation, Thor drank and drank and drank, but he was unable to empty the horn. He took another big draught, but again failed to empty the horn. Having failed to win the athletic events as well as the drinking challenge, Thor was shamed before Skrymir.

The next morning as Thor and Loki were leaving, Skrymir joined them for some distance. As he bid them farewell, Skrymir admitted that he had deceived them with trickery. He had hidden the end of the ale horn in the ocean! Although it had appeared that Thor's great drinking had accomplished little, he had actually consumed so much that he caused the sea to drop, thus starting the lowering and raising of the tides.

GERMANIC HEAVEN

By the way, the word "German" actually comes from the Celtic word for screamer. I thought you'd like to know. But our story is from ancient Germania, where Wodan was the head god, similar to the Norse god Odin. He held court in the great hall of Valhalla. Wednesdays were sacred to him; in fact, Wednesday comes from "Wodan's day."

When great German heroes were killed in battle, the Valkyries would bring the slain heroes to Wodan's hall. There they would feast at banquets and continue to battle with each other as they had on Earth. Only, in Valhalla, mead and beer had the power to heal their wounds instantly, preserving their combative bliss for all time.

BEER SAINTS

Yes, there are saints who have performed miracles with beer! Saint Bridget, who was born in 439 and died around 520, once changed water into beer. While she was nursing lepers, they implored her for beer, but there was none to be had. By the sheer strength of her blessing, she changed the water that was being readied for a bath into an excellent beer and served it to those who were thirsty. This miracle was accomplished by her faith and reliance on Christ, who had changed water into wine in Galilee.

Saint Columbanus, born in Ireland in 560, performed his miracle in Germania. He was left with only two loaves of bread and a little beer, so he prayed to Christ: "O Christ, Thou who multipliedest the loaves, mayest Thou also multiply the bread and beer." The beer doubled in quantity.

During his proselytizing in Germania, Columbanus was also said to have come across some local people about to perform a ceremony to Wodan. These people had filled a large wooden vessel with twenty pails of beer for sacrifice to the pagan god. After learning this, Columbanus blew on the cask, and it exploded; all the beer was lost. It should be noted that Columbanus was not a foe of beer; rather he was upset that these heathens were sacrificing the beer to a heathen god.

Columbanus' autobiography includes several references to beer. For example, he tells us that "Beer was boiled out of the juice of the corn and of barley, such as it is similarly prepared by other peoples, by the Scordisci, a people in Upper Pannonia, by the Dardanis, a people in Upper Moesia, and by the peoples dwelling on the shores of the ocean in Gaul, Britain, Hibernia, and Germania."

GAMBRINUS: THE PATRON SAINT OF BEER

Across northern Europe, Gambrinus is considered the patron saint and guardian of brewers. Unfortunately, there is no consensus on

A statue of Gambrinus.

who Gambrinus was, or how he became the protector of beer. One story tells us that Gambrinus was John I (Jan Primus), the Duke of Brabant, who was killed in a knight's tournament in 1294. John I was very heroic and terribly popular in both Brabant (Belgium) and Cologne. He was even admitted to the brewer's guild of Cologne. His picture hung in the guild there as well as in the brewer's guild in Brussels. How he became known as a saint of brewing is still unknown.

A German writer, Aventinus, wrote in 1554 that Gambrinus lived about 1730 B.C. with his consort, the Egyptian goddess Isis. He said Gambrinus invented beer. Another historian believes there was a mix-up in names between Gambrinus and Osiris, since Osiris was (a) an Egyptian diety and (b) also claimed to have invented beer.

Yet another account gives the honor to John the Intrepid (Jan Intrepidus) who lived from 1371 to 1419 and was the founder of the Order of the Hops. He became ruler of the Flemish during a war with Liege—a war centered around the fact that the Bishop of Liege was losing tax revenues because he had a tax on gruit (spices used in beer), and hopped beers were becoming more prevalent. It is possible that this Jan was chosen by the brewers of hopped beer as their protector.

THE HINDU GOD INDRA AND BEER

The oldest Hindu book is the *Rig-Veda* (hymn-Veda) which is considered a sacred work. It names Soma as the creator and father of the gods, the one who confers immortality upon both gods and men.

Soma also happens to be a plant that can be crushed with grain and added to milk to ferment it. Soma-milk was very powerful, exciting to those who drank it. It was believed to impart power to the gods. After consuming soma-milk, a person would be able to see and communicate with the gods, be inspired by them, and perhaps become like them. Soma was often offered to the gods.

The greatest Hindu god, Indra, was most attentive to mortals under the influence of Soma. One song goes as follows: "Come hither, O Indra, and intoxicate thyself. Drink of the Soma, O Soma drinker; thine intoxication is what gives us abundance of cows." Indra, it was believed, could not perform great deeds unless he was intoxicated. For example, "When he [Indra] combated against the withholder of rain (Vritra), in his inebriation, the refreshing rain rushed down the declivity like rivers."

There appears to be no doubt that early Hindu people were well aware of the intoxicating effect of Soma. Apparently, they were happy to have their gods come down to revel with them and partake in their festivities: "May Indra rejoice to his satisfaction in the pressed juice, mixed with milk, like Hotri at a morning service. . . . May the delightful drops of Soma delight thee, the drops made by us, well-made, and heaven directed, yes, made of milk."

BREWER'S COFFEE

During the Gold Rush in California, many breweries opened in the San Francisco area to make and ship beer up to thirsty miners in the Sierra Nevada mountains. The process of mining, and especially the heavy metals in the tailings of the processed ore, contaminated mountain water supplies. Thus, the miners couldn't use the water to make coffee. Beer, on the other hand, was a sterile product shipped up from the Bay Area, which had a clean water supply. It's been estimated that almost 75 percent of the beer shipped to the miners wasn't drunk straight, but was used in the brewing of coffee.

LIMEY

In 1779, the British Admiralty ordered all naval ships on foreign service to carry dehydrated malt as a remedy for scurvy. The malt took up far less space than barrels of beer. Grog (rum, cut with water) supplemented the malt for a time, but it was also eliminated once concentrated lime juice was made available to fight scurvy. The British practice of carrying lime juice on their ships gave rise to the American phrase "limey" during the American Revolutionary War. Just imagine—if the War of Independence had happened before lime juice had supplanted beer, the British might have been known as "hoppies"!

THE ORIGIN OF PICNICS

Our contemporary view of going an a picnic and bringing food and drink may have its origins in beer:

> The beer was not only made by the women, but was sold by them on the market, and ale-houses of unsavory reputation were also kept by women. These ale-houses were very much frequented by women of the lower classes. Samuelson, in *History of Drink,* says on the subject: "They spent much of their time in taverns and were of low morals." This practice grew until there were parties of them assembled who took with them the solid food for a meal:

Each of them brought forth ther dysch,

Sum brought flesh and sum fysch.

And this custom of each woman contributing her

share to the feast was the origin of our modern picnic.

(*One Hundred Years of Brewing*, 1903)

Picture

The ancient race of ale-drinking people who inhabited parts of Britain were called Picts. These people were small in stature but known to be very fierce. They also tattooed their entire bodies. The word "picture" derives from these tattooed people.

Whiskey

Whiskey is derived from the Gaelic, *usquebaugh,* which in turn is from *uisge* or "water" and *beatha* or "life." So, whiskey was considered the "water of life."

1890 Tradition for Pub Openings in Chicago

During the 1890s in Chicago, bars and saloons rarely closed. They were open seven days a week and on holidays. When a new saloon opened, the owner would walk down to the shore of Lake Michigan and toss the keys to the saloon in the water.

Beer as Building Material

In old England, beer-drinking parties helped raise money for maintaining churches. These gatherings were called "Church Ales" (ale here refers to a party rather than to the liquid). But ale did more than fund the construction. In the twelfth century, it was commonly believed that the mortar in bricks was stronger when beer was used instead of water, especially in church spires. References to this have been recorded by many churches, including this verse inscribed in the gallery of the church at Sygate in Norfolk:

God speed the plough
And give us good ale enow—
Be merry and glade
With good ale was this work made.

THE FIRST COMMERCIAL/PRIVATE BREWERIES IN THE UNITED STATES

As the New World was colonized, settlers either brewed beer for their own consumption or went to taverns where beer was brewed by the innkeeper. The first public brewery in America is thought to have been built in New Amsterdam, New York, by Director General Peter Minuit in 1630. This brewery stayed in business until 1638, when competition forced it out.

The first public brewery in New England, started in the Massachusetts Bay colony in 1637, was run by a Captain Sedgewick. In 1638, the first brewery in Connecticut was begun by Sergeant Baulston. Roger Williams, who later founded the colony of Rhode Island, actively and financially participated in the New Haven brewing project.

The first private brewery in the United States was established by Adrian Block and Hans Christiansen in 1612 in a log building in the Dutch colony of New Amsterdam.

FOSTER'S GIMMICK WITH ICE MAKES THEM A MAJOR PRODUCER

Foster's beer from Australia was actually founded by two American brothers, W. M. and R. R. Foster, in Melbourne, Australia, in 1886. Although there were other Melbourne breweries, the Foster brothers quickly became a roaring success by promising free ice to any retailer stocking their lager. Ice-cold Foster's soon became Australia's most popular drink.

GEORGE WASHINGTON'S
BEER RECIPE AND BEN FRANKLIN'S RECIPE

In a notebook kept by George Washington (now in the manuscript collection of the New York Public Library), an entry written when he was a colonel in 1737 contains the following recipe for beer:

TO MAKE A SMALL BEER

Take a large siffer [sifter] full of bran hops to your taste.
Boil these 3 hours then strain out 30 gallons into a cooler
put in 3 gallons molasses while the beer is scalding hot
or rather draw the Molasses into the cooler & st[r]ain the
bccr on it while boiling hot. Let this stand till it is little
more than blood warm then put in a quart of yea[s]t if
the weather is very cold cover it over with a blank[et]
& let it work in the cooler 24 hours then put it into the
cask—leave the bung [stopper] open till it is almost
done working—bottle it the day week it was brewed.

Another of our patriots, Ben Franklin, also had his hand in beer-making. He believed in temperance and abhorred drunkenness. As he said, "Eat not to dullness. Drink not to elevation." During the Revolutionary War, he spent time in France. On his return, he brought back the following recipe:

A WAY FOR MAKING BEER WITH ESSENCE OF SPRUCE

For a cask containing 80 bottles, take one pot of essence
and 13 pounds of molasses—or the same amount of
unrefined loaf sugar; mix them well together in 20 pints
of hot water: stir together until they make a foam,
then pour it into the cask you will then fill with
water: add a pint of good yeast, stir it well together

and let it stand for 2 or 3 days to ferment, after which close the cask, and after a few days it will be ready to be put into bottles, that must be tightly corked. Leave them 10 or 12 days in a cool cellar, after which the beer will be good to drink.

MAGNA CARTA: THE FIRST STANDARD MEASURE OF DRINK

Do you actually get a pint of beer when you order a pint? Sometimes foam takes up a good percentage of the volume, and sometimes bars use glassware that looks like it will hold a pint but actually holds less. In England, people are pushing for larger than pint-glasses with a pint line clearly marked on the side of the glass. The foam or head on the beer would have to start at or above the pint line, so that the drinker can be assured that he or she is receiving the full pint he or she has paid for.

In the past, there was no such thing as a standard measure, and that made it difficult to know whether you got what you paid for and for the government to collect the correct taxes. In 1215, the Magna Carta made the first recorded mention of a standard measure for drinks, changing practices forever: "Let there be one measure of wine throughout our realm, and one measure of ale … to wit the London quarter."

THE OLDEST-KNOWN BREWERIES IN THE WORLD

In the world—Weihenstephan, outside of Munich, was started in 1040

In North America—Molson was founded in 1786

SHAKESPEARE AND ALE

Yes, even William Shakespeare is associated with ale. In the Vale of Warwickshire, Avon, Shakespeare and some friends went to a Whitsun Ale celebration in the town of Bidford. Bidford ale was known for its strength. A group of Bidford men challenged Shakespeare and his friends to a drinking match. The local Bidford men won the contest, and Shakespeare and his companions headed home.

About a mile from Bidford, the strength of the ale overcame Shakespeare's group and forced them to stop. They all fell asleep under a crabapple tree and slept from Saturday night until Monday morning, when they were awakened by a local passerby. Shakespeare's friends encouraged him to return to Bidford and continue the drinking contest, but Shakespeare said he had had enough:

> "I have drunk with
> Piping Pebwoth, dancing Marston
> Haunted Hillbro', hungry Grafton,
> Dudging Exhall, papist Wixford,
> Beggerly Broom, and drunken Bidford."

All of the villages listed were visible from the site of the crabapple tree where the group had slept. The tree became known as Shakespeare's Crab.

ST. PATRICK AND BEER

One of the members of St. Patrick's household was a brewster named Mescan. During the life of St. Brigid, it was recorded that Mescan brewed ale to supply to churches in the neighborhood during Easter. In *The Humor of Drinking*, there is a poem by John Still called "St. Patrick":

> He preached then with wonderful force
> The ignorant natives a-teaching
> With a pint he wash'd down his discourse,
> "For," says he, "I detest your dry preaching."
> The people with wonderment struck,
> At a pastor so pious and civil,

Exclaimed, "We're for you, my old bucks,
And we pitch our blind gods to the devil,
Who dwells in hot water below."

BEER IS LIQUID BREAD

The Papyrus Zosimus, which dates to about 300 A.D., contained the
following directions for making *boozah*:

Take well-selected, fine barley, macerate it for a day
with water and then spread it for a day in a spot
where it is well exposed to a current of air. Then for
5 hours moisten the whole once more, and place it in
a vessel with handles, the bottom of which is pierced
after the manner of a sieve. [The meaning of the next
few lines is not intelligible, but according to Gruner it
was probably that the barley was dried in the sun so
that the husks, which are bitter and would impart a
like taste to the beer, would peel off.] The remainder
must be ground up and a dough formed with it, after
the yeast has been added, just as is done in bread
making. Next, the whole is put away in a warm place,
and as soon as fermentation has set in sufficiently, the
mass is squeezed through a cloth of course wool, or
else a fine sieve, and the sweet wort is gathered. But
others put the parched loaves into a vessel filled with
water, and subject this to some heating, but not
enough to bring it to a boil. Then they remove the
vessel from the fire, pour its contents into a sieve,
warm the liquid once more, and then put it aside.
(*The Origin and History of Beer and Brewing*)

This mash is a bread mash. The initial process of making bread is identical to the initial process of making beer; bread yeast also starts the familiar fermentation process. Thus beer can be viewed as liquid bread!

BEER AS MEDICINE

Beer was more than just a beverage. It was also used in religious ceremonies, and as a medicine to cure various illnesses. One of the earliest references to beer as medicine can be found is in the Ebers' Papyrus, which dates to about 7,000 years ago. This document lists about 100 remedies for ailments in which beer is a key ingredient!

In old England, beer was also believed to be a curative agent. In the *Eighth Book of Notable Things*, supposedly written in the sixteenth century, the following entries appear:

> **No. 45.** An excellent medicine and noble restorative
> for man or woman that is brought very low with sick-
> ness. Take two pounds of dates and wash them clean
> in Ale, then cut them and take out the stones and
> white skins, then cut them small, and beat them in
> a mortar, till they begin to work like wax, and then
> take a quart of Clarified Honey or Sugar, and half
> an ounce of the pod of Long pepper, as much Mace
> of Cloves, Nutmeg, and Cinnamon, of each one
> Drachm, as much of the powder of Lignum Aloes;
> beat all the Spices together and seeth the Dates with
> the Sugar or Honey with an easie fire, and let it seeth;
> cast in thereto a little Powder, by little and little, and
> stir it with a spatula of wood, and so do until it come
> to an Electuary, and then eat every morning and
> evening thereof, one ounce at a time, and it will

renew and restore again the complexion, be he never so low brought. This hath been proved, and it hath done good to many a Man and Woman.

No. 46. A notable Receipt for the black Jaundice. Take a Gallon of Ale, a Pint of Honey, and two Handfuls of Red Nettles, and take a penny-worth or two of Saffron, and boil it in the Ale, the Ale being first skimmed and then boil the Honey and nettles therein all together and strain it well, and every Morning take a good Drought thereof, for the space of a fortnight. For in that space (God Willing) it will clean and perfectly cure the black Jaundice.

No. 49. For a cough; Take a quart of Ale and put a handful of Red Sage into it, and boil it half away; strain it, and put to the Liquor a Quarter of a pound of Treacle, drink it warm going to bed.

Over the decades and centuries in England, different styles of beer led to improved medication. The book *London and Country Brewer*, written in 1744, extolled the benefit of a brown ale called Stitch. In the 1797 book *Medicina Nautica: An Essay on the Diseases of Seamen,* Thomas Trotter, M.D., describes how porter can help a seaman recover health, strength, and spirits.

In the United States, our forebears also utilized beer as a remedy. In 1801, the following was published in *American Herbal*:

Beer: Common malt beer is made of water, malt, and hops. Porter and ale [are] also made of the same ingredients. There are likewise other kinds of beer, as pumpkin beer, bran beer, spruce beer, etc.

Porter agrees with some constitutions, but not with others; and the same may be said of other malt liquors. It cured a young woman in Connecticut of the palpitation of the heart when other remedies were tried in vain.

Spruce beer is a very wholesome liquor, which is somewhat purgative, and very beneficial in scorbutic complaints. Different kinds of beer, ale, etc. are often prepared according to the prescriptions of the physicians, all of which, as well as pumpkin and bran beer, partake of the virtues of the ingredients put into such liquors.

CHRISTMAS IN DECEMBER DUE TO BEER

In the Northern Hemisphere, the end of December has always been a time of rejoicing. From summer through autumn, the sun continually gets lower in the sky, the days shorten, and the strength of the rays weakens. Ancient man noticed that after the winter solstice, the days started to get longer and the sun grew slowly stronger. As societies formed, formal holidays such as the Roman's Saturnalia, the first ten days after the winter solstice, were celebrated.

In ancient British society, the winter solstice celebration was loosely patterned after Scandinavian practices. Jul (Scandinavian for "winter solstice" and pronounced "yule") was a holiday steeped in tradition and full of superstitions about harvests in the new year. A yule log was brought into the local castle or manor house. If it was ignited by embers from the prior year's yule log, a good harvest was assured for the coming year. The embers of each year's yule log were carefully tended to keep them going until the next Jul celebration.

If the new yule log lit, the local people celebrated with specially brewed winter ales. They would take their celebratory brew out into the farm fields and anoint farm animals, fruit and nut trees, and the fields themselves in order to consecrate them for the coming year's harvest.

In Hampshire, England, a song is sung on Christmas Eve that extolls the practice of wassailing the fruit trees and planting grounds:

> Apples and pears with right good corn,
> Come in plenty to everyone,
> Eat and drink good cake and hot ale,
> Give Earth to drink and she'll not fail.

In the 600s, Pope Gregory the Great made many efforts to convert the peoples of Europe to Christianity. Pope Gregory found that if he associated local pagan celebrations with a Saint's Day, he could bring about conversions to Christianity. When he got to Britain, Pope Gregory tied the yule ceremony to Christ's birthday. Christmas had been celebrated in October, but the Pope changed it to late December to link the celebration to the winter solstice ceremony and its winter ales.

CHAPTER 15

THE SWEET SMELL OF SUCCESS

Beer makes you feel the way you ought to feel without beer.

—HENRY LAWSON

Success hasn't always been easy or obvious. I can't help but to think about a line from a Grateful Dead song, "What a long, strange, trip it's been." Considering that I hardly touched alcohol until a relatively advanced age, I find it amazing to see what's happened with our beer. Now, to be a certified beer judge and beer educator is a real twist of fate, but a great one. There are fringe benefits as well: I rarely have to buy a beer when I visit another brewing company!

It's been fun to see how interested other countries are in what's going on with specialty beers in the United States and, in particular, how our company and our beers are evolving. I spoke at the 1997 World Beer Symposium in Munich, right before Oktoberfest, and was amazed at the interest of the mostly European audience in what we were doing. Many of them found my Pete's Spectrum of Beers useful, and we've gotten requests for copies from around the world. We're absolutely shifting the center of the beer universe to the United States. It's fantastic to be part of this revolution!

In the beginning, Mark Bronder and I wanted to make world-class beer and make it available to as many people as possible. We also wanted not to take ourselves too seriously, right? One day, early on,

Mark asked me how I'd know if we were successful. I said that money would be a nice indicator of success, especially if I could send my kids through college, but that wasn't really how I measured success. After I thought about it for a while, I decided that my indicator would literally be a piece of trash. I imagined driving somewhere and pulling into a dirt parking lot. As I get out of the car, I look down at the dirt and see something shiny. When I look closer, I discover that this object is one of our bottle caps.

My first proof-positive that Wicked Ale was a success came in 1993 when I was camping with my wife and kids in northern California, Oregon, and Washington. We spent a night at Crater Lake National Park in Oregon and the next day drove back down to the interstate on a road that followed the Rogue River. All along the road there were signs for renting. We picked a store at random, and I went inside to fill out all the necessary paperwork. My son came running in and said, "Dad! Look what I found in the dirt of the parking lot!" In his hand he held one of our bottle caps. Someone had bought one of our beers and had thrown the cap away, only to have it be discovered by my son. That was it. He had found the first sign of our company's success, at least in my terms.

The second sign of success arrived in a totally different way. When I met Amy, she introduced me to the Grateful Dead. I had heard of them, but I wasn't familiar with their music. I had always assumed they were a heavy metal group and that I probably wouldn't like them, so I had never made an effort to listen to them. Amy loved them, and I soon got to know and love them as well. Nothing is as good as a live concert by the Dead. Their 1995 show at the Shoreline

BEER AS MONEY

Beer was so important in some cultures that it became a method of payment for goods and services. Cuneiform written on tablets from ancient Persia show that beer was used as a form of currency or barter. The ancient Persian word for beer was *kash* (cash).

In olden days in England, rents were frequently paid in ale. In 852, the Abbot of Peterborough rented out certain lands in return for two tuns of pure ale and ten mittans (measures) of Welsh ale.

Ale was also paid as a toll. A tenant in a Gloucestershire manor was customarily required to pay the lord of the manor a toll of 14 gallons of ale whenever the tenant brewed beer to sell. Similarly, wages were sometimes paid in ale. Some days of the year were voluntary work days for tenants, and if they worked, they were paid in ale and bread.

Amphitheater in Mountain View, California, is one I will never forget.
It was the first time I was able to see a Dead concert *and* have a Pete's
Wicked Ale on draught. Kind of sent
a chill up my spine, if you know what
I mean.

Before long, having Wicked
Ale in a bottle at a Dead show became
quite common. A lot of Deadheads
would buy beers like Wicked Ale or
Sierra Nevada pale ale and sell them in
the concert parking lot to make a little

Acquired at a Grateful Dead show in Mountain View, California—a melding of Phil Lesh, the bass player for the Dead, and our Wicked Ale label.

side money. I learned that whenever beer retailers found out that a
Dead concert was going to be given in their area, they order much
larger amounts of Wicked Ale and other distinctive beers to meet the
Deadhead demand.

People sometimes ask me how it feels to be famous. Honestly, I
never think about it—I truly don't believe that I'm famous. There
are times, however, when I feel like I've partially made it there. The
first time was at my favorite deli in the world, the Carnegie Deli on
Seventh Avenue in New York City. Whenever I've had to do business
in New York, I've taken the coast-to-coast Saturday night red-eye
flight out of San Francisco. By squeezing that Saturday night in, I
save about $1,000 in airfare. I'm cheap, and still do it! The red-eye
ritual means that I'm able to check into my hotel early Sunday
morning and then meet some of our sales guys for breakfast at the
Carnegie Deli. Well-prepared lox, onions, eggs, and a toasted bagel
always take away some of the sick feeling you get from being up
all night. The dining experience itself is usually pretty interesting

because all kinds of people wind up being seated right next to one another.

For years I begged Craig Sable, our sales guy, to call on the Carnegie Deli and see if he could get them to carry our beer in the restaurant. For years Craig blew me off because he thought it would be too much of a long shot for us. Finally, one Friday before a Saturday night red-eye trip, he made the call. It worked! In two minutes he convinced them to carry our Wicked Ale as their dark beer instead of Heineken's dark. By the time I arrived Sunday morning, the deli had already gone through several cases. We met with Sandy Levine, the general manager of the deli, and he was very happy with the results. They've been wonderful to us ever since. I've actually seen Sandy putting our table tents out on display. Believe me, it is seriously uplifting to see a general manager putting your point-of-sale materials out!

By the way, the Carnegie Deli also has pictures of celebrities hanging all over its walls. In 1995, my picture went up. It's in the back room, but it's there, nonetheless!

Once I met Sheila Himmel at a party just after she became the restaurant critic for the *San Jose Mercury News*. When I asked her how she liked her job, she said she loved it, and started telling me what it was like. I thought *I* had the most perfect job in the world, but Sheila's is a close second. I was curious about how she picked restaurants to review. There really was no science to it, she said. Most of the time other people suggested places she ought to check out.

I was curious whether she only looked for fancy restaurants to review; she said she'd try anything. Well, I love Middle Eastern food, and my favorite place for that fare is a Syrian doughnut store and restaurant in San Jose called Hayat's. Her review of it appeared three

weeks later. I loved the opening paragraph of the review. I guess some
people really do know me.

> Pete Slosberg, founder of Pete's Wicked Ale and man
> about Silicon Valley, told me the area's very best falafel
> could be found in a tiny, former doughnut shop in
> Santa Clara. But what does a beer guy know?
>
> *(San Jose Mercury News)*

What was even more fun was going to Hayat's a week or so
after the review. They had always known me as a loyal customer, but
had had no idea who I was. I wore a Pete's Wicked Ale T-shirt that
day. As usual, they thanked me for coming back, but the look in their
eyes when they connected the T-shirt to the restaurant review, was
one of pure shock. It's kind of cool to help others who are making
good products!

I must admit that when somebody, out of the blue, says my beer is
great, it really makes me feel good. In all my time at ROLM, and with
all of the traveling I did, I never heard anybody say that ROLM had
the best dial tone in the world. Yet, when somebody says that Pete's
Wicked Ale is the best beer in the world, I end up feeling pretty good.
To have a direct impact on someone's life, and a positive one at that,
says it all for me.

I'm a beer-can collector, and I go out of my way to look for
new cans in liquor stores and grocery stores wherever I happen to be.
One time, when I was in Hoffman Estates, a western suburb of Chicago,
I drove by a liquor store named Gold Eagle and decided to stop by
and check for new cans. Inside I spied a well-stocked shelf display of
Wicked Ale and thought to myself, "Fantastic!" As I walked around

the store, I saw not one, but two separate, large floor displays of Wicked Ale. This was hardly typical for us in the early days (and would be noteworthy even today). There were very few customers in the store and only one check-out person, so I asked her if I could talk to the manager or owner. She obliged and soon I was able to thank the manager profusely for giving us all of the displays. To my delight, he said it was his favorite beer and told me that his customers bought a lot of it. He was also interested in beer in general, so we spent half an hour chatting about my favorite subject. Towards the end of our conversation, I mentioned that I had recently gotten back from a trip to Germany, where I'd had the opportunity to try something called "smoke beer" in a small town called Bamberg. As we were talking about this unique style of beer, another customer came over and interrupted. "I just got back from a tour of duty in Germany, where I was stationed near Bamberg. I fell in love with that style as well," he said. Unfortunately, he hadn't been able to find this style in the United States, so he had settled on Pete's Wicked Ale as his next favorite beer in the world. The manager and I couldn't believe what this guy was saying. Smiling, the store manager said, "Please, may I introduce you to Pete?" A long pregnant pause. The customer couldn't believe it. Swinging out the old business card and driver's license finally convinced him of who I was!

It's funny how many of the people I've met over the years aren't convinced by a business card. You have to show that driver's license with the picture on it. A few years ago, I remember answering the company phone saying, "This is Pete, can I help you?" A woman's voice said, "So where is it?" Caught completely off guard, I asked her, "Where is what?" She was furious. "Don't you remember?" I'm wondering what's going on when she starts telling me how she met "Pete" from Pete's Brewing Company at a bar a couple of nights ago in North Carolina and how "Pete" had promised her all sorts of things. Now she wanted what the imposter had promised her. I never did find out exactly what that was before she hung up. I guess that photo ID is necessary after all.

When we began making Wicked Ale, I had to fight down this real
cold feeling inside, my worries over whether anyone else would like
my beer. Over the years, consumer reaction has taken many wild and
unexpected forms. At our first Great American
Beer Festival in 1987, the judges rated Pete's
Wicked Ale as the second-best ale in the country;
the attendees voted it number one. So, we know
then that real beer enthusiasts appreciated our
beer, but what about the general public? Around
1990, I got some independent confirmation,
directly from folks who had no idea who I was.

*Friend and investor
Bob Ropiak and me at
the Brooklyn Brewer's
Festival.*

My brother Steve worked for *The New
London Day*, a newspaper in New London,
Connecticut. A friend of his was working for
a paper in New York City and happened to be walking by a bar on the
lower Eastside when he noticed a sign in the window indicating that
they had Pete's Wicked Ale. At the time, we had just started shipping
beer to New York. The name of the bar was Brewski's Temple of Beer
Worship. Now is that a great name for a bar, or what? I mentally filed
it away and promised myself that if I ever got back to New York, I'd
go visit that bar. About nine months later, I was in New York and it
was snowing like a son of a gun even though it was March. I didn't
have a lot of free time, but I was deterimined to look up Brewski's
Temple of Beer Worship. The only thing I knew was that it was near
the corner of Second Avenue and Seventh Street. A cab took me there,
and I stepped out into snow and bitter cold wind.

I asked a couple crossing the intersection whether they
knew of any beer bars in the area. The woman said, "Yes, which one
are you lookin for?" I told her I wanted to find Brewski's Temple of
Beer Worship and she gleefully responded, "Come with us, we're

The "Brothers" at Burp Castle in New York City.

going right by it." Why was she so excited about Brewski's? As we walked, she said, "Brewski's is fantastic, they're one of the few places around that carries my favorite beer in the world, Pete's Wicked Ale!" I nearly fell over. So I did the Superman thing and opened my jacket, showing her the Pete's Wicked Ale T-shirt I was wearing, handed her my business card, and introduced myself. I don't know who was more stunned. Needless to say, we made each other's day!

The story of Brewski's Temple of Beer Worship didn't end there. I discovered that right next to Brewski's was a bar called the Burp Castle Temple of Beer Worship. It turned out that both are owned by the same guy! On my first visit, I only got to experience

Brewski's. It's a basic bar with a number of tap handles and lots of bottles of beer. Most of the bar staff at Brewski's didn't speak English. East Seventh Street had become a prominantly Ukrainian area, and most of the people working in the bar spoke only Ukrainian.

The Burp Castle turned out to be unique in a completely different way. At the 1994 Brooklyn Festival, our salesperson, David Glasser, introduced me to a number of guys who said they worked at the Burp Castle. One of them identified himself as Brother Alex, so I thought maybe he was in the clergy. These guys invited us to come by that evening for a beer. It was a long day, and when the exhibits shut down, David and I were tired, ready to grab a quick dinner and call it a night. As we closed up the booth, I remembered that we said we'd go by and visit the Burp Castle. It was 9:00 P.M. David agreed to stop by for one beer.

We arrived on East Seventh Street to find a small bar that appeared to have lit candles in it. Inside there was classical music playing, and the servers and bartenders were all dressed in monks' robes. Murals of various monastery scenes covered the walls, and there were candles on every table, along with signs reading "Whispering is allowed." This bar was different from anything else I had ever been in. Brother Patrick, the lead server, greeted us. Brother Alex was tending bar. They had eight beers on tap, two of which were ours. They must have had over 60 different bottles of Belgian beer on the menu. The whole bar was tiny, with maybe 10 to 15 tables.

> **SKÖL**
>
> One of the first kinds of drinking vessels were shells picked up at the seashore. Later on, skulls were used, either from animals or from a much-hated enemy killed in battle. The habit of drinking out of skulls continued for a long time, up through the Celts and later the Saxons of Britain. The name "scole" was given to a bowl that was shaped like a human skull cut in half. The Scandinavian word *sköl* is drived from this and is now a word of salutation before drinking.

For those who don't know much about Belgian beers, these are some of the most distinctive beer styles on earth. A tiny country with a population smaller than metropolitan New York, Belgium has over 1,400 different beers. In general, they are much stronger than other beers. Among my favorite Belgian beers is a beefy yet smooth beer called Scaldis. This beer is 12 percent alcohol by volume, best enjoyed when sipped slowly as you would a fine wine. Our colleagues in Belgium had experienced their own problems with Anheuser-Busch: In Belgium, their beer is called Bush, but AB wouldn't allow them to use that name in the United States, so they had renamed the beer after the river on which the brewery is located.

Autographed Burp Castle T-shirt with picture of Brother Patrick.

Anyway, David and I sat down, and the good brothers start shooing other customers out. It was about 10:00 P.M., their closing time, but they let the two of us stay. After a hectic day at the festival, to sit down and have a Scaldis while listening to classical music was hog heaven! We ended up staying till 3:00 A.M. At one point, Brother Patrick asked me if there was something special I wanted to listen to. For some reason, I really wanted to hear Beethoven's Fifth Piano Concerto. Brother Patrick went behind the bar to get the CD, but he came back deflated because he couldn't find it. We must have listened to Mozart or some other Beethoven pieces, but it didn't really matter because we were having such a good time together. We finally called it quits because we had appointments to keep that morning. (Morning, already?)

After a few hours of sleep, David and I made sales calls and stopped for lunch at a restaurant next to a Sam Goody's music store. On impulse, I ran into Sam Goody's, and emerged with a CD of Beethoven's Fifth Piano Concerto. When we delivered it to the Burp Castle that night, the good Brothers were blown away.

I must have been to the Burp Castle at least a half a dozen times since then, and every time I enter the bar, I hear Beethoven's

Fifth Piano Concerto playing. Coincidence? Maybe. Maybe not. But it sure makes me feel good.

So what is success? There is no one answer. Nor can success be viewed from any one level. Certainly, finding Wicked ale bottle caps in litter and draught Wicked Ale at a Grateful Dead concert rank way up there in signs of success.

Creating a product that people voluntarily tell me is their favorite beer in the world is pretty amazing. Most people go to work and never get such positive feedback on the fruits of their labor.

Most of all though, I view success as being able to enter a field that I never in my wildest dreams would guess I'd end up in; create something that people like; learn enough about a subject to become a world expert and educator; meet lots of interesting people; and have a lot of fun along the way.

REFLECTIONS

I wish we could all have good luck, all the time! I wish we had
wings! I wish rain water was beer!

—ROBERT BOLT, *A MAN FOR ALL SEASONS*

When you work at something, when you put that much
blood, sweat, and tears into it, you don't always get to meet
the customers who buy what you produce. At ROLM, I had some
great jobs, but God knows if anyone appreciated what I did. My boss
would give me a review and a salary increase maybe, but I never knew
if what I was doing had affected anyone in any way, shape, or form.
When I an have a real effect on someone—preferably a positive
effect—then I know I've done something.

To have somebody say to me that I've made their favorite
beer in the world, or one of their favorite beers in the world, is heaven.
In my first year of business, people came up to me and said Wicked
Ale was their favorite beer in the world. For me, well, that's what it's
all about.

I still get excited about talking about beer and its great
history. I feel immense satisfaction when people at my beer talks tell
me it's the first time they've ever understood anything about beer—
especially if they've been in the beer business for several decades and
have never heard any of the stories behind beer. Now they've learned
something from me, and they might pass it on to someone else or
simply be more willing to try new things. That makes me feel good.
And when I combine that with all the times people tell me, out of the

blue, that our beer is their favorite, I feel like I've done something important, that I've made a difference in their lives.

Is this a dream come true? Honestly, this was a dream of mine. All I wanted to do as a homebrewer was to experiment with great flavors and aromas and impress some friends. When Mark Bronder and I started Pete's Brewing Company, we wanted to make world-class beer and have some fun. We're on our way, but we've still got a long way to go. And as long as people want to try a great variety of beer and enjoy learning about beer, I'll keep making it and talking about it!

What's next? I love to drink great beer and eat good food. My suspicion is that a lot more can be done to educate the public about the incredible things you can do in cooking with beer. There have been a sprinkling of Brewmaster Dinners around the country, but the real potential has yet to be realized. And it's not just beer. I want to learn to play the bagpipes, earn my barbecue judge certification, speak German, become a paleontologist, and follow up on a whole slew of other dreams. I've got a huge backlog of fun things I'd like to do. That's why I took the chance and started Pete's Brewing Company with Mark. And who knows, by the time this book reaches you, you may have already heard about Mark and Pete's BBQ!

If I had to summarize everything about beer in one story, I would rely on John Barleycorn. Back in the early 1970s, one of the great English rock groups, Traffic (whose members included Steve Winwood and Dave Mason), recorded "John Barleycorn Must Die" as the title track for one of their hit record albums. The semi-understandable lyrics talked about killing, cutting, and then boiling this poor sot named John Barleycorn. In fact, the song is based on an old poem and isn't about killing anybody. *It's really the story of the planting, growing, harvesting of barley and the making of beer!* A chill went up my spine as I read the poem and realized that it was one of the best poems I had ever read:

JOHN BARLEY CORN
by Robert Burns

There were three kings into the east,
   Three kings both great and high,
And they have sworn a solemn oath
   John Barleycorn should die.

They took a plough and ploughed him down,   ***Planting the seed***
   Put clods upon his head;
And they have sworn a solemn oath
   John Barleycorn was dead.

But the cheerful spring came kindly on,
   And showers began to fall;   ***Spring rains***
And John Barleycorn got up again,
   And sure surprised them all.   ***Plants growing***

The sultry suns of summer came,
　　And he grew thick and strong;
His head weel armed wi' pointed spears,　　*Plants maturing*
　　That none should do him wrong.

The sober autumn entered mild,
　　When he grew wan and pale;
His bending joints and drooping head　　*Green plants drying out*
　　Showed he began to fail.

His color sicked more and more,
　　He faded into age;
And then his enemies began
　　To show their deadly rage.

They've taken a weapon, long and sharp,　　*Harvesting with knives*
　　And cut him at the knee;
Then tied him fast upon a cart
　　Like a rogue for forgerie.

They laid him down upon his back,
　　And cudgelled him full sore;
They hung him up before the storm,　　*Separating the barley*
　　And turned him o'er and o'er.　　　　*kernels*

They filled up some darksome pit,
　　With water to the brim;
They heaved in John Barleycorn,　　*Moistening the barley*
　　There let him sink or swim　　　　*for sprouting*

They laid him out upon the floor
  To work him further woe;
And still, as signs of life appeared,   *Sprouting*
  They tossed him to and fro.

They wasted, o'er a scorching flame,   *Drying out the malt*
  The marrow of his bones;
But a miller used him worst of all'
  For he crushed him 'tween two stones.   *Milling the malt*

And they have taken his very heart's blood, *Mashing the sugar out,*
  And drunk it round and round;   *then making beer*
And still the more and more they drank,
  Their joy did more abound.

John Barleycorn was a hero bold,
  Of noble enterprise;
For if you do but taste his blood
  'Twill make your courage rise.

'Twill make a man forget his woe;
  'Twill heighten all his joy;
'Twill make the widow's heart to sing,
  Though the tear was in her eye.

Then let us toast John Barleycorn,
  Each man's a glass in hand;
And may his great posterity
  Ne'er fail in old Scotland.

Perspectives change over time. These days when I see a pile of specialty beer litter on the sidewalk or gutter, I'm actually disappointed if there are no Wicked items among the clutter. Forget that single bottle cap; now we want our share of the trash! When I went to the last San Francisco Giants' baseball game of the 1997 season and passed a lot of empty beer bottles on the way to the parking lot, I had mixed emotions: The Giants won the division championship, but there were no Wicked bottles in the litter.

I guess the tag line from our 1994 television spots is still true: "We're not yet world famous." And we still have a long way to go.

Cheers, Pete

P.S. For the winter season, from a long time ago,

I WISH YOU A MERRY CHRISTMAS AND A HAPPY NEW YEAR,
WITH YOUR POCKETS FULL OF MONEY AND YOUR CELLAR FULL OF BEER.

I had the honor of throwing the opening pitch at the San Francisco Giants v. the Oakland A's spring season baseball game in Scottsdale, Arizona, in March of 1996.

BIBLIOGRAPHY

Ade, George. *The Old Time Saloon.* New York: Ray Long and Richard
R. Smith, Inc., 1931.

Anderson, Will. *The Great State of Maine Beer Book.* Portland, Maine:
Anderson and Sons Publishing Co., 1996.

Anon. *Every Man His Own Brewer; or a Compendium of the English
Brewery.* London, 1768.

Arno Press. *One Hundred Years of Brewing.* New York: H.S. Rich
and Co., 1903.

Arnold, John Paul. *Origin and History of Beer and Brewing.*
Chicago: Alumni Association of the Wahl-Henius Institute
of Fermentology, 1911.

Astley, T. *The London and Country Brewer.* London, 1750.

Aye, John. *The Humour of Drinking.* London: Universal Publications
Ltd., 1934.

Ball, Mia. *The Worshipful Company of Brewers.* London: Hutchinson
Benham Ltd., 1977.

Baron, Stanley. *Brewed in America.* Boston: Little, Brown,
and Co., 1962.

Barth, Heinrich J., Christine Klinke, and Claus Schmidt. *The Hop
Atlas.* Nuremburg, Germany: Joh. Barth and Sohn, 1994.

Bickerdyke, John. *The Curiosities of Ale and Beer.* London: Spring
Books, 1978.

Birmingham, Frederic. *Falstaff's Complete Beer Book*. New York: Universal-Award House, Inc., 1970.

Black, William. A *Practical Treatise on Brewing*. London: Smith, Elder and Co. Cornhill, 1840.

Bowering, Ian. *Brewing in Formosa*. Burnstown, Ontario, Canada: Ian Bowering and General Store Publishing House, 1995.

Brander, Michael. *The Life and Sport of the Inn*. New York: St. Martins Press, 1973.

Broderick, Harold. *The Practical Brewer*. Madison, Wisc.: Master Brewers Association of the Americas, 1977.

Brown, John Hull. *Early American Beverages*. New York: Bonanza Books, 1966.

Brown, B. Meredith. *The Brewers Art*. London: Naldrett Press Ltd., 1948.

Brown, Sanborn C. *Wines and Beers of Old New England*. Hanover, New Hampshire: The University Press of New England, 1978.

Burch, Byron. *Brewing Quality Beers*. Fulton, Calif.: Joby Books, 1986.

Butcher, Alan D. *Ale and Beer: A Curious History*. Toronto, 1989.

Cape, Jonathan. *A Book About Beer by a Drinker*. London: Jonathan Cape Ltd., 1934.

Cochran, Thomas. *The Pabst Brewing Company*. New York: University Press, 1948.

Cole, William. *Tavern Anecdotes and Sayings*. London, 1866.

Corran, H. S. *A History of Brewing*. North Pomfret, Vt.: David and Charles Ltd., 1975.

Dallas, John, and Charles McMaster. *The Beer Drinker's Companion*. Scotland: Edinburgh Publishing Co. Ltd., 1993.

Daniels, Ray. *Designing Great Beers*. Boulder, Colo.: Brewers Publications, 1996.

Dodsley, R., and J. Dodsley. "An Essay on Brewing." In Combrunes Book of Brewing. London: 1758.

Donnachie, Ian. *A History of the Brewing Industry in Scotland.*
    Edinburgh: John Donald Publishers Ltd., 1979.

Dornbusch, Horst D. *Prost!: The Story of German Beer.* Boulder, Colo.:
    Brewers Publications, 1997.

Downard, William. *The Cincinnati Brewing Industry.* Cincinnati,
    Ohio: Ohio University Press, 1973.

Duddington, G.L. *Plain Man's Guide to Beer.*

Dunkling, Leslie. *The Guinness Drinking Companion.* New York:
    Lyons and Burford, 1992.

Dunstan, Keith. *The Amber Nectar.* Ringwood, Victoria, Australia:
    Viking O'Neil, 1987.

Eames, Alan D. *The Secret Life of Beer.* Pownal, Vt.: Storey
    Communications, 1995.

Eckhardt, Fred. *A Treatise on Lager Beers.* Portland, Ore.: Hobby
    Winemaker, 1979.

——. *The Essentials of Beer Style.* Portland, Ore.: Fred Eckhardt
    Associates, 1989.

Endell, Fritz. *Old Tavern Signs.* New York: Houghton Mifflin Co.,
    1916. Detroit, Mich.: Singing Tree Press, 1968.

Fix, George. *Principles of Brewing Science.* Boulder, Colo.: Brewers
    Publications, 1989.

Fix, George, and Laurie Fix. *Oktoberfest, Vienna, Märzen.* Boulder,
    Colo.: Brewers Publications, 1991.

Forget, Carl. *Dictionary of Beer and Brewing.* Boulder, Colo.: Brewers
    Publications, 1988.

Foster, Terry. *Pale Ale.* Boulder, Colo.: Brewers Publications, 1990.

——. *Porter.* Boulder, Colo.: Brewers Publications, 1992.

French, Richard Valpy. *Nineteen Centuries of Drink in England.*
    London: Longman's Green and Co., 1884.

Gareth, John D. *A Good Head for Beer.* Great Britain: Starling Press
    Ltd., 1982.

Garetz, Mark. *Using Hops: The Complete Guide to Hops for the Craft Brewer.* Danville, Calif.: Hop Tech, 1994.

Glover, Brian. *Prince of Ales.* New Hampshire: Alan Sutton Publishing Inc., 1993.

——. *Brewing for Victory: Brewers, Beer, and Pubs in World War II.* Great Britain: Lutterworth Press, 1995.

Gourvish, T.R., and R.G. Wilson. *The British Brewing Industry 1830-1980.* Cambridge: Cambridge University Press, 1994.

Guinard, Jean-Xavier. *Lambic.* Boulder, Colo.: Brewers Publications, 1990.

Hackwood, Frederick. *Inns, Ales, and Drinking Customs of Old England.* London: Bracken Books, 1985.

Haiber, William P., and Robert Haiber. *A Short but Foamy History of Beer.* La Grangeville, New York: Info Devel Press, 1993.

Harrison, John. *Old British Beers and How to Make Them.* Great Britain: Durden Park Beer Circle, 1991.

Hart, George. *Egyptian Myths.* London: British Museum Press, 1993.

Hawkins, K.H., and C.L. Pass. *The Brewing Industry.* London: Heinemann Educational Books Ltd., 1979.

Hernon, Peter, and Terry Ganey. *Under the Influence.* New York: Simon and Schuster, 1991.

Higgins, Patrick, M.K. Gilmore, and P. Hertlein. *Homebrewers Recipe Guide.* New York: Simon and Schuster, 1996.

Hughes, E. *A Treatise on the Brewing of Beer.* London: Uxbridge, 1796.

Jackson, Michael. *Pocket Guide to Beer.* New York: Simon and Schuster, 1986.

——. *The New World Guide to Beer.* Philadelphia: Courage Books, 1988.

——. *Great Beers of Belgium.* Antwerp, Belgium: M.M.C.-CODA, 1992.

——. *Beer Companion.* Philadelphia: Running Press, 1993.

Johnson, Steve. *On Tap: The Guide to U.S. Brewpubs.* Clemson, South Carolina: WBR Publications, 1991.

——. *The On Tap Companion.* Clemson, South Carolina: WBR Publications, 1992.

King, Frank. *Beer Has a History.* London: Hutchinson's Scientific and Technical Publications, 1947.

Klein, Bob. *The Beer Lover's Rating Guide.* New York: Workman Publishing Co., Inc., 1995.

Laker, Joseph. *Entrepreneurship and the Development of the Japanese Beer Industry.* Submitted for Ph.d. dissertation. Bloomington: Indiana University, 1975.

La Pensee, Clive. *The Historical Companion to House Brewing.* Beverley, United Kingdom: Montag Publications, 1990.

Larwood, Jacob, and John Camden Hotten. *The History of Signboards.* London: John Camden Hotten, 1866.

Leverett, Brian. *Home Beer Making.* Dorchester, Dorset, Great Britain: Prism Press, 1980.

Lewis, Michael. *Stout.* Boulder, Colo.: Brewers Publications, 1995.

Line, Dave. *The Big Book of Brewing.* Andover, Hants, Great Britain: The "Amateur Winemaker" Publications Ltd., 1974.

Lipinsky, Bob, and Kathie Lipinsky. *The Complete Beverage Dictionary.* New York: Van Nostrand Reinhold, 1996.

Loftus, William. *The Brewer: A Familiar Treatise on the Art of Brewing.* London: W.R. Loftus, 1858.

——. The Maltster: *A Compendius Treatise on the Art of Malting.* London: W.R. Loftus, 1876.

Louie, Elaine. *Premier Beer: A Guide to America's Best Bottled Microbrews.* New York: Pocket Books, 1996.

MacCartie, J.C. *A Handbook for Australian Brewers.* Melbourne, Australia: Lawrence and O'Farrell, 1884.

Marchant, W.T. *In Praise of Ale.* London: George Redway, 1888. Detroit, Michigan: Singing Tree Press, 1968.

Matsunaga, Masahiro. *A Treasury of German Beer Labels.*

McClosky, Dennis. *365 Beertime Stories*. Burnstown, Ontario, Canada: General Store Publishing House Inc., 1989.

Molyneux F.G.S., and William Molyneux. *Burton-on-Trent: Its History, Its Waters, and Its Breweries*. London: Trubner and Co., 1869.

Monckton, H.A. *A History of English Ale and Beer*. London: The Bodley Head Ltd., 1966.

——. *The Story of British Beer*. Great Britain: H.A. Monckton, 1981.

——. *Whitbread's Breweries*. Great Britain: Publishing and Literary Services Ltd., 1984.

Morrice, Alexander. *A Treatise on Brewing*. London: Knight and Compton, 1802.

Nachel, Marty, and Steve Ettlinger. *Beer for Dummies*. Foster City, Calif.: IDG Books Worldwide, Inc., 1996.

Nordland, Odd. *Brewing and Beer Traditions in Norway*. Oslo: Universitetsforlaget, 1969.

Owens, Bill. *How to Build a Small Brewery*. Livermore, Calif.: Working Press, 1982.

Papazian, Charlie. *New Complete Joy of Homebrewing*. New York: Avon Books, 1984.

Pasteur, Louis. *Studies on Fermentation*. London: Macmillan and Co., 1876.

Pepper, Barrie. *The Bedside Book of Beer*. Great Britain: Alma Books Ltd., 1990.

Plavchan, Ronald Jan. *A History of Anheuser-Busch*. New York: Arno Press, 1969.

Powell, Stephen R. *Rushing the Growler*. New York: Apogee Design, 1996.

Protz, Roger. *The Great British Beer Book*. Great Britain: Inpact Book, 1987.

——. *Beer, Bed and Breakfast*. Great Britain: Robson Books, Ltd., 1988.

——. *The Ale Trail*. Kent, England: Eric Dobby Publishing, Ltd., 1995.

——. *The Ultimate Encyclopedia of Beer.* United Kingdom: Carlton Books Ltd., 1995.

Rajotte, Pierre. *Belgian Ale.* Boulder, Colo.: Brewers Publications, 1992.

Rhodes, Christine P. *Encyclopedia of Beer.* New York: Henry Holt and Co., 1995.

Ritchie, Berry. *An Uncommon Brewer: The Story of Whitbread.* London: James and James Ltd., 1992.

Romanko, Richard, and Howard Eismann. *Guide to American Hops Book III.* United States: Steiner Inc., 1986.

Ronnenberg, Herman. *Beer and Brewing in the Inland Northwest.* Moscow, Idaho: University of Idaho Press, 1993.

Salcedo, Nancy. *The Guzzlers Guide to California Beer.* Stinson Beach, Calif.: Nancy Salcedo, 1994.

Salem, Frederick William. *Beer: It's History and It's Economic Value as a National Beverage.* Hartford, Conn.: F.W. Salem and Co., 1880.

Schermerhorn, Candy. *Great American Beer Cookbook.* Boulder, Colo.: Brewers Publications, 1993.

Shay, Frank, and Helen Ramsey. *Drawn from the Wood.* New York: Gold Label Books, 1929.

Siebel, Dr. John E., and Anton Schwarz. *History of the Brewing Industry and Brewing Science in America.* Chicago: G.L. Peterson, 1933.

Smith, Gregg. *The Beer Enthusiast's Guide.* Pownal, Vt.: Storey Communications, 1994.

——. *Beer: A History of Suds and Civilization from Mesopotamia to Microbreweries.* New York: Avon Books, 1995.

Smith, Gregg, and Carrie Getty. *The Beer Drinker's Bible: Lore, Trivia, and History: Chapter and Verse.* Boulder, Colo.: Brewers Publications, 1997.

Spence, James. *Victory Beer Recipes: America's Best Homebrew.* Boulder, Colo.: Brewers Publications, 1994.

Steinberg. *Steinberg's Dictionary of British History.*

Strong, Stanley. *The Romance of Beer and Brewing.*

Thomas, Virginia. *Brewery Operations.* Vol. 7. Boulder, Colo.: Brewers Publications, 1991.

Tuck, John. *The Private Brewers Guide 1822.* Woodbridge, Conn.: Zymoscribe, 1995.

——. *American Beer, It's History and It's Manufacture.* New York: U.S. Brewers Association, 1909.

——. *Beer and Ale in Old New York and It's Environs.* New York: U.S. Brewers Association.

——. *Documentary History.* New York: U.S. Brewers Association, 1896.

Walsh, Peter. *Guinness.*

Watney, John. *Beer Is Best: A History of Beer.* London: Peter Owen Ltd., 1974.

Webb, Tim. *The CAMRA Good Beer Guide to Belgium and Holland.* St. Albans, Hertfordshire: Alma Books Ltd., 1992.

Weisberg, David. *50 Great Homebrewing Tips.* Peterborough, New Hampshire: Lampman Brewing Publications, 1994.

Wykes, Alan. *Ale and Hearty.* London: Jupiter Books, 1979.

Yenne, Bill, and Tom Debolski. *The Ultimate Book of Beer Trivia.* San Francisco, Calif.: Bluewood Books, 1994.

Young, Jimmy. *A Short History of Ale.* London: David and Charles, 1979.

INDEX